REBEL CHIEF

REBEL CHIEF

THE MOTLEY LIFE
of
COLONEL WILLIAM HOLLAND THOMAS, C. S. A.

Paul A. Thomsen

A TOM DOHERTY ASSOCIATES BOOK

New York

REBEL CHIEF: THE MOTLEY LIFE OF
COLONEL WILLIAM HOLLAND THOMAS, C.S.A.

Book design by Mary A. Wirth

A Forge Book
Published by Tom Doherty Associates, LLC
175 Fifth Avenue
New York, NY 10010

www.tor.com

Forge® is a registered trademark of Tom Doherty Associates, LLC.

Library of Congress Cataloging-in-Publication Data

Thomsen, Paul A.
    Rebel chief : the motley life of Colonel William Holland Thomas, C.S.A. / Paul
A. Thomsen.
    "A Tom Doherty Associates book."
    ISBN-13: 978-0-765-30959-4
    ISBN-10: 0-765-30959-9
    1. Thomas, William Holland, 1805–1893. 2. Soldiers—Confederate States of
America—Biography. 3. Confederate States of America. Army—Biography. 4.
Cherokee Indians—Biography. I. Title.

E467.1.T46T47 2004
973.7'42'092—dc22   2004010063

First Hardcover Edition: September 2004
First Trade Paperback Edition: November 2006

Printed in the United States of America

0 9 8 7 6 5 4 3 2 1

For Liz

ACKNOWLEDGMENTS

Despite unforeseen obstacles, nay-sayers, and periodic deficits of desirable choices, the fortunate among us manage to muddle through our daily chores and trials with a little support from those who for some reason care for us. When one is granted an opportunity to contribute to something extraordinary, that person can either fail outright, suffer under the creative crucible in attempting to reap their reward, or draw strength from their supporters and friends.

This work would not have been possible without the assistance of a collection of extraordinary individuals, institutions, and information repositories. I wish to express my gratitude towards the orchestrators of Georgia University's Digital Library of Georgia and the on-line GALILEO Project for providing this poor historian with easy access to digitized copies of the hundreds of archived manuscripts and papers concerning William Holland Thomas and his contemporaries' dealings with southern leadership and the federal government on behalf of the North Carolina Cherokee. I am also grateful for the efforts of the University of Georgia's Hargrett Rare Book and Manuscript Library, the University of Tennessee's Hoskins Special Collections Library, the North Carolina Museum of the Cherokee Indian, and the Tennessee State Library and Archive for providing much of the digital archive's material readily available for study. I also share a deep appreciation for the efforts of the United States Army's Center for Military History and the University of North Carolina at Chapel Hill Library, as well as the Gutenberg Digital Archives, the National Parks Service Civil War Soldiers and Sailors database, and the Library of Congress's American Memory Digital Archive to widely disseminate some of the historical gems of American history to the on-line community. My deep appreciation also goes to the North Carolina Supreme Court Library, Cathy Martin of the North Carolina Legislative Library, the National Archives, and the Special Collections Department of Duke University for supplying me with key points of information on Colonel Thomas's many varied private and public profit-making ventures.

On a more personal level, I wish to express deep appreciation towards Mattie Russell for her lengthy research scholarship on Thomas, David Powell and Will Terdoslavich for their eleventh-hour assistance puzzling out the sourcing for the almost phantomlike actions of the Thomas Legion's war-ending activities, and Dr. Eugenio Baban for his medical insight into the symptomology of tertiary syphilis. Furthermore, this work would not have been possible without the assistance of my readers Kevin Loughnane, Suman Sabastin, Philip Abramson, Vincent Scutaro, Dorothy Siminski, Joshua Spivak, Lin Ying Goodson, Sofia Belenky, Margery Smith, Arne Israel, Martha Seelenberger, Scott Sendrow, Joe Ferlazzo, and Art De-Cesario, as well as the support and encouragement of Brenda Lacy, Mike Dockett, Joanne Coniglio, Andrew Chazen, Donna Alston,

Fred Wilken, Melissa Parker, Christopher Osgood, Portia Cook-Dyrenforth, Jeff Sandgrund, Elizabeth Early, Jonathan Early, Lauren Sullivan, Kevin Kelly, Nancy Melissas, Dyanne Norris, Kent Stridiron, Katalena Grieco, Bob Reives, Lynda Hernandez, Robert Muccigrosso, James Johnson, Leonard Gordon, Hans Trefousse, Peter Mastrocovi, Anthony Cassea, Michael Wikowski, Dennis Showalter, William R. Forstchen, Miguel de Cervantes Saavedra, Brooklyn Parks Commissioner Julius Speigel, New York Parks Commissioner Adrian Benepe, my agent, Frank Weimann, my editor, Brian M. Thomsen, and my parents, Arthur and Eileen Thomsen. Finally, I extend my deepest, most heartfelt gratitude to Elizabeth A. Crefin for her years of keeping the wolves at bay with the words ". . . I know you can."

AUTHOR'S NOTE

For a person many have considered an obscure figure there is a sizable amount of disparate and, at some points, even contradictory information regarding the life of Colonel William Holland Thomas.

Yet, Thomas's life personifies many of the conflicts that shaped modern America: frontiersman versus urban dweller, Anglo settler versus Native American inhabitants, state governance versus federal rule, North versus South, independent businessman versus cartel establishment, old money versus upwardly mobile entrepreneur.

The recording of Cherokee history and American interaction

with the Native Americans of the North Carolina region have led to several different ways of spelling the same names. The names of Cherokee Nationals and Eastern Band members are those found in most common usage.

CONTENTS

INTRODUCTION

U nlike many children born into American families a generation after the Revolutionary War, William Holland Thomas did not exclusively confine his interests to a specialization of farming, mercantilism, the sciences, or the practice of law.

By poor fortune or fate, the young man's birth in the remote Western North Carolina outback had severely limited his options. With an interest in the life beyond his small rural locale, within a few years Thomas had ably managed to fill many of the local jobs necessary for Western North Carolina growth and eventual prosperity. Before long, Thomas became the backcountry's small store manager, merchant, legal consultant, franchise owner, lobbyist, state senator, and colonel in the Confederate States of America. In his spare time, he was also an Agent of the Eastern Band of Cherokee, served as their regional public relations expert, and, eventually, became their Chief.

Despite the complexities his numerous occupations carried, William Holland Thomas was motivated by simple objectives. Born on the frontier of North Carolina to parents struggling to carve out a new future in the mountain outback, instead finding only tragedy and isolation, William Thomas was forced to relentlessly pursue the seemingly never-ending goal of fiscal security and familial accomplishment. Throughout his life, he would struggle with fears of failure and with the urban preconceptions of others. His ardent desire to protect his family (blood, inherited, and adopted) would lead him to great challenges, exotic vistas, influential people, and dangerous frontier situations.

In recognition of this collection of responsibilities assumed by the formally unschooled Thomas, past historians such as E. Stanley Godbold Jr., Mattie Russell, and John Finger have marveled at the character of the man's complexity. Indeed, William Thomas was a unique spirit among the North Carolina outback populace and, one might even say, a man ahead of his time. Yet, Thomas can also be viewed in the greater context of the continuously evolving country his parents' generation had struggled to create. Gifted with the ability to anticipate potential markets, he rivaled the coastal aristocracy in business prowess and, in a few years, was able to parlay a few inherited holdings into a small fortune covering land, chattel, and legal claims. When Thomas saw an opportunity, he took it, made it his own, paid off his debts, and reallocated his now expanded resources into even greater projects. To the frustration of many contemporaries, in business and in politics, he was always one step ahead of his counterparts.

Still, Thomas was more than a simple "jack-of-all-trades" and consummate politician. He was an archetype of the future American entrepreneur, constantly keeping his eye on his investments and modifying them to the changing world around him. As a driven businessman, Thomas knew what raw materials moved best in urban or foreign markets and the cost-effectiveness of obtaining the encouragement of refined products for his more frequent customers. Similarly, as a frontier franchise owner Thomas's lifestyle must have been the envy of the more adventurous urban shopkeepers, dealing on a daily basis with a plethora of exotic clientele and suppliers (including frontiersman and Cherokee warrior, the region's coastal economic aristocracy, and urban New York suppliers). As legal counsel to neighbors and regional Cherokee, he moved to take advantage of national events such as Supreme Court decisions, the federal government's Removal Program, the flight of fugitive Native Americans, and the ever shifting sands of Washington 1850s politics to produce the most beneficial outcome for his clients. Finally, as an elected official and military officer, Thomas worked tirelessly to enhance his contemporaries' economic standing, his own potential for future profits, and the security of his client neighbors (Thomas may have been many things, but an altruist he was not).

Having forged most of his amassed fortune with his own blood, sweat, and luck, Thomas knew the dangers of missteps, damaged relations, and lost opportunities. Unlike his more well-known impetuous contemporaries Davy Crockett and Sam Houston, William Thomas took caution in planning his strategies. Borrowing from his long-time colleague John Caldwell Calhoun (the preeminent arguer for southern rights), in the pursuit of many of his goals, Thomas often appeared as a cool and dispassionate but persuasive man in the midst of the most turbulent of situations.

Yet, the North Carolinian was also given to excess where his friends and family were concerned. In his youth, like many future pioneers, Thomas was captivated by the allure of gold fever stalking the Cherokee Nation's lands in Georgia. As a consultant to the Eastern Band Cherokee, several times the man exceeded his mandate to become their investor, economic advisor, and public relations liaison with the American settlers as well as governmental authorities. As their financier, he envisioned a safe haven of privately bought and held Native American land called the Qualla Boundary, which would deeply strain his own invested finances to the breaking point several times. In his declining years, much like Cervante's Don Quixote of La Mancha, Thomas would publicly manifest these impulses in darker moments (violent altercations, written denunciations of his detractors, and verbal castigations of long-standing friends), but his community would overlook the episodes of madness in favor of remembering the amiable, just, and noble businessman who had accomplished so much for Western North Carolina.

Time has taken many of the self-described "merchant's"[1] more guarded moments into obscurity. As a businessman with diversified interests, he relied largely on memory. As a result, Thomas kept few records of his daily business activities and even fewer mentionings of personal thoughts or social experiences. Those which he did keep were often lost to fires, thieves, and enemy raiding parties. The few diaries, which remain as a window into Thomas's travels, are replete with abbreviated entries, mathematical calculations, and non se-quiturs, undoubtedly meant to be for William Thomas alone as aids of recollection rather than vehicles for rumination and exposition.

Yet, those surviving sources illustrate that there was far more to the backcountry businessman than met the eye. In birth, William Holland Thomas was a poor child, but, in the relentless pursuit of his dreams, fueled by his deep-seated fears of failure, the North Carolin-ian shaped and was shaped by the world-changing events around him that affected his Western North Carolina home and his adopted brethren among the Eastern Band of North Carolina Cherokee.

AUTHOR'S NOTE: The material upon which this work is largely based is derived from an abundance of William Thomas's surviving digitally preserved notes, legal documents, and correspondence mated to period sources of the surrounding region and supplemented with the exhaustive doctoral research work of Mattie Russell.

CHAPTER ONE

THE COLONIAL
FRONTIER

O n February 5th, 1805,[2] Temperance Thomas gave birth to her only child, William Holland Thomas, in a small house on the western mountainous frontier of North Carolina.[3] The birth had been a brief but welcome respite from recent troubles plaguing the small family.

While the woodland mountain landscape of the Southern Appalachians conveyed a natural presence of serenity and majesty for centuries to explorers and passing travelers, the region's rugged features remained a constant reminder for the thirty-year-old mother that life on the frontier was as perilous as it was beautiful. Having immigrated to the Virginian colony with her family from England's Newcastle on the Tyne, Temperance Thomas (born Temperance

Colvard in 1775)[4] was familiar with the trials and troubles of relocat-
ing to unfamiliar locale, but 'unlike the predominantly urbanized
rolling green countryside of Virginia, much of North Carolina had
never been formally surveyed at this time, much less been traveled by
anyone other than seasoned hunters, trackers, adventurers, and members of the receding native populace.

Likely lured by the promise of "A country, whose inhabitants may
enjoy a Life of the greatest Ease and Satisfaction, and pass away their
Hours in solid Contentment,"[5] in the summer of 1804 the newly wedded couple of Temperance and Richard Thomas had moved from the
relatively urban state of Virginia to the untamed North Carolina outback. With Temperance already several months pregnant, the couple
planned to carve out a prosperous future for their new family in the
seemingly idyllic land. However, rather than finding a utopia populated by 1709 adventurer John Lawson's[6] advertised "Darlings of an
English Nature,"[7] the couple settled into a stark landscape replete
with wilderness hazards and the inherent cruelties of frontier society.

The "savage and less than civilized" region* was populated by
frontiersmen, rogues, and native tribes. Far from the advertised land of
leisure, the countryside was bereft of such basic amenities as a regional
post office (by comparable standards, the State of Virginia already held
a fully functional and expansive postal service) and a network of commercially navigable roads.[8] Stripped of ready communication to the
outside world, the expectant couple was deprived of reliable support
from close and caring family members for the preparation for the
birthing and raising of their new child. The spartan life grew vastly
more difficult for the wife when Richard Thomas died in a wilderness
accident shortly before the birth of their son.[9] Apart from a few of
Richard's friends and shared relatives, Temperance and her newborn
son, William Holland,† were left to their own devices in the wilderness.

Contrary to the appealing images promulgated by both intrepid

---

* By European standards.
† William Holland Thomas was likely named after Temperance's father (first
name) and her mother (middle name), respectively.[10]

adventurers and the state's resident aristocracy (clustered along the coastline), North Carolina's largely uneducated populace, undeveloped infrastructure, and underutilized land gave reason to label the region "the poorest state in the union."[11] The seemingly luckless territory held an abundance of inland resources that, under other circumstances, would have attracted several lucrative investors,[12] but since there were negligible means of reaching the exploitable areas by water (few of the state's numerous waterways could accommodate the larger vessels that would make the site commercially feasible) or by roadway (many of the state's roadways had been supplied to service either military needs or already-established short-distance civilian commerce between cities, towns, and states). Even the region's most highly prized commodity, the sticky, smelly sealant tar (made possible by the abundance of pine trees), barely managed to maintain the interest of visiting high volume traders.

As limited outside interest in the colony's resources had stagnated the growth of North Carolina's economy, first by the British and later by the region's victorious colonial gentry[13] whose sole focus was on short-term gains, instead of investing deeply in the meager profits of early western expansionism, generations of wealthy businessmen and overseas capitalists relegated their meager liquid capital towards the greater potential returns of an expanded coastal port and refinery production facilities. Deprived of attention and the defense of a watchful militia guard, the area's native Cherokee tribes and a lawless collection of frontier farmers, hunters, and traders called the Over-Mountain Men retained dominion over Western North Carolina, the then-poorest region of the poorest American state.

With the conclusion of the American Revolution, control over the backcountry began to gravitate eastward. Realizing the large taxable income an immigrant populace could bring to their state coffers and affiliated businesses, the now independent state's victorious coastal Patriot leadership was eager to change the Tories' indifference and neglect of the western region into profitability for the state. Where their former British overlords had failed to secure permanent settlement with survey reports and published travelogues, the southern elite succeeded, enticing adventurous masses to make the Tar Heel State their new home with incentive offers of inexpensive and occasionally free land grants. Facing pricier land in the more developed coastal territories,[14] within a few short years, Scotch Highlanders and Lowlanders, French, Huguenot, and German immigrants joined a steady stream of poor and middle class men and women like Richard and Temperance Thomas from neighboring American colonies in taming the wilderness lands in the shadows of the Appalachian Mountains.[15]

Although the record is unclear as to the motivations or circumstances of his crossing,* the future father of William Thomas had immigrated to the American colonies prior to the onset of the American Revolution. When the war came, young Richard enlisted in the Continental Army for a standard three-year term at Culpeper County, Virginia.[17] Although many details of his years of service remain a mystery, the Welsh-born Thomas was assigned to the riflemen of the Eleventh Virginia Regiment.[18]

The Eleventh Virginia Regiment (formed shortly after the fall of New York in September 1776) was assigned to the Continental Army on December 27th, 1776. The contingent consisted of five companies containing remnants of the Maryland and Virginia Rifle Regiment, four other companies mustered from Amelia, Loudon, Prince William, and Frederick counties, respectively, and Colonel Daniel Morgan's renowned Independent Rifle Company.[19] While briefly held under the command of the proven and now legendary guerrilla war–fighting tactician Colonel Daniel Morgan,[20] the man left his mark of swift and steady combat effectiveness on the regiment throughout its many reorganizations and redesignations.†[21]

---

* According to E. Stanley Godbold Jr. and Mattie Russell, Richard Thomas was born during the mid-1700s in the English town of Dover.[16]

† One of Colonel Morgan's favorite tactics involved the employment of a line of riflemen to winnow British lines at long range. As they closed, the colonel would then order his snipers to fall behind the ranks of the pike-and-bayonet-bearing infantry, who could then provide covering fire for the detachment's escape or charge the advancing British line and engage the enemy in hand-to-hand combat.

During his service to the Patriot cause, Richard Thomas was taken prisoner on August 1ˢᵗ, 1776, in an unspecified action, and he remained in British captivity until September 1ˢᵗ, 1777.[22] Whether the colonial escaped or was released by his captors is ambiguous, but records clearly indicated that, rather than remain on the sidelines for the remainder of the conflict, Richard Thomas rejoined the Eleventh Virginia (reconstituted and restructured several times since his first enlistment) and took part in their march against British-contested North Carolina and the region's rising tide of Tory dissidence.[23]

With the betrayal of General Benedict Arnold at West Point in September of 1780, many in the occupied sector of the northern and southern regions began losing hope that the colonials might ever achieve a decisive victory against their British occupiers. Instigated by the propagandist machinations of British major Patrick Ferguson,[24] North and South Carolina's Tory militia ranks swelled with new recruits.

Conversely, as the month progressed, the long anticipated "sudden disintegration" of the warring rebel forces before the might of the British Empire seemed less and less imminent among the upper echelon of the occupying red-clad army. Consequently, as progress in the war's prosecution slowed, the well-respected Major Ferguson's southern duties became of greater necessity to the war effort. In discharging his duties with characteristic zeal, however, the British officer had in due course provoked the ire of regional colonial forces and neutral disinterested residents alike by threatening the region's Over-Mountain Men (who had previously chosen to remain neutral during the War of Independence) "that if they did not desist from their opposition to the British arms, and take protection under his standard, he would march his army over the mountains, hang their leaders and lay their country waste with fire and sword."[25]

Thus, when their Virginian colonial brethren marched into the region, the two forces linked up and swiftly moved across the rain-soaked countryside to neutralize Ferguson's faction. Acting in consonance, they trapped the enemy at North Carolina's Kings Mountain, and, under Colonel William Campbell's direction, Richard Thomas and his companions surrounded the mountain.

There they waited.

At approximately three o'clock on October 7th, 1780, the combined might of the Continentals and the Over-Mountain Men was then brought to bear against the ill-prepared mixed British and Tory force exposed at the mountain's top. The enemy was forced to endure a withering hail of fire from all quarters as the rebels and mountain men ascended the mountainside time and again in an ever tightening ring. A few of the besieging units were briefly rebuffed by enemy bayonets, but, after several minutes of sustained fire, the British-Tory lines buckled, fell back, and, minutes later, Major Ferguson, outmaneuvered and outgunned, was shot from his horse and died in an apparent escape attempt.

Ignoring cries of surrender from the decapitated enemy force, the colonials and Over-Mountain Men, mindful of the "mercy" the British had shown surrendering Continental forces at the Waxhaws, reportedly offered a group of survivors "Tarleton's Quarter" and laid waste to the enemy's ranks.[26] Colonel Campbell's Virginians suffered the most severe Patriot loss of the engagement (thirteen reported officers killed or dying), but the total of ninety killed or wounded Patriots had been deemed well worth the elimination of Major Patrick Ferguson's complement of 1,125 men from the theater of operations.[27] On May 12th, 1780 the Eleventh Virginia Regiment was captured by the British Army at Charleston, South Carolina, and the contingent was officially disbanded on January 1st, 1781.[28]

After the war, Richard Thomas returned to Virginia, where he engaged in business[29] and fell in love with a lady twenty-five years his junior, Temperance Colvert, and on May 6th, 1804, the two were married in Richmond. With few prospects in the increasingly economically demanding state of postwar Virginia, Richard and a now pregnant Temperance accepted North Carolina's veteran-aimed land grant reward (offered in the postwar years to those who had defended North Carolina during the War of Independence),[30] and traveling with fellow veterans and cousins John and George Strothers, the couple crossed the Blue Ridge Mountains into Western North Carolina within the year.

The couple settled on a 228-acre plot near Raccoon Creek,[31] where they lived in relative peace in the shadows of the Smoky Mountains until Richard's untimely death.

As with much of the history concerning William Thomas's parentage, there are conflicting accounts as to how the family patriarch met his end. One story relates that the man drowned in a flash flood, which had suddenly engulfed the Big Pigeon River he and one of his cousins had been crossing, while a second story reports that he drowned somewhere in the northern region of Georgia in the conduct of some business.[32] A third family story just claimed Richard Thomas was trying to return to Virginia when he drowned.[33] Regardless of the location, Richard Thomas's demise left his pregnant wife an empty grave (as her husband's body had never been recovered), an inherited farm to run, and an expectant child to birth and (should the two survive the ordeal) clothe, feed, and educate.

Removed from the comforts of her family's Virginia home, Temperance Thomas raised young William in the remote mountain landscape of the Upper Piedmont. Richard had chosen a good home for his family, and granted clean mountain air and water, the two led healthier early lives than most city families. Above the stagnant insect-ridden waters of the Lower Piedmont, but below the area's mountainous primary snow belt, the Thomas family farm held protection from the more severe weather patterns. By North Carolina standards, the soil was modestly arable and well situated to produce an even annual yield capable of supporting the small family throughout the year and, if fortunate, a modest surplus for bartering or storage.

Beyond each settler's day-to-day concerns remained the persistent fear of the unknown and concerns for the security of oneself, one's family, and one's property. While mother and son could always flee to the safety of the Strothers brothers or Temperance's brother-in-law, David Nelson (living on nearby Jonathan's Creek), in case of unforeseen trouble, the distances involved and the intervening physical obstacles that needed to be crossed made such an eventuality only a remote possibility.

While a number of dangerous two- and four-legged animals continued to roam the Appalachian Mountains as William Thomas learned to crawl and walk, luckily for the widowed mother and her son, the hopes of North Carolina's coastal leaders were slowly becoming reality[34] with the rise of settlements throughout the state's interior, and "persons of the meaner Sort"[35] who had long inhabited the region were diminishing in the face of the nation's expanding frontier. Hoping to discourage a reoccurrence, many of Western North Carolina's newest neighbors assisted in the formation of several tracts of land into allotments such as Mount Prospect County (which would later be reshaped and renamed into Haywood County[36] and, later still, become the county seat of Waynesville[37]). Given defined boundaries, the leaders then elected to fill essential bureaucratic administrative posts with a sheriff, court clerk, county constable, coroner, and register of deeds.[38] These civil servants then, in turn, fostered the promulgation of documentation as dictated by the local elite (largely in the form of business contracts, marriage certificates, land deeds, and treaty documents) and, consequently, spurred the erection of such needed public facilities as jails and courthouses in order to encourage the frontiersmen to either settle down and grow educated in the ways of civility or remove themselves to parts less traveled.

William took up tending to his mother's home and farm property at an early age, but beyond the potential of a farming life, there seemed little prospect for betterment in the young boy's future.[39] For most children of Western North Carolina families, formal education and social refinement were considered unattainable concepts. Indeed, to compensate for their deficit in funds, books, schools, and formal teachers, period parents and associate workers followed the old practice of apprenticeship, allowing children in just a few years to learn a trade that would provide future fiscal stability for themselves and, at the same time, grant the community the continuance of much-needed services after the master had retired or died.

Temperance taught the small blue-eyed boy the foundation of his education in reading, writing, arithmetic, and the rites of his Christian heritage. While Thomas remained a poor speller and an occasionally illegible writer for the extent of his life, William's mother soon discovered the young boy was a quick study with a particular affinity for numbers and complex equations. Whereas most rural boys were apprenticed to carpenters, tailors, weavers, or blacksmiths or served as tenant farmers with their families, somehow young William remained apart from the county seat's clannish craftsmen. His own chance of escaping the hand-to-mouth existence of an Appalachian farmer would lie in William's own talents, helped by some generosity and a bit of luck.

Encouraged by the boy's mathematical abilities, as young William approached adolescence, Temperance Thomas honed her son's skills into marketable assets that eventually attracted the attention of one of the region's more successful store owners, Felix Hampton Walker Jr., whom William Holland Thomas would watch, listen to, and learn from, possibly to grow into a man of similar accomplishment.

CHAPTER TWO

THE MOUNTAIN STORES

In 1818, at the age of twelve, William Holland Thomas signed himself over to the influential Felix Hampton Walker Jr., of Haywood County. In exchange for three years of daily service at the businessman's Soco Creek trading post, the young man was promised a supply of clothes, sleeping space in the small wooden riverside store, and a hundred dollars to be collected upon the completion of his contract.[40]

This agreement seemed an amiable exchange of goods and services in a period when indentured servitude, tenant farming, and slavery were fairly commonplace. Temperance Thomas likely saw more potential in the man to whom she had allowed her son to be apprenticed than the meritorious points of the contract both parties had signed or the illusory emotional benefits of a quasi father figure. On the surface, Felix Hampton Walker Jr. was an accomplished merchant from whom the young William Thomas would surely have learned a great deal about minding a frontier store, trading goods, keeping inventory, and other assorted shop-tending duties, but the respected businessman also held a close affiliation with an extraordinary local figure, Felix Walker *Sr.*

While Walker Junior was an achiever of local renown, his accomplishments realistically paled in comparison with his own father's veteran acts. In his younger days, Felix Walker Sr. had served as a traveling companion to the legendary explorer Daniel Boone[41] and, during the American Revolutionary War, had stood post with a token colonial force on the Carolina frontier as a deterrent to potential British-organized Native American raiders. Shortly after the war, Felix Walker Sr. had risen to prominence as a local political leader, and, by the time Thomas entered the Walker family's service, the aging man had capped his civil service career with an election to the United States Congress.

In those early decades of the nineteenth century, William Thomas's opportunities for social advancement seemed nearly limitless. While Felix Hampton Walker Jr. had yet to achieve the heights his father had attained, the Thomas family probably saw the telltale signs of the businessman's seemingly inevitable ascension behind "Old Oil Jug" Walker's own success.[42] Observing the success of the father and the rising status of his apparent protégé son, the backcountry family would have easily deduced that such a relationship could only help the boy and his mother. As a result, young William's granted service apparently also implied the promise of a marketable position of prominence, influence, status, and, if taken under the wing of Walker, an exploitable series of contacts and upwardly mobile relationships.

When William Thomas moved into the Soco Creek store, it seemed neither mother nor son could have asked for a more promising opportunity, . . . but the position was also far from easy. Though a far cry from the elegant shops of North Carolina's sprawling coastal port cities, Walker's Soco Creek store functioned on two regionally equally important levels. First, the outpost served as the frontline of the landowner's frontier trading operations through which raw goods might be funneled to other business outlets (for greater profits) in exchange for daily fare and token finery shipped from the coastal facilities. In doing so, the mountain store became an essential hub for regional news and sundries and a provider of morsels from the city centers many regional settlers had exchanged for the mountain frontier. Located on the southern bank of Soco Creek (a small body of water referred to as Sagwa'hi [One Place] by native Cherokee and which feeds into the southwestern Oconaluftee River),[43] the store furnished imported goods from the coastline and northern states and bartered for comparably valued goods. With few other consumer choices available to the Haywood County community, the store probably also provided its daily clientele with surplus perishable farm goods, such as apples, assorted vegetables, rye, oats, and honey.[44]

When William Thomas began manning the store, he realized Soco Creek's importance in servicing Haywood County's diverse clientele and exotic suppliers who stretched from the eastern coastline to the wilderness homes of the neighboring Appalachian and Blue Ridge Mountains. In earning a steady income from residential purchases and refined goods (brought from the coast in exchange for the raw supplies his clientele offered as currency), William Thomas was often tasked to mind the Soco Creek facility while Felix Hampton Walker Jr. traveled in search of greater wealth, leisure, and luxury and more genteel means of obtaining status. Often unsupervised for lengthy periods, Thomas managed the Soco Creek store's daily operations, handled local transactions, and even bargained for exotic flora and fauna and other lucrative commodities. As Walker's absences increased, William Thomas's responsibilities grew to the point where the young man was essentially running Walker's satellite store's entire business.

Although it was by no means an idea original to either Western

North Carolina or Walker Junior, the merchant venue also took advantage of the previously unanswered need many local families had for a supplemental income from the vast untapped resources of a pristine wilderness. Whereas large farms and plantations had already begun to yield sizable profits in other regions of North Carolina and across other southern states, the westward rocky woodland terrain inherently limited agricultural development to a smattering of small farms and a few fixed strips of level, cleared, and arable land. In keeping with a few of the regional traditions of the fading Over-Mountain Men and Native Americans of the receding Cherokee Nation,[45] many locals and adventurers alike often carried hunting kits up the Smoky Mountains' ancient footpaths and across the wilderness trails of the largely untamed territories of Tennessee and Georgia in search of sustenance and enterprise. Once the survival-pressed hunter had traveled a sufficient distance, he (or, sometimes, she) would then seek out his (or her) potential prey (often in pursuit of such indigenous fauna as deer, Canadian lynx, woodchucks, elk, opossums, and beavers),[46] down the game, and return home with the kill's prized meat and pelts.

When the hunters were successful in their venture and/or lucky enough to find rarer mountain-growing commodities (such as apples, peaches, and grapes, which thrived in the mountains' temperate or "brushy" range),[47] shopkeepers like Thomas often offered the hunters a decent price for their bounty.

While the hunting of an elk, deer, or several small red foxes might stave off hunger or supplement the income of a mountain or valley family for a considerable period of time, the traders and "Mountaineers of the South"[48] with whom William Thomas most often dealt were consummate experts in their game. The Cherokee natives and the backwoodsmen who inhabited the mountain area had been hunting not single animals but entire herds at a time for generations. In the 1700s one traveler explained: "[W]hen these savages go a hunting they commonly go out in great numbers and often times a great many Day's Journey from home, beginning at the coming of the Winter; . . . 'Tis then they burn the Woods, by setting Fire to the Leaves and wither'd Bent and Grass . . . . drive the Deer and other Game into small Necks of Land and Isthmis's where they kill and destroy what they please . . ."[49] (methods of stalking that Thomas would remember and draw upon to greater advantage later in life with far more "civilized" prey).

After the long hunt, the native parties of tribal men, women, and children separated the skins or furs from the edible meat and packed them away as storage to see their community through the coming winter weather when foraging and game would be scarce. With the coming of the Europeans, however, the natives began gravitating towards the new settlements on the periphery of their ancient hunting grounds, and before long the indigenous populace saw the Europeans' demand for their easily obtained wares and quickly converted their surplus with the neighboring populace's available supply of novel luxuries (largely rum).[50] With the expansion of European trading companies into the region and independently sponsored residential ventures after the American Revolutionary War, the Cherokee and several smaller regional tribes rapidly became a reliable source of inland-lying game and resources.

While neither supplier nor business owner grew wealthy through such commercial venues, Felix Hampton Walker Jr.'s enterprise was relatively prosperous. With the proximity of several vital water sources near Waynesville as well as the well-trafficked Appalachian Trail (along the modern North Carolina–Tennessee border), the Indian Gap Trail (near the turbulent Little Pigeon River), and the Soco Gap (found a few miles north of the store at the head of Soco Creek), traffic through the Soco Creek area must have been quite considerable.

Among the many goods William Thomas cataloged, inventoried, and sold, few were more sought after than the region's naturally growing medicinal herbs and roots.[51] Whereas many locals supplied an adequate amount of Smoky Mountain game, few settlers were schooled in the difference between much sought after exotic plant life and common floral underbrush, and fewer could pull it from the ground, and fewer still could, without damaging the find, transport the greenery overland for sale at a marketable price (as with most modern produce, the greener the item the longer the shelf life).

Utilizing the healing/curative properties of local flora and fauna for centuries, the Cherokee people inhabiting the Smoky Mountain region rapidly grew into the roles of herbal providers and medicinal guides for settlers and traders. While certain types of plant life, such as ginseng (purported by some to extend life and talked about by others as having a special tranquilizing property of making an ingestor's most irritable of wives tolerable),[52] were valued as highly as ten cents a pound along the coastline and in overseas markets,[53] the Cherokee taught their new neighbors some of the more practical uses for the local plant life, including the use of Red-Root (similar to Spearmint) for sore mouths,[54] ginger tea with red pepper poultice for sore throats,[55] peppermint for cholic,[56] and Dog-Wood for use as a makeshift antiseptic.[57] Their herbalist knowledge was so widely sought after that, by the time of the Civil War, many of the group's backwoods treatments and cures were marketed in bound wilderness survival guides.[58]

Regardless of the profits and stored sundries, life for the young mountain merchant must have been starkly different from that at his mother's warm home and farm. His employer came and went with little warning. His suppliers, ranging from the few remaining Over-Mountain Men, to Native Americans, to coastal associates of Walker, lived a perpetually transitory existence and his customers were equally unpredictable, making life at the Soco Creek store alternatingly solitary and tempestuous. Still, the teenager showed patience and understanding beyond his years, weathering the day-to-day store running with little recorded trouble.

Prior to the completion of his contract, Thomas received a minor reprieve from the often solitary existence of frontier business in the form of a supplemental worker, a young Cherokee male. The Cherokee (likely from the nearby Indiantown settlement) became fast friends with the similarly aged settler's child,[59] and with the assistance of his newfound companion William Thomas learned the language and dialect of the local Cherokee in both spoken and written form. In time, he also learned many of the tribe's customs, legends, and histories, including tales of the world's creation,[60] their origins in the lands of the rising sun,[61] the mystical creatures which stalked through the bald patches of the nearby Smoky Mountains (referred to as Shaconage or the "Mountains of the Blue Smoke" by the Cherokee),[62] the different histories of the animals who were once men,[63] the coming of Hernando de Soto's Spanish Expedition,[64] and the ambush the Cherokee had enacted long ago against invading Shawano at the nearby Soco Gap (known by local natives as Ahalunun'yi or Ambush Place).[65] The sharing between the two had been so extensive that, by the end of his three year contract, young William Thomas had learned more about his surroundings, the trading business, and the region's inhabitants than most other settlers in the region knew.

Despite his native education and diligence to his shop duties, William Thomas had little of substance to show for his three years of dedicated daily and nightly service. Still, the young man had made himself a productive member of the community and a key player in his superior's business enterprise, and, in light of his demonstrated skill and competence, Thomas reasonably expected to have his contract renewed with expanded duties and entitlements as he neared its completion.

Instead, in 1821 Felix Hampton Walker Jr. approached the boy with a substantial problem. While the businessman had been pursuing his father's course of studying law in hopes of a second, more upwardly mobile, career, Walker had invariably let his company's bookkeeping fall by the wayside. Before the elder businessman could right himself, Thomas's employer was mired in debt, and with creditors already hounding the congressman's son for returns on their substantial investments, Felix Hampton Walker Jr. was unable to pay William Thomas his contractually obligated $100. The second blow came when Walker informed Thomas that the Soco Creek store was going to be closed and liquidated. Furthermore, the anxious businessman revealed that he was speedily entertaining future business ventures in regions other than North Carolina.[66]

As a result of Walker Junior's fiscal irresponsibility and subsequent flight out of state, William Holland Thomas was broke, unemployed, past the prime age of apprenticeship, unqualified for most other forms of work, and bereft of the influence the Walker family might have otherwise brought for himself and his mother. With nowhere else to turn, the young man left the Soco Creek store and returned to his mother's home on Raccoon Creek.

Temperance Thomas welcomed her unlucky son home with open arms. While the news of the betrayal was, indeed, a sour and devastating blow to both mother and son, young William's store experience actually offered the family a means of escape from their shared bleak future. One day, shortly after William's sullen return, Temperance presented her son with the means to make it happen. Guided by the faith of a mother in the untapped potential of her progeny, Temperance had disposed of some farmland property she had acquired and applied the modest sum to her son's first business venture (and likely last chance of escaping the mundanity of farm life[67]). Within a year, the mother watched her sixteen-year-old William open his own store amidst his most popular Soco Creek suppliers, the pure-blooded Native American Cherokee of Indiantown (within the confines of the modern day Qualla Boundary).

Punished as a collective for their aggressive actions by North Carolina settlers (led by American Revolutionary colonel John Sevier and his neighbors), many of the Cherokee Nation beat a grudging retreat beyond the mountains into the Georgian and Tennessee territories, but a few among the Nation chose to remain on the other side of the mountain. Minor fractures, which had long existed within the collective, were rapidly brought to the forefront of tribal politics.[68] When the matters were not acceptably addressed, several pure-blooded members of the Cherokee Nations, including Subchief Euchella and Chief Yonaguska, chose to remove themselves from their colleagues and follow a path they felt would ensure the survival of their ancient beliefs and traditions before the advance of the region's new settlers. In a rather short amount of time, they engineered private agreements with members of the newly formed United States of America, sold the land upon which they had settled, formally severed ties with leadership of the Cherokee Nation, and, taking up new tracts of their ancient tribal land around Indiantown (later named Qualla Town), began to assimilate with the settler's western society.

The little doubt which may have surrounded the young Caucasian man's presence among the Cherokee seemed to evaporate as William Holland Thomas demonstrated his cultural sensitivity and his acquired mercantile skills learned on Soco Creek. He was courteous, respectful, and trusting of his new neighbors, and the young man's command of Cherokee language won more than just acceptance and a fiscally prosperous trading relationship with the natives. It literally opened a door the Thomases likely thought had closed with Walker Jr.'s economic failure.

Chief Yonaguska (known by some as Drowning Bear),[69] the leader of the self-exiled tribe,[70] had been watching William Thomas for some time, and had heard others speak well of the short, blue-eyed Caucasian and, may have even engaged in some minor business with the unknowing Thomas during his tenure minding Walker Jr.'s Soco Creek store.[71] In assimilating much of the native Cherokee culture in the past handful of years and treating the Chief's Cherokee with a respect and deference their own tribal brothers had not cared to offer, Chief Yonaguska saw the young man as not only a friend to the tribe but also a symbol of their ideological difference from their divorced brethren and one who, perhaps, presented tangible examples of the future the Chief wished to create for his faithful Cherokee brothers and sisters.

Through his observations Chief Yonaguska saw something within the backwoods merchant that his brethren could appreciably utilize. Knowing about the early loss of Richard Thomas, Chief Yonaguska (apparently unbeknownst to the young man) campaigned long and hard among the subchiefs and headmen of his tribe for William

Thomas's adoption into the tribe.[72] When a consensus was reached, as Thomas was fatherless, the tribe next proclaimed the young man an orphan under Cherokee law. Speaking for the Eastern Band, Chief Yonaguska then granted the young man sanctuary as part of his family (the Chief's family enveloped the several thousand Eastern Band members under his protection).[73] At the close of the proceedings, Chief Yonaguska bestowed upon the absent William Thomas his new name to be spoken among his Cherokee followers, "*Wil-Usdi* (meaning Little Will)."[74] After the proceedings, Thomas was notified of his candidacy, sponsor, and acceptance into the tribe.

Although he had not sought inclusion with the Cherokee, William Thomas understood the realities of tribal politics, the ramifications of the secrecy surrounding the entire process, and, above all, the honor which Chief Yonaguska bestowed upon him. He came to see the Cherokee Chief as an honorable man, a replacement father figure, a contemporary, and in viewing the unexplored path upon which Yonaguska's tribe had embarked, a leader of a noble cause worthy of any assistance he could provide.

As the months passed, time and again William Thomas's continued mercantile successes were further reassurance that he had made the proper choice in placing his first store (with expanded goods and services beyond those of the old Soco Creek trading post) in Indiantown. Before long, five more stores scattered about the North Carolina outback would follow his Indiantown success made possible largely by Cherokee hands.

CHAPTER THREE

SON, BROTHER, AND AGENT

As the young merchant was preparing to open his Indiantown store, in 1821 William Holland Thomas received a most unexpected letter from his former employer, Felix Hampton Walker Jr., dated May 31, 1821, and postmarked "Hinds County, Mississippi." It seems the fugitive had apparently successfully traveled far and fast from his creditors.

Thomas had not heard a word from the disgraced businessman since the abrupt termination of William's work contract without compensation several months earlier and his subsequent flight for parts less traveled. With literacy viewed as a convenience (compared to the regionally necessary skills of farming and hunting), formal correspondence to Western North Carolina was sporadic and costly.

In the letter, Felix Hampton Walker Jr. related to William Thomas that his losses did not end with the demise of his business enterprise. Rather than share in their relative's disgrace, the majority of Walker's own family distanced themselves from the failed business owner and his self-made fiscal crisis.[75] When Walker was next forced to choose between flight and prison, his getaway dually alienated the friends he had made and encouraged his famous family (likely fearing *they* might become targets for hungry creditors) to abandon Walker to his own devices. In the end, Walker was left without money, influence, and a family willing to listen to his pleas.[76]

"Nothing but a bad course of conduct on your part," Walker Junior assured the young William, "will cit [cut] asunder those ties of friendship that seems to have commenicled [commenced] with your childhood and have been growing stronger and stronger Ever since."[77]

Isolated from his family and hounded by business associates, Felix Hampton Walker Jr. finally turned to *his* former protégé for commiseration and support. Yet, Felix Hampton Walker's words also conveyed something more than a fugitive's search for friends. The document clearly conveyed, implied between the carefully crafted words of a legal student, that the failed businessman was also the bearer of a guilty conscience. The man was seeking the forgiveness of the boy he had inadvertently wronged and then abandoned with due haste.

"Your honesty of heart and sprightly genius will ever endear you to me," Walker continued. "I have often wished that you could have come with me[,] but since my arrival here have thought that perhaps it is well or better for you to stay with your mother a few year[s] longer, although that is a bad country for Education[.] [H]owever[,] you need not take up the bad habits of the vulgar class of Mankind. . . . It is my wish for you to come and Study the law or any thing that will be best adapted to your talents . . ."

While Felix Hampton Walker Jr.'s foibles, familial inadequacies, and business failures were not uncommon for the period, his misfortune had also afforded his former employee certain benefits to be embraced. Although William Thomas never rekindled his business association with his former employer, the man's abject failure had not only allowed Thomas the impetus to open his own store but also engendered a sustaining compensatory gift in lieu of the debt Walker carried with his former employee. In his expression of guilt over abandoning the boy, Walker had begged his former employee to accept possession of his small law library (several volumes of legal text in size).[78]

While other more wealthy families of the period afforded their sons (such as Felix Hampton Walker Jr.) legal materials with which they might study or affiliations with a practicing lawyer who might take a promising child under his wing, the meager Thomas family was neither wealthy nor part of a booming populace that demanded a surplus of courtroom counselors. The timely receipt of Walker's legal volumes granted William Thomas a boon as great as the Raccoon Creek land grant offered his father.

The books were readily accepted.

As a resident of Haywood County's seat of Waynesville, William Thomas had been exposed to the region's judicial proceedings (a common form of backcountry entertainment), but in living among the Upper Piedmont and Mountain regions of North Carolina he had almost unilaterally removed the prospect of a formal legal education or a future arguing points of legal order before a courtroom audience. While William Thomas had little hope of becoming a practicing lawyer, Walker's legal volumes offered the young shop owner and his mother insurance of the potential of achieving a respectable professional practice that would both service their region's legal needs and supplement the family's store income against competitors, insufficient stock, and harsh weather.

While the unexpected gift had indeed been timely, William Thomas was just one among a number of other young men turning to the law as a means of escaping the agrarian life of their parents and neighbors.[79] By the 1820s alone, there was such an excess of self-charged legal professionals in North Carolina that one long-practicing lawyer critically wrote: "The profession of Law is becoming daily fashionable. It is the denier resort in this state of every S–O–B, who fails in every other attempt at subsistence."[80]

As North Carolina's backcountry populace continued to grow with the arrival of new settlers, the attraction of a legal practice, which, only a generation prior, inspired America's founding fathers on their revolutionary course, began to dim in the eyes of many elder North Carolina residents who had once placed their learned country lawyers and local judiciary in the highest esteem. When the area's populace rose to a sustainable communal level, a sector of residents (previously relegated to the pursuit of game or farmable produce) was relatively free to pursue their own interests. A number of locals did turn their extra time to increasing their family farm's yields, but others, much to the dismay of their elders, took advantage of the "revolutionary" legal and political freedoms their parents had won from the British Empire and her civil services.

While a number of North Carolina's more socially conscious residents winced when they passed their appointed judiciary members as these professionals drove their own wagons home to plow their own fields,[81] young men like William Holland Thomas were free to try their hand at the formerly aristocratic profession without regard for the social caveats or imperial prerequisites of prior generations.

Yet, the young businessman seemed to realize his own limits.

Rather than attempting to apprentice himself with a practice or vie for a court case that might bring him precedent-making (or -breaking) fame, Thomas bypassed the weaker aspects of his home-schooling for a legal course of self-education and practice that would suit his more systematic thinking. Instead of studying to pass the local court's licensing requirements like most of his legal-minded contemporaries[82] (the establishment of a Bar Examination for Attorneys was still many years away) or attempt to apprentice himself as a clerk, the young man applied his studied knowledge to the application of legal contracts and filed claims.

After a brief period of self-study, the young man began to actively assimilate the form, syntax, function, and structure of the legal profession. Within a matter of months, his self-learned knowledge was applied to contracts and depositions being entered as legally binding documentation, and shortly thereafter his skills were brought to bear in regional land speculation and the filing of personal claims against individuals, businesses, and government entities. Eventually, traveling throughout the region in the representation of neighbors' interests over various legal disputes, the young man proved himself to be a valuable member of the Western North Carolina community, with many appreciative friends.

While the bestowed legal library proved to be of far greater economic worth to William Thomas than Walker's contractually promised hundred dollars, the bound set's usefulness did not end with the completion of Thomas's studies or his personal business pursuits. It also allowed him entree to the leadership of the Eastern Band of North Carolina Cherokee.

While William Thomas had pursued his course of self-taught legal studies and service to the surrounding community's legal needs, Chief Yonaguska of the Eastern Band continued to watch his now adopted son with great interest. Although illiterate, the aging chief knew the value of the written English word and had embraced its binding power as few Native Americans had before him. The leader of the Eastern Band had experienced firsthand the consequences of unhonored pledges and treaty vagaries exploited time and again by signatories for ephemeral political gains.

Chief Yonaguska had been born during the intervening years between the French and Indian War and the American Revolution. As a young boy, he had fled with his Cherokee tribe when settlers, seeking unchecked expansion and tacit security, launched a preemptive attack on the mountain regions in 1780. Led by American Revolutionary North Carolina settler John Sevier, a Patriot column marched into Cherokee territory and laid waste to nearly forty Native American settlements. At the conclusion of the campaign, Yonaguska's people received the following note:

> Chiefs and Warriors—
>   We came into your country to fight your young men, we have killed not a few of them, and destroyed your Towns. . . . We are now satisfied with what is done, and may convince your nation that we can distress them much at any time they are so foolish to engage in a war against us.
>   If you desire peace, as we have understood you do, we, out of pity, to your women and children, are disposed to treat with you on that subject, and take you into friendship once more. . . .
>   If we receive no answer to this message until the time . . . expires, we shall conclude you intend to continue to be our enemies, which will compel us to send another Strong force into your Country, who will come prepared to stay a long time, and take possession though as conquered by us, without making any distribution to you for lands.[83]

Ill-equipped to effectively counter the threat, the then-youthful Yonaguska witnessed his demoralized superiors capitulating to the insurgents' demands and watched firsthand the almost inevitable decline of the Cherokee Nation as they abandoned much of North Carolina to the region's increasing number of settlers. As time passed, the young Native American grew increasingly mindful in observing, listening to, and understanding the relationship between his superiors *and* the settlers. Yet, as a follower of the Cherokee Nation, he could do little to change the destructive path he saw his brethren pursuing. When Yonaguska eventually became the Chief of his people, however, the young man surprised his contemporaries with his brashness.

The Cherokee leader understood the methods of his tribe's adversaries (both among the settlers and within his own Cherokee Nation). Chief Yonaguska well understood the binding power of the written word and the disadvanges his brothers fostered in proposing vague terms to state and federal entities, thinking they could attain a better deal with each succeeding reevaluation. Having watched the borders of the Cherokee Nation steadily recede with each passing year (metaphorically as well as literally), Chief Yonaguska knew it was only a matter of time before the settlers would surround the Cherokee, grow weary of their games, and use the newly founded United States legislative and judicial system to bring about a final resolution to their sitiuation, one that would be dictated by the United States' desires alone.

FUELED BY PERSONAL ILL FEELINGS towards the rising tide of youthful leadership of the Cherokee Nation (primarily John Ross) and sensing the approaching storm of western encroachment, in 1821 Chief Yonaguska withdrew from the autonomous body of Native Americans and, followed by fifty other Cherokee families, sowed his fate with the newcomers.[84]

Instead of following a few Cherokee Nationals volunteering to make a peaceful settlement across the mountains in Tennessee, Georgia, or Arkansas, the seceded Cherokee of Chief Yonaguska invoked a minor proviso in an 1819 treaty agreement to first gain exclusive legally binding use of a government-sanctioned stretch of North Carolina land between the Oconaluftee and Tuckasegee Rivers as their new reservation.[85] A few years later, Chief Yonaguska sold the reservation for $1,300 and reinvested the money in another allotment of property deep within the century-old colonized area of Western North Carolina, later called Indiantown (note: In keeping pace with their movements, the seceded Cherokee also went by several succeeding names, including the Oconaluftee Indians or Lufty Indians, the Eastern Band, and the Qualla Indians).[86]

Chief Yonaguska's actions rankled many of his former brethren within the Nation, but the personal opinions of his former peers mattered little before the profitability and the now established legal precedent of their land occupation/ownership. As the seceded Chief and his followers had gambled, the American legislative and judicial systems indeed worked in the interest of the accepting Cherokee.

The rogue leader realized, however, that the moves meant little if they could not be intelligently argued by legal representation favorable to the new Eastern Band of North Carolina Cherokee.

While the Eastern Band remained a vital part of the region's trading system, Chief Yonaguska knew the group of several thousand largely uneducated Cherokee could not realistically defeat an organized aggressor like Sevier or, should the state try to renege on their agreement, represent themselves against a politically savvy American leadership and their legal representation. Reluctantly, the Eastern Band's leadership conceded they would need to employ an American professional as a safeguard against falling into the disorder of their brethren in the Cherokee Nation. Recent experience of other Cherokee tribes had proven there was cause for caution. While President George Washington's Indian Affairs Advisor and first Cherokee Agent, Benjamin Hawkins, had obtained initially favorable compensation on the Cherokee Nation's behalf during the drawing of the 1785 Treaty of Hopewell (in the form of tools, land, and societal infrastructure for those who would take them), several subsequent Cherokee agents and administrators were less interested in improving the lives of Native Americans and more interested in serving the second generation Patriot cause[87] in "enrolling [Cherokee] immigrants pretty fast and great exertions are making for their departure"[88] to distant westward locales.[89]

In 1829, as a deterrent to their enemies and affiliates on both sides of the Appalachian Mountains, Chief Yonaguska and his councilors contracted John L. Dillard as their legal counsel and first Cherokee Agent of the Eastern Band.[90] While the period of time for which the Eastern Band had contracted Dillard was decidedly brief, the leadership's effort at deterrence, open experimentation with the intricacies of the United States government, and veiled testing of a non-Cherokee's deference in pursuing the Eastern Band's agenda remained a quantified success. They had given John Dillard authority to deal with governmental issues affecting the Cherokee of Indiantown, their legal status, their solubility, and their territorial retention.

During Dillard's tenure of office, the Eastern Band's legal and social standing remained relatively positive. As successful as Dillard was in administering to the needs of the Eastern Band, however, the man was still an outsider capable of fickle moments and swaying allegiances. Chief Yonaguska and his leadership needed someone to whom they could entrust the very security of their collective and who could help to ensure the tribe's longevity in Western North Carolina. A wily politician in his own regard, Chief Yonaguska had already groomed and deftly maneuvered his best candidate for the communally accepted post: William Holland Thomas.

When Dillard's contract ended, Chief Yonaguska offered the position to the business associate and new legal practitioner. As he was an adopted son of the Chief, a Cherokee brother, a local shop owner with a long-standing history of deference towards the Cherokee as well as a heavy reliance on Cherokee commerce, and a proven working knowledge of North Carolina's legal system, few could have faulted the Chief's timely selection, but, unlike the secretive beneficence that Chief Yonaguska had woven to ensnare William Thomas as a member of the Eastern Band, the position was Thomas's alone to accept or deny.

As the young man found, however, Chief Yonaguska's shrewd politicking had not been limited to the maneuvering of his tribal council and community into a position of blind acceptance. Apart from the economic dependence of Cherokee-borne and -bought supplies, Thomas may also have shared Felix Hampton Walker Jr.'s depths of ill-placed guilt and desire for reconciliation. In several respects, Thomas had, however inadvertently, contributed to the destabilization of the Cherokee Nation.

The Raccoon Creek land granted to Richard Thomas for his military service in the American Revolution had once been property of the Cherokee Nation, as had the tracts of land purchased for William's store, as had the recently acquired homestead Temperance was fashioning for the two in the Soco Creek area.[91] Raised on his mother's Protestant morality, the young man likely saw Chief Yonaguska's offer as much a means of guilt assuagement and misplaced penitence as a sound investment in the community that had offered William and, by association, Temperance shelter from failure. Much like Felix Hampton Walker's letter, Thomas's father figure's offer was also a vote of confidence firmly placed on the shoulders of a mildly insecure young man.

In the young man's mind, there could be no other way.

Among the Western North Carolina populace, Chief Yonaguska was ubiquitously considered a wily old man with a sage mind and a gifted understanding of Anglo and Native American cultures.[92]

William Holland Thomas followed the lead of his adopted father and accepted the position as Agent of the Eastern Band.

CHAPTER FOUR

EXPANDING INTERESTS

As time passed, William Holland Thomas found increasing rewards in his endeavors as a trader, as a Cherokee, and as an Eastern Band advocate, but the young professional was only beginning to feel the weight of his newfound responsibilities.

In less than a decade Thomas had managed to turn his Indiantown store into a thriving success. Trying to keep abreast of potential competitors in the late 1820s, he started looking for ways to enhance and expand his mercantile assets. The young man eventually found potential in a store and tannery on nearby Scotts Creek, North Carolina. After evaluating the logistics of the venture coupled with the demands of his first store, William Thomas then approached the business partnership of William Welch and James Robert Love Sr.

about the prospect of trading his proven managerial skills in exchange for the experience he might gain in the running of their trading facility. With little to lose from the deal, the Welch-Love partnership agreed to Thomas's proposal.

Often working from sketchy records or remembered inventories, William Thomas poured his little remaining spare time into both store facilities, and by the early 1830s the joined profits of his first store and the subsequent partial profits from his Indiantown venture (as well as likely earnings from several recent land and slave market transactions) enabled Thomas to buy out both Welch's and Love's interest in the Scotts Creek location. The venture was hard earned but rapidly became a lucrative source of supplemental revenue as well as customer services (in a business where skins were surplus commodity and refined garments a largely imported luxury, the tanning facility rapidly became a prized jewel in William Thomas's growing North Carolina enterprise).[93] Furthermore, when the Scotts Creek and Indiantown stores began earning a greater degree of profitability, the merchant hired Allen Fisher and Johnson W. King to run each facility, respectively.[94]

While William Thomas continued to expand his trading business whenever an opportunity arose (eventually managing to turn one profit-making store into a chain of seven facilities scattered throughout Western North Carolina), the businessman made a point of sharing his good fortune with his Eastern Band brethren. As an adopted son of the Chief and a proven member of the Haywood County community, Thomas felt a certain responsibility for the regional Cherokee and did his best to return the generosity they had shown him in his company's formative years.[95] When he received news of one member's financial hardship, Thomas would make a point to seek out the individual, inquiring "if the destitute had been furnished and . . . was sufficient to supply their wants."[96] If they were not, the businessman often removed stock from one of his holdings and distributed the sundries to ease the burden of his Cherokee neighbors. Should an Eastern Band member need Thomas's support while he was away on business, he left standing orders with his staff that his adopted brothers were to be granted clothes,[97] corn,[98] grain,[99] or other essentials of regional life available and that the purchase were to be logged in the store's records under the respective Native American's line of credit.[100] Years often passed before the businessman received even a modicum of monetary remuneration for his generosity, but William Thomas's credit policy remained a cornerstone of his mercantile ventures long after the Civil War.

Over the years the young man continued to refine his business plans and philanthropic efforts, but events taking place beyond the Appalachian Mountains in the State of Georgia overshadowed the man's prosperity. For decades, Georgia's populace had coveted the fertile soil that had been given to the Cherokee by President George Washington and their intermediary, Indian Agent Benjamin Hawkins. While the land remained geographically within the boundaries of the State of Georgia, the 1791 Treaty of Holston had granted the Nation sovereign status. As the United States began to expand into the interior of the North American continent, Georgia's leadership began to threaten the stability of the region and the entire southern Native American populace with dubius internal policies and fallacious legal practices.[101]

The Georgian-based followers of Principal Chief John Ross (the majority holder of the factionalized Cherokee Nation) viewed themselves as a sovereign Native American nation recognized by the first President of the United States, George Washington. However, the Cherokee Nation remained a loose knit confederation of small tribes that demanded constant attention as well as ample federal governmental personnel, time, and money for the conduct of regional business with the Native Americans.[102] Although President Washington had pledged the "[American] Government would do full justice to the Cherokee,"[103] years of being referred to as "Children"[104] and treated as geopolitical pawns of imperial neighbors (namely the hemisphere's French, British, and Spanish forces) and more militant

tribes (especially the Creek), led many within the Cherokee Nation
to deduce that the controlling leadership of the United States of
America desired they be sent elsewhere.[105] In preferring to follow the
strict interpretation of the word "nation," the Cherokee Nation consistently made their opposition to dealing with the corrupt purposes
of the Georgia legislature clearly understood. With the Cherokee
lacking legal and political representation and a means of forcing the
federal government to acknowledge their plight (outside of total
war), the situation was ripe for Georgia's exploitation.

Utilizing the cries of their citizenry for greater tracts of quality
land as leverage, Georgia's leadership actively stonewalled Cherokee
National efforts to apprehend treaty violators already hunting, pro-
specting, and settling on their sovereign territory (alluded to in the
1785 Treaty of Hopewell[106] and laid out in detail with the 1791 Treaty
of Holston).[107] Later, when the Cherokee petitioned the United States
Congress for action, the state successfully and systematically dually
undermined the responding federal investigative efforts as well as the
legislature's long-standing relatively untroubled relationship with the
Cherokee Nation through, at first, a stance of willful ignorance and
then, subsequently, the raising of an argument which the northern
states long had thought had been settled with the establishment of the
Constitution of the United States of America, the issue of federal governance against a state's individual interests or a citizen's essential
freedoms.

Thus, by the late 1820s, as William Thomas saw to his new Eastern Band charges, the Cherokee attempted to move the issue to the
national level, . . . but Georgia's leadership had already adroitly assessed the situation. Since the nation's inception, the leadership of the
United States remained largely divided between northern views of
urbanization and southern agrarian views (largely centered on the
electoral power held by slave owners). Still, the rapid succession of
unpredictable foreign and domestic events was beginning to tear the
young republic apart over the intricacies of American expansionism.
The War of 1812 had been born as much out of a desire for Canadian

land as hawkish imperialism and the rights of the sea. The Louisiana Purchase had recently brought uncounted raw acreage to the United States. The 1819 Spanish ceding of Florida and issuance of the 1820 Monroe Doctrine promised even greater profits for the country in the Mexican Gulf and South American markets. The country's elected representatives were veritably swimming in found acreage but were at a loss as to how the surplus would be parceled into territories and their pending status as free or slave states, and the situation was further exacerbated by several recent backroom negotiations and Supreme Court rulings.

During the course of his education, William Thomas had studied the federal government's interaction with the Cherokee Nation and the Eastern Band. While some were straightforward, others were vague, and still others when viewed in a greater context were almost entirely byzantine to the understanding. In the 1824 *Euchella v. Welsh* case, the State Supreme Court firmly upheld the status of the Cherokee Nation as a sovereign state, but instead of removing the encroaching settlers from Cherokee land, the state was instructed to grant the affected Cherokee Nation's members the value of the land and to entitle them to adequate territorial compensation elsewhere in the state.[108]

In 1829 William Thomas heard about the discovery of gold in several Cherokee Nation–controlled areas near Dahlonega, Georgia. By the following year, roughly four thousand nonindigenous people had moved on the state-coveted land with intentions of permanent settlement.[109] Within nine months, approximately $230,000 had been mined from the area and deposited in the nearby Georgia town of Augusta.[110] Remarking that "gold was the only thing to afford a subject of conversation for gentlemen,"[111] William Thomas packed his bags, put his business affairs in order, and set out on what would become one of his many trips over the Appalachian Mountains and into Georgia.

While North Carolina and Georgia's countryside was long known for its natural beauty, most intrastate and interstate travel was not undertaken lightly. On his various business and legal excursions,

Thomas sometimes traveled by horse-drawn wagon (frequently laden with tradable goods) or, when journeying between urban localities, sometimes indulged in the use of a carriage. However, the dirt roads between Haywood County and New Echota, where the delegates of the Cherokee Nation and the United States were set to gather, made a saddled horse the most easy form of rapid transport available to the man.

Where Cherokee mythology often spoke of spectral lights that were sometimes spotted crossing bare patches in mountaintop foliage (allegedly the spirits of Cherokee murdered in long past combat)[112] and tradition held that Cherokee mothers (fearing their children might be kidnapped by creatures and drawn into nearby lakes) mandated they be woken before dawn,[113] the few surviving accounts of William Holland Thomas's travels attest to other naturally occurring dangers. On the road, travelers were subject to the privations of not only weather and accidental mishaps (like the one that claimed Richard Thomas's life) but also the removal of such creature comforts as companionship, a warm bath, a soft bed, and a set of prepared meals. In their place Thomas often found loneliness, wet clothes, soft, muddy ground, sore joints, periodic illness, mountain predators (including bears, mountain lions, wildcats, and wolf packs),[114] and sometimes hunger. At one point, the young businessman even found himself sharing a bedroll and campfire with a four-foot, eight-inch-long rattlesnake, which he hurriedly killed.[115]

Yet, William Thomas and many others like him actively chose to spend much of their lives on the open road in pursuit of fame, fortune, and peace. William Thomas undoubtedly enjoyed the quiet of the wilderness. If he desired a change in diet, he could, as his long-time suppliers had, take advantage of the indigenous fauna or fish in a nearby stream. With taverns a very scarce commodity along nineteenth century urban roadsides, as night neared, Thomas would often find a place to settle down in the wilderness. Making camp, he would bed down, write in his journal or compose letters to colleagues by the light of a small fire, and fall asleep beneath the stars. The isolation between towns and passing fellow travelers may have given the young businessman ample opportunity to contemplate and relax, but the Mountain region's urban areas also held an allure for the young North Carolinian.

A consummate salesman, William Thomas put aside his advocacy of Cherokee issues when a good bargain, advantageous contact, or profitable business venture could be found.

Arriving on Cherokee National land, William Thomas began investigating the veracity of the rumors he had heard (it is unclear how much geologic knowledge Thomas actually acquired, but the surviving remnants of the eager businessman's journals describe the North Carolinian over the course of his stay as having conducted several "experiments" along the Valley River in his search for gold[116]). Using his Cherokee affiliations, William Thomas arranged to stay with local Cherokee resident Chunaluska. Over the course of the evening, the North Carolinian subsequently discovered through a friend of his host, named Wilnote, that "there was a lead mine not far from his house on the other side of the river . . . and a silver mine also in the same neighborhood."[117] Thomas then analyzed the samples he had collected and, apparently, verified the rumors. There was untapped gold potential within the boundaries of the Georgia-locked Cherokee Nation, but, as Thomas was rapidly made aware by his contacts, not a single speck of gold dust could be recovered from the reservation without the expressed approval of the Cherokee leadership. The businessman hastily secured the promise of samples from his contacts for study to be obtained upon his next trip through the area[118] and rapidly made for the capital of the Cherokee Nation, the town of New Echota.

When Thomas reached the convergence of the Conasauga and Coosawatee Rivers (near the modern site of Calhoun, Georgia), the Cherokee Agent was greeted by a modernized Cherokee National capital. In the space of a few decades, the Cherokee Nation had attempted a rapid transformation into a faded copy of the United States government as an initial stop-gap against baseless racist charges of "red man . . . savagery,"[119] against the growing machinations of Georgia's leadership, and against the increasing treaty violations of would-be settlers encroaching on the Nation's sovereign territory.

By the end of the 1810s, the remaining chiefs of the Nation had drafted a constitution (strikingly similar to the one governing the United States of America), elected a presidential figure in the form of Principal Chief John Ross (to speak for the Cherokee Nation as one voice), enacted the institution of a tax limited to supporting roadway construction and a bicameral legislature with upper and lower houses (whose representatives were derived from the segmenting and redistricting of the remaining Cherokee Nation's tribal landholdings). It remained to be seen, however, whether the creation of a centralized power would work for the Cherokee and work against the threats to the Nation's sovereignty or hasten the demise of the ancient Native American cultural identity.

Arriving in the capital, William Holland Thomas assumed the posture that he could offer the regional Cherokee a similar deal to the one he had worked out with Welch and Love Senior for the Scotts Creek store, allowing both Thomas (who would supply the labor and supplies) and the Cherokee Nation (who would supply the legal authority) to mutually profit from the American society's obsession with gold.

The businessman was sorely disappointed.

"I found to my great astonishment," Thomas later wrote, "that their [Georgia's] law respecting minerals [as it applied to the Cherokee Nation] was different from what I had heard. . . . Instead of each individual being entitled to work two years at any mines [he] might find[,] all mines were considered as the property of the nation and no individual had any right to work at any of them."[120]

As Georgia waited for the requested presence of two United States Army companies (out of South Carolina) for the purpose of conducting period patrols of the area, Thomas realized that he had hit an impasse. He could not circumvent the will of the state surrounding the Nation without antagonizing his own charges within the Eastern

Band. Instead, he decided to tackle the matter with his legal skills, but there too his aspirations met with an unproductive end.

In showing around his test results to various officials in the hopes of gaining supporters to lift the ban, Thomas introduced his idea of exploitation to the wrong individuals. Within a matter of months thousands of illegal operations began "to sprout like a contagion"[121] throughout the region. The United States Army increased their patrols, and, in response, the Cherokee Nation reciprocated with the creation of a group of Light Horse mounted guards. After several dubious attempts to win support from the local Cherokee tribes (an effort made further impractical by Chief Yonaguska's adoption of Thomas),[122] however, William Thomas abandoned his fleeting dream of mineral speculation and returned home to North Carolina tired, annoyed, and empty-handed, leaving both himself and his Cherokee no richer from the resources of the land than they were before.

CHAPTER FIVE

REMOVAL

Shortly after William Holland Thomas had recrossed the Appalachian Mountains back into North Carolina and had once more settled into life at home, the situation with the Cherokee Nation and the State of Georgia reached a critical point.

Contrary to the treatment the Eastern Band received from the State of North Carolina, Georgia anxiously and actively coveted the fertile lands of the Cherokee Nation. The United States government's successful relationship with the Nation had always rankled the populace of Georgia. In a handful of treaties Georgia's leadership believed they had lost dignity, integrity, and key fertile soil to a Native American populace they were convinced was unilaterally inferior to themselves. With the security of several states at risk from potential Native

American uprisings and guerrilla actions (both remote possibilities), Georgia allowed the cultivation of a perceived imbalance of safe settlements over swaths of prized territory.

As the country entered a phase of rapid expansionism, Georgia's leadership bided its time. Then, coincidentally, gold was discovered behind the borders of the Cherokee Nation. With a keen sense of timing, advocates began associating the issue of Cherokee National sovereignty with the increasing congressional burden of legislating America's rapid expansion westward. They would first induce the Cherokee to leave willingly, but failing that, Georgia intended to force a removal of the Native Americans at the expense of the Cherokee's former allies within the federal government. In a handful of moves orchestrated beyond the reach of the Cherokee leadership (as they were not entitled to congressional representation), the situation started bearing fruit as Georgia's leadership pressed the Washington politicos to support their claim of territorial supremacy (several decades later the concept came to be referred to as eminent domain).

Relatively safe behind North Carolina's mountain border, William Thomas and Chief Yonaguska watched as Georgia's elected officials enacted a series of highly dubious moves. First, they permitted settlers to begin occupying Cherokee land (in direct opposition to the guarantees of prior treaties). Next, they began harassing members of the Cherokee Nation with informal bands of anti–Native American settlers. Third, as the Cherokee leadership responded to the assaults by invoking their influence with the United States government, Georgia began to position the arrival of federal soldiers to patrol the region as a means to both reinforce their own constituents' biases and claim their own lands were now insecure (due to the alleged rising level of "hostility" with the Cherokee Nation). Finally, through the misrepresentation of alleged Cherokee/settler incidents, the illegal imposition of limitations upon Cherokee entitlements, and the arrests of both guests and Cherokee Nationals on sovereign Cherokee territory, the State of Georgia began to gain the upper political hand with the steadily growing ambivalent members of the United States

Congress and, as expected, the Cherokee people continued to unwittingly aid their aggressors.

"The country is patrolled by them [Georgian paramilitary forces] in every direction," the delegates reported to Congress, "often traveling thirty miles by night to strike terror and dismay wherever it is believed the slightest degree of unwillingness prevails to acknowledge and bow in submission to the 'sovereignty' of the State. The gold miles [mines] have been seized upon by them, and the benefits of their mother earth, where, from immemorial years, the Cherokees have dwelt, denied them, at the hazard of bloodshed or four years' imprisonment at hard labor, in the walls of the penitentiary."[123]

The Cherokee Nation's options, however, were limited. Fractures among the Nation's tribes, which had begun prior to Chief Yonaguska's secession, began to split the Cherokee into two divergent philosophical and political camps, one led by Principal Chief John Ross, a rather wealthy pale-complexioned Cherokee half-breed from Lookout Mountain, Tennessee, and the other led by a half-blooded Cherokee from Georgia named Major Ridge.[124] The son of a Scotch Loyalist and a mother of one quarter Cherokee blood, Principal Chief Ross may not have been as pure-blooded a Cherokee as Chief Yonaguska but had served beside then–future president Andrew Jackson at the 1814 Battle of Horseshoe Bend. Holding a penchant for politics and a mind for business, the Principal Chief of the Cherokee Nation remained ardently committed to retaining his people's contiguity on their ancestral eastern lands and, by default, was a potential enemy of the Eastern Band.

In almost every way, Major Ridge was Principal Chief Ross's opposite number. Born and raised in what was then the State of Georgia (his birth area is now part of modern Tennessee), Major Ridge also distinguished himself as a soldier during the Creek War of 1814. An articulate and thoughtful speaker, he was eventually elevated to the level of office holder within the Cherokee Council and began speaking out as a counterpoint to his Principal Chief's argument, maintaining that open opposition to the United States would be a foolhardy venture that offered the Cherokee Nation little more than continued trouble.

With their options becoming increasingly limited, neither faction seemed capable of moving to even marginally accommodate the other, let alone the American people, as Chief Yonaguska had decades prior. Full capitulation with Georgia's desires, many thought, would likely bring about civil war among the Cherokee tribes. Partial capitulation meant a sorely wounded Cherokee government. The taking up of arms was seen by the realistically minded Cherokee Nationals as a suicidal move when contemplated against their likely wartime adversaries; the efficient destructiveness of federal troops supported Georgia's quasi-militia elements.

The situation looked desperate, but there was one other option. With few places to turn to, the Cherokee Nation reluctantly embraced the path of legal action taken by Chief Yonaguska and Chief Euchella to interdict Georgia's intentions. After withstanding the necessary appeals process, in 1831 the first Cherokee National test case, *Cherokee Nation v. Georgia*, reached the Supreme Court. Although the case dealt directly with the allegedly unlawful arrest, detention, trial, and subsequent execution of a Cherokee National by authorities of the State of Georgia, the Cherokee community hoped the Court would see fit to definitively establish the Cherokee Nation's sovereignty before the American populace and thus end several decades of legal and political ambiguity. The results, however, were not entirely what the Nation intended.

In *Cherokee Nation v. Georgia*, Supreme Court Justice John Marshall, speaking for the court, answered the Cherokee Nation's concerns in the following manner:

> The Cherokee Nation is not a foreign state in the sense in which the term "foreign state" is used in the Constitution of the United States.
> . . . The Cherokees are a State. They have been uniformly treated as a State since the settlement of our country. The

numerous treaties made with them by the United States recognize them as a people capable of maintaining the relations of
peace and war; of being responsible in their political character
for any violation of their engagements, or for any aggression
committed on the citizens of the United States by any individual of their community. Laws have been enacted in the spirit of
these treaties.[125]

The ruling was a severe blow to the Cherokee. Unlike the Eastern Band who had been granted their land rights in 1783 by the State
of North Carolina,[126] the Cherokee Nation existed by the sufferance
and enforcement of federal treaty signatories. While *Cherokee Nation v.
Georgia* had technically been found in favor of the Cherokee claimant
(an unlawfully imprisoned and executed Cherokee National), Justice
Marshall had also ruled *against* the Cherokee Nation. In his appraisal,
they were not an established foreign power with its own unimpeach-
able sovereignty (as was, for example, held by the nations of Europe).
In effect, Marshall had dually limited the Cherokee Nation's ability
to legally defend itself and handed the State of Georgia the means by
which they could absorb and eliminate the Cherokee problem within
their borders. Chief Yonaguska and his legal council had apparently
been wise in breaking away from the Nation and aligning with the
state of North Carolina.

Before a broad, sweeping expansionist policy could be imple-
mented, however, the Supreme Court revisited the issue of Cherokee sovereignty in the next judicial term with *Worcester v. Georgia*.
While the 1832 case directly related to the fate of two missionaries
claiming unlawful arrest by Georgia authorities on Cherokee land, Justice Marshall took the opportunity to codify his prior decision, saying:

> Certain it is that our history furnishes no example, from the first
> settlement of our country, of any attempt, on the part of the
> Crown, to interfere with the internal affairs of the Indians farther
> than to keep out the agents of foreign powers who, as traders or
> otherwise, might seduct them into foreign alliances. . . .

. . . . To construe the expression "managing all their affairs" into a surrender of self-government would be a perversion of their necessary meaning, and a departure from the construction which has been uniformly put on them. . . . Is it credible that they could have considered themselves as surrendering to the United States the right to dictate their future cessions and the terms on which they should be made, or to compel their submission to the violence of disorderly and licentious intruders? It is equally inconceivable that they could have supposed themselves, by a phrase thus slipped into an article on another and most interesting subject, to have divested themselves of the right of self-government on subjects not connected with trade. Such a measure could not be "for their benefit and comfort," or for "the prevention of injuries and oppression.". . . . It would convert a treaty of peace covertly into an act annihilating the political existence of one of the parties. Had such a result been intended, it would have been openly avowed.[127]

Instead of complementing their previous term's decision, the Supreme Court had openly challenged the actions of the State of Georgia. In the new legal opinion, Justice Marshall branded Georgia's actions as illegal and gross violations of the spirit of the Cherokee Nation's past treaties with the United States. Much to the Cherokee Nation's tacit relief, the Court also ordered the southern state to desist in the pursuit of similar actions to their decidedly illegal ends.

Yet, at a pivotal moment in the history of the Court and the United States of America, Georgia refused to bend to the Court's mandate. While the law resoundingly fell on the side of the Cherokee Nation, the Court held no power to enforce the laws it interpreted. The State of Georgia would not abandon its efforts. Congress would not intercede.[128] The President of the United States, soldier-turned-politico Andrew Jackson, followed suit, reportedly saying, "John Marshall has made his decision; now let him enforce it."[129] The boldness of Georgia's leadership had managed to successfully embarrass the northern states into, rather than embarking upon yet another Indian war (having just waged war against the Creeks in 1814 and the Seminoles in 1818) or, worse, a civil war fought over states' rights (recently narrowly averted by the Missouri Compromise), complicit acquiescence, causing a gathering of Cherokee chiefs to surmise that "in the vehemence of her [Georgia's] thirst for sovereignty . . . our treaties become obsolete; the protection guaranteed by them withdrawn; our property confiscated to lawless *bandittie*, and our necks placed under the foot of Georgia."[130]

Still, there was little to be gained from removing the Eastern Band from their Indiantown home and sending them westward with the Cherokee Nation. Unlike Georgia's neighboring Cherokee Nation who had long suffered the impracticality of a confederated government, Chief Yonaguska's Eastern Band and the few remaining pockets of Cherokee within the mountains and in the south (near Asheville) had remained a matter of indifference for North Carolina. In November 1811 it had been "the sundry inhabitants of North Carolina"[131] who had asked the United States House of Representatives to remove "the whites from the Territory secured by the treaty to the Cherokee Indians."[132] Although the issue was subsequently removed to the desk of the Secretary of War, neither the Cherokee nor the state had pushed to resolve the incident with the force of arms.

In stark contrast to the subject of the landmark 1831 Supreme Court case *Cherokee Nation v. Georgia*, not one of Chief Yonaguska's Cherokee had given cause to be questioned, detained, jailed, or executed by any authorities.[133] Rather, the Eastern Band inhabited land obtained and supported through their own funds with the consent of the North Carolina government. Furthermore, not a single valuable commodity had been found on the land belonging to the Eastern Band. Conversely, members of the Eastern Band unarguably held a place of acceptance among the Western North Carolina community.

For the Eastern Band, the rule of law and contractual restraint had successfully replaced rifle barrels and the sharp ends of bayonets. Apart from the Cherokee Nation across the mountains, Chief Yonaguska's Cherokee followers had been allowed by his disassociative actions the chance to both politically distance themselves from the Georgia quarrel and meld with the North Carolina communities being formed around them. Whereas the Cherokee Nation's populace by virtue of the Supreme Court's decisions was considered a tribe apart from the state which surrounded them and hence held no sway in changing the outcome through local elections, the Eastern Band demonstrated daily their value to the economy of Western North Carolina in providing needed goods and services to such businesses as Walker's Soco Creek store and Thomas's Indiantown and Scotts Creek holdings. In addition, many were paid for manual labor for regional farms and showed a growing deftness with handcrafts and metalwork.[134] Contrary to the diminished Cherokee National lobby, by his growing number of well-positioned regional contacts and frequent trips through neighboring states (including the North Carolina coastal region, Georgia's various cities and townships, the former swamplands of Washington, D.C. [then named Washington City], and the New York area)[135] Thomas was beginning to illustrate the value of a trusted Caucasian Cherokee Agent in keeping the Eastern Band's efforts from easily being dismissed by either North Carolina's authorities, the United States Congress, or the Indian Affairs Office.[136]

In choosing not to test the limits of North Carolina's coastal aristocracy with active lobbying efforts, federal bargaining actions, or the desire for the entrance of a greater stabilizing force than the local constabulary, the Cherokee under Chief Yonaguska's and William Holland Thomas's care had managed to escape the fate of the Cherokee Nation, . . . but neither William Thomas nor the Eastern Band was in a position to gloat.[137] Were North Carolina's coastal aristocracy to see the Cherokee as a potential threat to regional stability or, perhaps, see material benefit in their collective incarceration, removal, or termination, there would be relatively little any Cherokee Agent or businessman could enact to win a decisive reversal.

Realizing the Eastern Band's survival necessitated the walking of a fine line, Thomas methodically assessed the situation and initiated a series of actions designed to further ingratiate his adopted brethren with the federal, state, and local entities concerning the presence of the Eastern Band within North Carolina. First, Thomas collected a series of testimonials and affidavits from his cultivated business and political contacts (including Nimrod Jarrett and James R. Love Sr.), attesting that the Eastern Band's Cherokee were productive members of North Carolina society.[138] Guarding against the uninitiated (recent settlers, avaricious land developers, and eager politicians) who might feel threatened by living next to a community of Native Americans, Thomas next solicited the sworn testimony of several neighbors and staff members in support of Chief Yonaguska's Cherokee.[139] Finally, hoping to both quell a minor disharmony within the Nation and provide whichever governmental entities that might wish to test the Eastern Band's trust in beneficent federal-run initiatives (in stark contrast to the arguments of the Cherokee Nation's Principal Chief Ross) William Thomas filed several claims on the behalf of a few dissatisfied Eastern Band members wishing to remove to the west with the rest of the Cherokee Nation. (Moreover, Thomas asked for a small portion of the awarded removal cost to defray his incurred business expenses.)[140] As a result, in the space of a few months, the thirty-something businessman had managed to turn an insular-appearing Indiantown settlement into a happy and contented Western North Carolina community indistinguishable from its neighbors.

Yet, the impending 1835 confiscation of the Cherokee Nation's land and their citizenry's relocation westward forced the Cherokee Agent of the Eastern Band to play a more direct role in the Georgia and Washington–based negotiations over the Treaty of New Echota, which detailed the finer points of the United States' Native American removal plan. Acting on behalf of Chief Yonaguska, William Thomas projected an ameliorating influence on a few of the Cherokee Nation and United States' governmental representatives, meeting with members of each group during stopovers in Washington. In the process, Thomas forged a friendship with Cherokee National Major Ridge (while, simultaneously, making a crucial enemy of Ridge's adversary, Principal Chief John Ross) and strengthened his already amiable bonds with several civil servants, including Reverend John Freeman Schermerhorn (who, among other functions, served as a negotiator and signatory of the Treaty of New Echota) and North Carolina congressional representative James Graham.[141]

The North Carolinian, however, also had ulterior motives.

Thomas was already a skilled, opportunistic businessman and charismatic bargainer, but in Washington he was foremost an agent of his adopted father and an advocate of Eastern Band security. Realizing Principal Chief Ross's position of Cherokee National contiguous sovereignty was undefendable, in the space of a few weeks Thomas gained the grudging acceptance of several otherwise occupied colleagues to leave the Eastern Band afield of the issues of Cherokee National legal sovereignty, territorial security, and population relocation.[142] As Thomas receded from the foreground of the treaty discussions, he initiated several carefully worded proposals to the group (considered minor by comparison to the plentitude of weighty treaty issues) and pressed for their acceptance.

One by one, Thomas's backroom manueverings were rewarded.

Not only did he secure the acceptance from all parties (and the State of North Carolina) that the North Carolina Cherokee were an issue separate from the Cherokee Nation, but he also gained the key acceptance of his colleagues to include in the treaty the allowance for "those individuals and families . . . *averse* to a *removal* to the Cherokee country west of the Mississippi and are *desirous* to become *citizens* of the *States* where they *reside,* and such as are qualified to take care of themselves and their property, shall be entitled to *receive their due portion of all the personal benefits accruing under this treaty,* for their *claims, improvements,* and *per capita* . . ."[143] Next, Cherokee Agent Thomas bolstered his clients' legal position with the allowance of "preemption rights to each head of the family who remained east 460 acres of land."[144] Finally, Thomas pushed past the politics, egotism, and self-interest to befriend the man who had made the treaty proposal happen, Major Ridge, and thus succeeded in making inroads with the anti-Ross faction.

Meeting several times with Major Ridge, Thomas gained several concessions from Principal Chief Ross's Cherokee adversary. In seeming opposition to his prior accepted proposals, Thomas was granted by Ridge (1) the agreement that the Eastern Band would share all land belonging to the Cherokee Nation and awarded annuity sums, (2) the security that any future sale or transfer of Cherokee land also be shared among the Eastern Band, (3) the awarding of $53.33⅓ for those wishing to move west, (4) the use of Cherokee National grounds for hunting, and (5) the allowance of obtaining several biblical texts written in Cherokee that Ridge's group produced to facilitate Cherokee-English bilinguality.[145] The backroom promises would not only ensure a continued relationship between the two entities but also ensured that Thomas's brethren would not be burned as he had been in his first major business dealing with Felix Hampton Walker.

If Principal Chief Ross moved against Thomas, the Eastern Band would have an ally and if the federal government decided to renege on their agreement, the group would at least be assured the same removal awards as their cultural contemporaries.

WHEN THE TREATY WAS FINALIZED and the removal started, William Holland Thomas, given his newfound standing, saw a new opportunity to ingratiate himself with the federal government, sooth the sore feelings of the Cherokee being removed from their Georgia land, and earn a greater profit for his expanding chain of stores. During his 1829 Georgia excursion, Thomas had hoped to reap a substantial profit from gold deposits. As greater and greater numbers of United States Army personnel moved into the largely rural region of the Georgia–North Carolina border, the more modest intentioned Thomas traveled to North Carolina's Murphy County and, purchasing a small plot of land on the outskirts of Fort Butler, promptly began setting up shop.[146] Planning to order finery from his other stores, William Thomas began marketing himself as a provider of urban goods for the legions of salary-encumbered soldiers posted to the region's fortifications, the departing Cherokee, and the promised forthcoming waves of Georgia and southern North Carolina settlers.

Having already purchased a large stock of corn, blankets, and clothes for the Cherokee being removed by the federal troops, in an attempt to ingratiate himself with the receding Cherokee Nation and their handlers,[147] Thomas subsequently moved to secure the support of the nearby fort's commander, the breveted Brigadier General John Ellis Wool. William Thomas presented himself to the regional commander as a simple businessman with altruistic tendencies, but Brigadier General Wool did not share the North Carolinian's assessment.

As a career officer, the brigadier general had raised volunteers against the British in the War of 1812 and was wounded in the service of the United States in April of 1812 at Queenston Heights. Rising through the ranks, the young officer rapidly earned a reputation as a watchful and dedicated soldier who excelled at turning problematic situations to his country's advantage. Brigadier General Wool went where he had been ordered by his superiors without question, but the man enjoyed neither the task of securing the removal of the Cherokee Nation nor dealing with those he considered the "corrupt agents of the Government."[148]

"If I could, and I could not do them a greater kindness," he once remarked, "I would remove every Indian to-morrow, beyond the reach of the white man, who like vultures, are watching, ready to pounce upon their prey, and strip them of every thing they have or expect from the Government of United States."[149]

Wary of creating situations that might bring his command trouble, Brigadier General John Wool was mindful of the presence of yet another Causasian ready to make a quick dollar on his troubled charges. While Brigadier General Wool apparently was skeptical of Thomas and his motivations (having heard rumors casting Thomas as an opportunistic businessman and Cherokee "friend" but ultimately a friend serving his own financial interests),[150] there was little the military officer could do to stop William Holland Thomas. With Brigadier General Wool bargaining that it would be better to keep an eye on Thomas, the store's construction was allowed with one stipulation: the proprietor could not sell any form of alcohol to members of the United States Army under the brigadier general's command.

In February 1837 Thomas readily agreed and began managing the construction of his new store on the Hiwassee River. Prior to the store's completion, however, a contingent of soldiers arrived on the scene. Indicating that they were under the command of Brigadier General Wool, they instructed Thomas that work on the store be stopped immediately, as the dwelling was being constructed less than one mile from an active military post. Thomas ignored the order and continued the raising of his Murphy County store. A few days later, the contingent returned to the Hiwassee site and tore the structure down.

Unknowing of Brigadier General Wool's inaccurate intelligence concerning the young businessman, Thomas was stunned at the reversal. Instead of challenging the reversal, William Thomas wisely discharged his workforce, begged his leave of the troops, and secured a new set of quarters nearby to store his belongings and stockpiled supplies. When Thomas tried to rectify the situation with the brigadier general, the North Carolinian found the military officer had recently vacated his supervisory position. Upon further investigation, Thomas found that the ranking commanding officer at New Echota, a Colonel William Lindsay, had a vested interest in two of the regional stores with which William Thomas would be competing.[151]

The businessman tried to prove his honorable motivations to the military authorities through the use of petitions similar in content to the ones he had recently used in the defense of the Eastern Band, but the regional military authorities were initially lukewarm. After several months of campaigning and the committing of certain indiscretions by the other businesses (providing customers with prohibited alcohol), however, Colonel Lindsay (later rejoined by Brigadier General John Wool) reassessed the situation and allowed William Thomas to once again set up a trading post in Murphy County. While Thomas's business ethics were ultimately vindicated, the costly battle to prove himself would remain a constant struggle for the North Carolinian and the Eastern Band to overcome in the decades ahead, as old and new enemies moved to cast a dark shadow of doubt on the man's ulterior motivations.

CHAPTER SIX

TSALI

While Chief Yonaguska's foresight and William Holland Thomas's surrepetitious efforts as the Eastern Band's Cherokee Agent had managed to deliver the North Carolina Native Americans from the fate of the Cherokee Nation, in 1838 the Removal Program brought forward a new danger for the man's clients and new possibilities for himself.

Thomas and his brethren sympathized with their former Cherokee affiliates and regional acquaintances (a number of Cherokee Nationals living beyond Eastern Band territory in the State of North Carolina), but there was little they could do without endangering themselves. Although the businessman had traveled through the region several times throughout the removal negotiation period and had spoken with many of the key treaty players and offered his opinions to the proper ears and had seen that the government-fostered/ Cherokee-furnished document provided for his Eastern Band clientele, Cherokee Agent Thomas was appropriately absent from the signing of the Treaty of New Echota on December 29th, 1835.

In withdrawing from the legally valid removal, William Thomas effectively distanced the Eastern Band from the issue of removal, the personalities controlling the Cherokee Nation, and the troublesome treaty itself. Still, the potential of an explosive meeting between short-tempered Native Americans and an overzealous group of Georgia militia realistically threatened the meticulously achieved neutrality of the North Carolina Cherokee. Even the military agreed that any rash action involving the Native American populace on either side of the Appalachians engendered the very real possibility of initiating a cycle of violence, retribution, counterretribution, wholesale slaughter, and genocide.

"I have deemed it my duty to present these facts to the General-in Chief, in order that he may be on his guard against misrepresentations," Brigadier General John Wool wrote to his superiors, "and to apprize him that a people so determined in their opposition, and so unwilling to leave their native country, require to be urged but one step further to raise the tomahawk and scalping knife. That we shall have difficulty with them which may lead to the shedding of blood, I have little doubt. . . . It requires, I assure you, only the torch to be applied, and we have a bloody war on our hands. . . ."[152]

Since the onset of the nineteenth century, the federal government had encouraged the peaceful exchange of eastern Native American–held land for untouched western territory, but once Georgia (and, subsequently, Alabama) began forcing the removal of Native American occupants at the threat of rifle barrel and bayonet point, many among the military and civilian agencies felt the situation would inevitably deteriorate into violence perpetrated by an unarguably previously peaceful populace attempting to defend their ancestral lands. In an effort to alleviate the situation, many military officers (themselves feeling at odds with the moral ambiguity of their orders) began securing the contested areas with frequent patrols, fixed assembly/evacuation areas within the shadow of manned and fortified defensive structures (including Fort Newman, Fort Buffington, and Fort Campbell), and served as public buffers between regional Native Americans and their Georgian aggressors when the need arose. The laudable efforts, however, were minuscule when compared with the size, scope, and temper of the process. Everyone concerned knew it would only be a matter of time before something went violently wrong.

Major Ridge had signed the Treaty of New Echota legitimizing removal for the Cherokee Nation against the wishes of his numerous brethren (a price for which a group of his countrymen would later ensure he pay). In doing so, the man had consciously chosen the path of peaceful removal over the course of genocidal fury a minority had advocated. Similarly, Principal Chief John Ross, who had lobbied long and hard against removal within the Nation and in numerous trips to the Washington area, had eventually acceded to the point where Georgia had given the Nation little choice. To preserve the lives of his constituency, Principal Chief Ross grudgingly followed Major Ridge into Cherokee National removal, but both leaders knew they could not affirm the uniform resolve of their Cherokee Nationals to embrace the lesser of Georgia's proffered two evils. For that matter, neither leading faction could realistically guarantee the conduct of their own membership, let alone the visceral motivations of their own lesser government competitors. There was only faith, hope, good intentions, and guarded optimism.

Breveted Brigadier General Wool also struggled to maintain a non-confrontational posture and to maintain a relatively secure environment in which the Cherokee might could gather their belongings, dispose of their non-essential possessions, and begin their trek westward. His efforts met with some initial success, keeping overeager settlers and the shady businessmen of the sort he had mistaken William Thomas for embodying in check.[153] The military officer's efforts initially granted a relative peace to the potentially catastrophic situation. Still, the avaricious Georgian leadership and their less disciplined military volunteers were hard to manage.

Shortly after attaining temporary command of the removal from Brigadier General Wool, Colonel William Lindsay elevated the severity of the removal situation with the calling of an extraordinary number of volunteers to the region to erroneously impress upon the Cherokee that "resistance on the part of the Indians would have been madness."[154] While the federal troops (largely hailing from outside the contested region) were generally sympathetic to the plight of the Native Americans and listened to their commanding officer's orders to "carry out the general object with the greatest promptitude and certainty, and with the least possible distress to the Indians . . ."[155] the presence of Georgian troops only served to rankle the Cherokee. Not only were the Georgian volunteers largely desirous of relocation duty over "literally calling us to the grave"[156] in Florida's brewing Seminole War, but also a past history of hostilities between the two parties and the promise of personal advancement offered the volunteers a personal incentive in the elimination of a Cherokee presence within the state's borders. This situation needed to be monitored.

Having received assurances that no member of the Eastern Band would "remove west to their home in that country as they made it their choice,"[157] William Holland Thomas paid little attention to the removal process beyond his business concerns. Chief Yonaguska had refused to sign the Treaty of New Echota (when approached by Thomas's friend and colleague Reverend John Freeman Schermerhorn), as much a final symbolic gesture of disassociation from the faltering Cherokee Nation as a means of stalling the federal government until a better offer came to the table.[158] On the other hand, the Cherokee who wished to leave were departing with his legal assistance. Furthermore, Thomas's smooth handling of previous Cherokee treaties, the accompanying legal documentation pertaining to the Eastern Band's lack of violence or illegal activities, and positive influence within the Western North Carolina region had sufficiently insulated his

Cherokee brethren from every foreseeable potential threat to the Eastern Band's contiguous integrity.

In the fall of 1838, however, federal soldiers entered North Carolina in search of a renegade group of Cherokee warriors. Bearing orders from Brigadier General Wool's permanent successor, breveted United States Army major general Winfield "Old Fuss and Feathers" Scott, they explained that a number of Cherokee Nationals had fled the military's Removal Program (including prior Supreme Court plaintiff Euchella). According to a November 9th, 1838, memorandum, the stout army general had been granted numbers from the Cherokee Agency showing that only 11,721 of the 12,608 Native Americans involved in the removal had actually been verified as having settled in the western territory.[159] The rest were missing.

The Virginia-born Winfield Scott had enlisted in the cavalry in 1807 and, like Brigadier General John Ellis Wool, had distinguished himself in the War of 1812, but Scott also knew captivity firsthand, having been held as a prisoner-of-war in October 1813 at Queenston. Though later exchanged for another prisoner and fast-tracked for promotion to the rank of brigadier general (after sustaining wounds in the May 27th, 1813, capture of Fort George), the Removal Program's new commanding officer was keenly aware of the perspectives one gains at both ends of a bayonet. Furthermore, having recently suffered the inanity of South Carolinian partisanship in the 1832 Nullification Controversy *and* the deleterious battlefield conditions of the Seminole War, Major General Scott brought to the removal process the experience of a judicious administrator and a seasoned combat officer and a presence that discouraged Georgian intervention into his regional military operations and jurisdiction.[160] Similarly, having traveled through the area prior to his elevation to command the removal,[161] the stout man was not going to be dissuaded from carrying out his orders by either Georgia's leadership or their volunteers who, according to Major General Scott, "vowed never to return [home] without having killed at least one Indian."[162]

Shortly after assuming command, the major general took corrective measures to offset Colonel Lindsay's prior orders. As winter months neared, Major General Scott ordered that the region's Native American populace be granted medical aid and food (in the form of hard bread, flour, and/or corn).[163] Following the lead of Brigadier General Wool, the commanding officer also felt that "acts of harshness and cruelty on the part of our troops may lead, step by step, to delays, to impatience, and exasperation, and, in the end, to a general war and carnage."[164] As a result, he issued clear orders to his troops, stating: "Every possible kindness, compatible with the necessity of removal, must, therefore, be shown by the troops, and, if, in the ranks, a despicable individual should be found, capable of inflicting injury or insult on any Cherokee man, woman or child it wanted, it is hereby made the special duty of the nearest good officer or man, instantly to interpose, and to seize and consign the guilty wretch to the severest penalty of the laws."[165]

In the course of his investigation into the illegal flight of several Cherokee Nationals from military custody, Major General Scott heard rumors that the fugitives might have taken refuge in the nearby Smoky Mountains and among the Eastern Band settlement, but as the situation of removal grew increasingly complex, the task of hunting down fugitive Native American families grew to be a strain on the stout military commander's resources. Deeming the pursuit of fugitives a lower priority than the orchestration of the rallying points, disembarkation times, and supervised removal trails, Major General Scott left the hundreds of fleeing "poor creatures"[166] to find lives for themselves where they could. Yet, when two of his soldiers were slain and one wounded in the performance of his duty,[167] the Cherokee National Tsali[168] and his entire family became the subjects of a regional manhunt.[169]

Hearing of William Holland Thomas's reputation with the United States government and the Cherokee, Major General Winfield Scott directed a small detachment of soldiers to engage Thomas with the purpose of obtaining assistance in finding the murderer.

Hoping to "prevent the other [C]herokees remaining east from unit-
ing with them [Tsali's supposed renegades], and protect the lives
and property in the adjacent county,"[170] Thomas agreed to the major
general's request and traveled with Colonel W. S. Foster and the
Fourth Regiment of the United States Army to nearby Augusta for a
conference with the stout major general.

At the Augusta headquarters, Major General Winfield Scott impressed upon the businessman his desire to rapidly apprehend Tsali
and his family (which included his wife, brother, and three sons and
their families).[171] The major general then outlined a plan through
which he would utilize William Thomas's regional Cherokee contacts
to ascertain the location of Tsali and send the businessman in with a
proposition that Tsali surrender himself, his sons, and his brother for
punishment in exchange for the lives of his family members (and the
understood lives of the other fugitives encamped atop the Smoky
Mountains). If Tsali rebuked the offer, the army would then pour into
the mountain camp and apprehend the entire lot by force of arms.

The plan was sound, but Thomas was unconvinced of the merits of his involvement in the military action. Responding to the businessman's implications, Major General Scott told Thomas that he
would be "liberally compensated by the Government."[172]

In later recollection of the exchange, William Thomas explained,
"I would not consent to run so great a risque [risk] of losing my life,
for any compensation he would be justified in giving me, because if
I then as [a] hireling lost my life[,] it would be said I was influenced
to run the risque [risk] by [unintelligible]. . . ."[173]

Although guarded against fraud by North Carolina's legislature
(early in the removal debate, the state enacted legislation to legally
and fiscally safeguard their own interests against the self-serving actions of individuals trying to accrue portions of Cherokee land/com-
pensation through misrepresentation),[174] William Thomas implicitly
understood the ramifications of having an unchecked military presence roaming the mountains behind the home of the Eastern Band. It
was not a situation to be desired, but the businessman gambled that

the army major general would not be inclined to unleash such a destructive force upon the Georgia–North Carolina border if a better option presented itself. Since Thomas had been called for an audience with the major general, the businessman likely realized the bargaining power of his position and played his hand for all he could gain. Instead of looking for monetary compensation, William Thomas, holding a greater appreciation for the military life (since his initial dealings with Brigadier General Wool) and understanding of Washington politics (since the Treaty of New Echota), chose to place the military commander in the debt of himself and, by association, Chief Yonaguska's Eastern Band.

Disregarding the transitory reward of monetary remuneration, the businessman volunteered his services as intermediary and pathfinder in favor of a future testament imparted by Major General Scott regarding William Thomas's good character. In advance of Colonel Foster's contingent, Thomas (likely accompanied by a handful of soldiers from First United States Dragoons and under the command of Second Lieutenant Andrew J. Smith)[175] made for the Smoky Mountain camp of the refugee Chief Euchella. (In later recollection William Thomas admitted Euchella "had[,] but little left to make life desirable."[176]) Over the course of reacquainting himself with his adopted father's old friend turned fugitive, Thomas learned the bitter reason. Euchella was suffering the loss of his wife and brother due to the bitter existence of mountain fugitives.[177]

For a while the businessman listened to the aging man talk about how Tsali's group was, as Major General Scott had feared, attempting to gather an army from the ranks of the fugitive Cherokee. They were ready to "sell their lives as dear as they could to the whites. . . ."[178]

When he sensed an opening, the adopted son of Chief Yonaguska explained to the bereaved fugitive the dawning prosperity of the Eastern Band, the new laws that had been passed by the North Carolina General Assembly protecting the Cherokee from theft and fraud,[179] and the accommodations that could be made for the man who had preceded Chief Yonaguska in breaking from the Cherokee Nation.

Appealing to the man's honor, Thomas eventually convinced Eu-chella and his followers (a group of fugitives who had come from nearby encampments to hear the two men speak) to forsake Tsali's renegades for the protection of North Carolina's Eastern Band.[180]

As proof of their shifted allegiance, Euchella's people offered up the location of Tsali to William Thomas, who in turn relayed the po-sition to his army associates. Rather than chance any further compli-cations involving Tsali's capture (and the potential of compromising not only the recently secured integrity of Euchella's group but that of Chief Yonaguska's Eastern Band as well), the businessman abruptly reneged on his promise to deliver the ultimatum to Tsali's growing contingent to remain behind with Euchella's people to facilitate their assimilation within North Carolina.

The army found Tsali where Thomas's information had indi-cated and offered the men of the immediate family the choice of sur-render. They accepted and were eventually brought before a firing squad manned by their own Cherokee brethren.[181] In the following months, the fugitive Cherokee atop the Smoky Mountains were al-lowed to peacefully integrate with the Eastern Band and the sur-rounding North Carolina community.

After the Tsali incident, the removal continued without further violence, but the disruption had managed to cast the light of practi-cality on the program's less enthusiastic supporters. As the first hard figures detailing the removal's costs in manpower, accommodations, and fiscal appropriations came to light, the data was viewed in stark contrast to the promised gains of the removal. Upon further inspec-tion, the cruel disparity was soon discovered. The process of tracking down Cherokee runaways was abandoned.

Contrary to the cold, bitter silence the Cherokee Nation's leaders offered the federal government and the military,[182] for his part, William Holland Thomas earned experience in dealing with the mil-itary, the reward of welcoming an old friend into the company of the Eastern Band, and, most of all, the respect of Major General and fu-ture Lincoln Administration Commander of the Army Winfield Scott.

CHAPTER SEVEN

MANAGEMENT

I n 1839, after spending several years living at his stores, on the road, or on one of his mother's recently purchased real estate holdings, William Holland Thomas moved his mother and himself into a permanent residence on the southern shore of the Tuckasegee River. The mother and son named the thousand-acre estate reportedly collected by Thomas as compensation for a bad debt[183] Stekoa Fields in remembrance of the pre–American Revolutionary era Cherokee township that had once been located on the land. With the assistance of his slave stock, staffers, and surplus store supplies, the man orchestrated the transformation of a modest rural plot into a sizable agrarian refuge replete with earthen cellar, a makeshift irrigation/plumbing system, and a scenic vista of the nearby river.

It was his intention that the place, located relatively near his Indiantown holding, might serve as a periodic escape from the trappings of his mercantile trade, but, in the months and years that followed the Tsali incident, the young businessman's idle thoughts continued to return to the potential vulnerability of his adopted brethren among the Eastern Band.

Thomas's brush with Major General Winfield Scott had benefitted the opportunist businessman, the Eastern Band, and those fugitive Cherokee who had forsaken the life of the hunted for the promise of security within the confines of the State of North Carolina. Yet, the potential for disaster remained. Tsali's murder, flight, and potential insurrection had also illustrated the extent of the Eastern Band's vulnerability to the perceptions, predilections, and privations of the American people. Even though Chief Yonaguska and his tribal leadership had divined a way to escape the fate of the Cherokee Nation's factionalism and the Eastern Band's Cherokee agents had managed to save the community from the repercussions of the fugitive status of Euchella's people and the forced relocation of the remainder of the Nation, the tribe's continued existence remained closely linked with the seemingly fickle nature of the federal government and the disinterested sufferance of North Carolina's coastal leadership. William Thomas knew that in order to remain on their land his Cherokee brethren would need to adopt a balance between the cultivated settler culture and the distinct nature of their own heritage.[184]

Moving with the efficiency of a shrewd administrator, Thomas established a post office in his old Indiantown store.[185] While increasing his own business's efficiency (and potentially drawing a greater number of influential non–Native American neighbors to the Cherokee land), this move also gave the man a bureaucratically founded reason for renaming Indiantown something decidedly less exclusionary and less "Indian." As a result of the additional federal service provided, the settlement was officially renamed Quallatown for an elderly Cherokee woman (who had long inhabited the property) and the surrounding Eastern Band reservation came to be popularly referred to as the Qualla Boundary.[186] As Thomas was given additional official opportunities (either through the institution of federally mandated census-takings or through the filing of legal actions on behalf of Eastern Band members), he segmented the surrounding Cherokee territory into the named townships of Alarka (on the banks of the Tennessee River in Macon County), Aquona (found along the Nantihyala River in Macon County), Stekioh (a short distance from the new Thomas homestead near Quallatown), and Cheoih (on the Cheoih River in Macon County).[187] As Quallatown similarly grew into the Qualla Boundary, William Thomas subsequently divided the land initially into several additional settlements (including Bird Town, Yellow Hill, Paint Town, Wolf Town, and Big Cove).[188]

Next, he petitioned both North Carolina's regional authorities and the state legislature for the construction of a proposed "Ocanaluftee Turnpike" through the area and across the mountains into Georgia. However, after several attempts, as Western North Carolina was still considered far too remote and far less economically viable than other regions, he received only vague promises of pending road work improvements. Undeterred by the distantly held opinions, the businessman responded with the institution of several construction plans that would make not only his own property but also the landholdings of the Eastern Band more palatable to skeptical state investors who failed to share Thomas's vision of the untapped wealth of traffic that would transit between Georgia and Tennessee hidden behind the Appalachian Mountains.

Instructing his Murphy store staffer J. W. King to be mindful "that the lumber be good quality [and] plank well seasoned,"[189] William Thomas ordered the erection of a store house at his Murphy locale as well as the completion of a house and a meeting house and the maintenance of a sawmill at Quallatown.[190] Heeding the United States' wishes and imposed requirements that "if individuals are desirous of remaining, they must purchase residences for themselves,"[191] Thomas also started accruing backcountry real estate for his adopted tribe.[192] As the law remained decidedly grey as to additional private Cherokee land grants to the already established Eastern Band reservation, Thomas (the contracted Cherokee Agent and an indisputable United States citizen) worked out a system with Chief Yonaguska so that private area land, obtained parcel by parcel as they became available, was then bought in advance from William Thomas for the Eastern Band and the allotments placed under his name in trust for Chief Yonaguska's followers. The land could then be utilized by the Eastern Band of Cherokee as legitimately documented private real estate holdings beyond the restrictions of a government-allotted reservation and, at the same time, remain the irrevocable communal property of the Eastern Band.

As the Quallatown community began resembling other prominent urban centers, Thomas turned his attention to addressing social and cultural issues, but, for all of their political foresight and fiscal savvy, the North Carolina Cherokee were, according to one 1808 observer, "at least twenty years behind"[193] the Cherokee of other regions. In relying on oral communication as a means of retaining their heritage and socio-cultural identity, the regional Native American populace had been slow to adapt to the written style of communication brought by the Europeans.

Relegated to the status of "savages"[194] and "Red Men,"[195] the Cherokee began actively combating the settlers' allegations of primitive thought and backwards cultural motion shortly after the turn of the nineteenth century with the creation and implementation of a written form of the Cherokee language (courtesy of Cherokee National and Ridge supporter Sequoya).[196] The language, when published in bilingual (Cherokee-English) newspapers and distributed throughout the Cherokee Nation,[197] enabled a dramatic educational transformation among most regional Cherokee tribes.

Chief Yonaguska's followers, however, had seceded from the Cherokee Nation several years prior to the widespread implementation of Sequoya's syllabary. Eastern Band sovereignty had already been threatened when a contingent within the 1828 North Carolina Assembly referred to the North Carolina Cherokee in a report to the

United States Congress, saying that "the red men are not within the pale of civilization, they are not under the restraint of morality, nor the influence of religion. . . ."[198] Deprived of the Cherokee Nation's limited advances, Eastern Band members drew dangerously close to being identified by the notions of their jaded critics as "unlettered people"[199] and, hence, as undesirable an element as the Over-Mountain Men and outlaws who had previously controlled Western North Carolina.

While several missionary groups (notably the Moravians, Methodists, and Baptists)[200] had made their way into the country's southern interior during the colonial era and the succeeding periods of "mental improvement"[201] through Great Awakening revivalism, few had managed to retain the ongoing interests of the Cherokee citizenry. Those few whose teachings and supplies intrigued the Southern Cherokee were occasionally asked to remain, answering questions, demonstrating the preferred western way of using English speech and written language, the finer skills of construction, farming, herding, and the fashioning of clothes, besides the preaching of their own monotheistic doctrine. However, once either the missionaries realized they were being had or their usefulness to the tribe had noticeably declined, the Christian emissaries were encouraged to leave. This later changed, however, as greater numbers of Cherokee began to intermarry with the encroaching European (as well as later American hunters and settlers), bringing more permanent teaching assets and formal Christian practices to the mainstream Cherokee in the formal settings of missionary schools.[202]

The same could not be said of the Eastern Band's otherwise proactive membership. To William Holland Thomas, the introduction of the regimentation, rote, and formulaic environment of the Christian religion seemed to be the only way he could counter the bitter taste of the Eastern Band's presently disorganized but equally bitter opposers. While a Christianized Eastern Band would appeal to their American neighbors, the Cherokee who had escaped the rising tide of Christianity within the Cherokee Nation were not as enthusiastic.

Conversely, as a collection of largely pure-blooded Cherokee immersed in the ancient teachings of their tribe (far removed from Christian influences), the Eastern Band of North Carolina suffered the social privations of near isolationism again. Undesirous of converts to their religion, the group remained a numerically minor North Carolina community with limited exposure to the skills of the evolving modernized world. Uninterested in Christianity and inhabiting a remote region with an initially spartan populace, Chief Yonaguska's people attracted scant missionaries and teachers endowed with hardy dispositions to weather the climate and render their intellectual services for more than a few months at a time. Even with Thomas's own liquid assets, the Eastern Band met with repeated instances of grievous disappointment as one promising teacher after another chose to move away in search of a more urban environment and the promise of greater profit to be found in a growing populace.

Although Thomas's aging Chief was an open-minded opportunist and a social progressive in many ways, he remained deeply rooted in the centuries-old philosophy and cosmology of his ancestors and largely suspicious of missionaries.[203] After listening to his slave, Cudjo, read the Book of Matthew from a proffered Christian Bible, for example, Chief Yonaguska once remarked, "Well, it seems to be a good book—strange that the white people are not better, after having had it so long."[204] Thomas, himself a somewhat reluctant child of his parent's Protestant beliefs, however, saw the immediate benefits of a Christian affiliation and began lobbying for the creation of a Cherokee church congregation with regular services.

When the proposal was accepted, Thomas instructed his brethren in the pageantry of the singing, reading, and preaching of the Christian word, and when he felt confident the performance would be acceptable to an outside audience, he sent out invitations to key regional neighbors and North Carolina elite to attend the Eastern Band's annual Green Corn Dance (a several day and night long fertility/harvest festival similar to their settlement neighbors' own yearly Corn Shucking parties).[205] When the appointed day came, Thomas maneuvered his brethren into providing an albeit theologically questionable but seemingly necessary performance for the enjoyment of their Caucasian audience, which included the influential businessmen, southern politicians, and the son of a long-time Thomas business associate and noted southern nullifier, John Caldwell Calhoun,[206] succeeding in making his group that much more socially accepted.

After their repeated successes in the public relations arenas, Thomas redoubled his efforts at integration. Affording the Eastern Band his personal experience in the diplomatic trade, the young North Carolinian crafted a positive shift in perception towards the Eastern Band (now largely viewed as a distinct subculture within their state), softening the potentially problematic aspects of their history into more benign skills and modernizing the parameters of their ancient traditions without altering their central themes or cultural distinctiveness.

Chief Yonaguska's followers continued to prove themselves as consummate hunters, bringing down in just one year 540 deer, seventy-eight bears, eighteen wolves, and two panthers,[207] but with Thomas's assistance, the tribal warriors and hunters adapted themselves to the newer advancements in rifle technology. In a move towards Eastern Band self-sufficiency, the Eastern Band of North Carolina Cherokee began producing and dyeing their own clothes, herding a number of pigs and sheep, as well as some cattle,[208] and laid down small farm plots (averaging 9.67 acres in size)[209] similar to their neighbors' for the yielding of corn, wheat, rye, and a few vegetables.[210]

As William Thomas and Chief Yonaguska had hoped, the Eastern Band eagerly took to their newfound skills. Before long, the adopted son of the Cherokee's advocacy towards western education (reading, writing, and mathematics) bore visible fruit in several Cherokee, such as Salola (Squirrel), who on his own took up the study of the practical points of engineering and metallurgy, and after a considerable amount of personal effort, trial and error, the Native American was producing not only farm equipment for the region but also patent-worthy improvements upon nationally available hunting rifles.

Yet, for all of William Thomas's efforts, Chief Yonaguska and his followers continued to remain in very real danger of sharing the Cherokee Nation's fate because of a shared long-standing personal vice, alcoholism. First introduced to liquor in the exchange of gathered surplus raw materials for rum, inebriated Native Americans were soon typified by chroniclers as slow-thinking creatures and, by wilderness travelers as tell-tale indicators of nearby "place[s] of Refreshment."[211] As the settlers made inroads, industrious traders like Walker and Thomas replaced happenstantial exchanges between trappers and travelers with fixed frontier stores erected along the borders of established Native American territory, some of which escalated into the realm of widespread social stereotype with the opening of stores for the explicit purpose of "vending spirituous liquors,"[212] which eventually contributed to Georgia's successful removal scheme.[213]

Although the Eastern Band was not removed with the Cherokee Nation, William Thomas, himself an initial purveyor of liquor to local Cherokee, recognized the deleterious effects of alcohol consumption on the general health of his brethren when he entered the position of Cherokee Agent. As with their spiritual issues, there was little Thomas could do, however, regarding the Eastern Band's addiction and susceptibility to a small vocal group of local critics[214] until the businessman changed the habits of the group's most well known drunk, his adopted father.

According to William Thomas's shared reminiscences with James Mooney, Chief Yonaguska was "somewhat addicted to liquor,"[215] but there are several indications in the historical record that the Cherokee Chief was something more than an occasional alcohol abuser. In one instance, at the age of sixty, Chief Yonaguska fell into "a severe sickness, terminating in a trance, during which his people mourned him as dead."[216] Chief Yonaguska, sources relate, awoke either twenty-four or fifteen days later (depending on the version of the story) outstretched upon a bier, awaiting the conclusion of tribal funerary services.[217] Rising before the assemblage, the Cherokee Chief reported that he had had one of his "visions"[218] with the Great Spirit.[219]

Although the documented situation appeared to hold spiritual validity for the Chief's Cherokee followers, a more worldly traveler like William Thomas (and an occasional imbiber himself) likely saw his adopted father's plight with a more scientific mind as an alcohol-induced coma.[220] It would take nearly a decade of discussion, but by late 1838 Thomas had convinced Chief Yonaguska to assemble the Eastern Band at the Qualla Boundary meeting house for a heated discussion on the subject of temperance.

At the gathering, the Cherokee Agent listened to his adopted father rail against the poisoning influence of alcohol on the Eastern Band and their fellow Native Americans. Chief Yonaguska then turned to William Thomas to ask the businessman to draw up a document pledging all signatories to perpetual sobriety, with those signatories who relapsed slated to be fined a sum of two shillings (that would then be tasked for use in purchasing new land for the Cherokee tribe). After affixing his name to the document, the Cherokee Chief stepped aside and subsequently watched as his followers likewise took the temperance pledge.

While one account brought before Congress reported that "an army of whiskey shops are situated on the line which divides the lands of Indians from whites"[221] in the western territory of the transplanted Cherokee Nation, Thomas continued to reinforce the temperance efforts of his adopted father. Thomas had applauded the initial Cherokee assemblage's efforts and relentlessly continued to utilize the issue on his trips beyond Haywood County to accrue public support for the Eastern Band. He eventually attended further tribal sobriety meetings.[222] When away on business, he also instructed his staff through correspondence to remind his brethren that they "must not get drunk,"[223] but the businessman also continued to provide ample availability of the source of the Eastern Band's vice. Long after the taking of the pledge, however, the opportunist's chain of stores continued to stock and sell a ready supply of liquor to his customers. Furthermore, not only did Thomas persist in his own moderate intake of alcohol on the road and at home, but he also, reportedly, allowed the consumption of alcohol at several tribal occasions (though the privilege was apparently never abused).[224]

With the returns on claims, the businessman continued to reinvest his time and money into the expanding interests of the Eastern Band. By the 1840s, William Thomas and the Eastern Band received their reward from the federal government. Not only had the action of removal proved to be a fiscal and logistical waste of governmental resources that eliminated further forced removal speculation, but the elite of Washington City had also conceded that "valuable improvements have been made on the [Qualla Boundary] lands."[225]

The Cherokee of the Eastern Band could remain in the shadows of the Smoky Mountains for as long as they desired.

CHAPTER EIGHT

ADVOCACY

As the danger of removal ebbed with the retasking and reallocation of United States Army assets (ordered to return to old posts, oversee positions farther along the Trail of Tears, or man new fortifications on American's western and southern frontiers) and civilian governmental Indian Affairs entities (ordered to new assignments out west or instructed to return home and file their reports), William Holland Thomas attempted to once more settle into his role as a private businessman, but the North Carolinian could no longer distance himself from his role as Cherokee Agent or adopted child of Chief Yonaguska, unlike his store business or other private profit-making ventures. For Thomas, the Eastern Band had become his extended family. His good fortunes were theirs, and, conversely, their problems were now entirely his own to manage or solve.

Although Chief Yonaguska's followers had been made relatively secure from summary criticism and the swift execution of removal through the implementation of Thomas's socialization policies, the Eastern Band remained on relatively unsteady economic and legal ground as far as its critics were concerned. As a group, the Eastern Band remained among the poorest elements of Western North Carolina society, and for decades many of the Cherokee continuously relied on Thomas's good graces for the provision of food, clothing, and legal services. Much of the land Thomas obtained for his brethren was paid from his own largely undocumented assets to be transferred to the Cherokee when they could pay the balance of the cost (an issue that would plague both parties in the years after the War of the Rebellion). Furthermore, as his involvement with breveted Brigadier General Wool attested, William Thomas's personal, legal, and business interests were rapidly becoming publicly associated (some might claim even interchangeable) with his motivations in representing his Cherokee brethren as their contractual Agent and public advocate.

Instead of distancing himself from the Eastern Band's legal affairs or seeking out a competent legal assistant who would allow Thomas to spend more time raising store profits and acquiring land for his Cherokee brethren, William Thomas intensified his efforts as Cherokee Agent and took on the additional position of political advocate on behalf of the Eastern Band.

Almost overnight, Thomas adopted a new, more proactive strategy. If he worked the situation and current political climate to his advantage, Thomas could dually recoup his dwindling investments through business contacts made in the service of the Eastern Band and through opportunities encountered in his regional travels (and through Thomas's charged rate of ten percent per claim filed) and thus ensure the longevity of the Cherokee under the shadows of the Smoky Mountains regardless of the fickle nature of politics.

Throughout the late 1830s and the 1840s, William Thomas continued to file personal claims for Cherokee like Scroop Enloe[226] and Betsy Woodward,[227] who sought their treaty-stipulated expenses to subsidize their desired relocation westward, but the developing legal expert also expanded his legal services to include other clients like mixed-blood Valley Town resident John Welch,[228] settler neighbor William Cunningham,[229] and other regional businessmen reportedly wronged by the United States Army malappropriations of private resources in their pursuit of a speedy Cherokee removal.[230]

A long-standing friend and mercantilist associate, William Thomas easily routed Welch's compensatory claim (engendering a reported loss of $3,990 in valuables)[231] along the same route as his Cherokee claims (as both went through the Department of War, before proceeding to their separate offices). William Cunningham's claim was another matter. In the man's attempt to fulfill his business obligation of delivering wagons stocked with goods to a rallying point for the Cherokee Removal, Cunningham had been stopped by a soldier, told to remove himself from the vehicle, and forced to allow the procession of his goods to continue, as Thomas later summarized, "entrusted to the care of a waggon [wagon] master in whom he had no confidence . . . to travel over a road almost impassable. . . ."[232] The two had apparently turned to arguing, and as a result the United States Army refused to pay the man the difference of $437.50 for his services.[233] It was William Thomas's job to see if the claim could be handled without the invocation of the onerous civilian court system. It would be a long, hard claim.

While William Thomas continued to represent Cunningham's claim and other similar claims on his frequent business trips,[234] the North Carolinian was reassured that he was proceeding as a competent legal professional when he suddenly began to receive a steady influx of documentation concerning the original set of removal claims he had filed a few years prior. Looking over the documentation, Thomas realized the delay. The claims were being approved as rapidly as the methodical machine of Washington bureaucracy could judge and grant them valid status. Similarly, as the federal government rewarded his lobbying efforts with small personal claims (averaging initially about six hundred dollars each),[235] other attorneys and agents began to approach the talented businessman, bequeathing to him their powers of attorney and hoping that Thomas would have equal success with their Cherokee clientele.[236] As a result, by November of 1839, William Thomas had managed to obtain $135,000 in removal awards for his Cherokee clients (and a fee of $15,000 for himself).[237]

Allowed the comfort of dealing with claimants and their related parties through correspondence (made relatively simple now that his Qualla Boundary post office was running with a local by the name of Jesse Silier as Postmaster),[238] the businessman was once more able to entertain the notion of exclusively managing his store chain. Spending some nights at his stores, William Thomas paid as many bills as he could, reallocated supplies from one store to another, and, in consultation with each establishment's record of transactions, ensured that his employees were being honest as well as faithful to their employer's wishes.[239] Occasionally staying at home when rest was needed, Thomas continued to oversee the management of the Stekoa Fields estate. The lonely businessman also saw to the needs of his mother and two children he had reportedly informally adopted: two sons (Andrew Patton and William Hyde), and an adopted daughter (known only as Angelina),[240] . . . but the life of a merchant meant constant movement and the occupation of an agent engendered traveling to distant locales, leaving the North Carolinian more at home on the open road than either at home with his mother or pulling inventory at one of his stores.

While on the road, the bachelor continued to visit the prospering cities of Raleigh, Charleston, Washington, and Philadelphia, but, according to his diary, William Thomas also traveled as far north as New York and Niagara Falls in search of sellable commodities (such as bacon,[241] pink root,[242] tobacco,[243] and ginseng[244]), profit-making business ventures, and changes of scenery. While largely dedicated to obtaining and transporting goods for his store[245] (including the rare backwoods commodity of published books)[246] which he conveyed via horse, wagon, and, sometimes, schooner, William Thomas also brokered occasional transactions for influential clients (including the depositing of credit at various banks along his travel routes), obtaining sorely needed cash to help stabilize his region's barter-dependent economy and overseeing the liquidation of several Welch and Love business assets.[247] The vital merchant also continued to indulge in the more lucrative aspects of land speculation and slave trading during the antebellum period, but as much as the businessman earned on his own, the North Carolinian remained deeply attracted to the more lucrative contacts he had made during his periods of active service to the Eastern Band.

During one of his buying and claim-filing trips, William Holland Thomas ran into an old acquaintance from his earlier governmental discussions over the 1835 Treaty of New Echota, former United States Commissioner to the Cherokee Reverend John Freeman Schermerhorn of New York. A member of the old Dutch Schermerhorn family[248] which had colonized much of the New York area during the late 1600s, the Schenectady-born reverend had moved his way up the social ladder through the administration of missionary activities. Oddly enough, Reverend Schermerhorn had been granted the position of overseeing the legal ramifications of the Cherokee Removal by the Jackson Administration as a shallow, placative gesture. As an ardent believer in missionary activities and moralistic Christian ethics, within a few months Reverend Schermerhorn managed to facilitate the largely peaceful transition of a Native American populace elsewhere, proving his personal worth to William Thomas and the Eastern Band as not only an honorable man but, more important, a proven friend of the Cherokee.

After the two colleagues discussed recent matters concerning the Cherokee Nation, the Eastern Band, and the backroom machinations of the Washingtonian bureaucratic machine, the conversation turned to matters of investment and real estate. Reverend Schermerhorn revealed that he was aware of a parcel of undisclosed land in which he was interested but was also short on the funds to secure it. The North Carolinian had occasionally utilized others' funds for business ventures that he, himself, deemed worthy of yielding a sizable return, having witnessed the deleterious effects of debt. William Thomas was also habitually free with his criticisms of others' financial problems, including glibly replying to a prospective client, "I would advise the doing all you can . . . to extricate yourself from embarrassment,"[249] but Reverend Schermerhorn seemed different.

At first, Thomas offered the man a hundred dollars, but then, reconsidering the deal's prospective gains, Thomas gave the man $200 for their prospective shared land purchase.[250] The reverend accepted his offer and the two parted company, expecting to see each other on their next trip to Washington, but Reverend Schermerhorn was nowhere to be found. Thomas waited for news from the man or the purchased parcel's deed sent through the mail, but no letters or packages from the New Yorker were received by the Qualla Boundary's post office in the following weeks or months.

Before the businessman could look into what had happened to his absent partner and funds, however, William Thomas was once more besieged by a series of unexpected difficulties. Returning home from a business trip, Thomas was forced to deal with the desertion of one of his store clerks from his post for an indeterminate amount of time.*[251] With his store still intact, the man was willing to forgive the transgression and moved on to Eastern Band business.

Soon, however, the Washington office was sending Thomas requests for documentation concerning the present and projected future status of Chief Yonaguska's Eastern Band. As had occurred with Major General Winfield Scott's count of the Native Americans traveling west on the Trail of Tears, Washington's political leaders were pressing for the establishment of census-taking operations to be analyzed against the concurrently created North Carolina Cherokee

---

* ". . . I had hoped better things," Thomas admonished the man's brother. "My experience has long since taught me to believe all persons are liable to err, therefore small ones may be overlooked where integrity is not involved."[252]

Removal enrollment lists. In a hasty effort at crisis management, Thomas, knowing that a lack of sufficient readable documentation would likely place his Cherokee clients in jeopardy as well as cause a substantial monetary loss (specifically, removal awards, legal fees, and lost store assets), ordered a few of his trading post staffers away from their daily positions to cull from the man's records and those of the surrounding towns the requested data.

The staff's assignment, covering a large swath of Western North Carolina, was haphazard and, admittedly, incomplete, but when William Thomas deemed that enough information had been gathered to satisfy Washington, he submitted the findings in list form (resembling several pages in length detailing family units in each Qualla Boundary town under Thomas's care)[253] to Commissioner T. Hartley Crawford of the Indian Affairs office, . . . but the process of paperwork and record keeping did not end there. As new information became available, Thomas then sent the accrued information along to the commissioner or his superior, the Secretary of War.[254] While the practice would later land Thomas in deep trouble, the Washington officials seemed to be appreciative of the additional effort and ameliorative of the Cherokee Agent's speedy desire to please his Washington handlers with tales of "the sweet shrub . . . and . . . rich pasturage"[255] of the forming Qualla Boundary set in stark contrast to "the army of whiskey shops" along the borders of the Cherokee Nation.[256]

Yet, once more, Thomas was given cause to doubt himself when he learned of the existence of a small vocal minority inhabiting the surrounding regions desiring a return to the forced removal practices of years past.

The recent spells of bitter weather and poor economic outlook in the urbanizing region had seemed to rekindle in a few less fortunate and less educated backcountry residents the old familiar sentiments of xenophobic division, disassociation, and blame upon those who were outwardly different from themselves. Following the sentiments of their fathers and grandfathers and eventually sons and grandsons in their persecution of regional slaves and freemen, the vocal minority chose to take out their misdirected anger and economic frustrations upon the region's most visible alien cultural group and ready source of cheap agrarian labor, Chief Yonaguska's Cherokee.

Over the years, Thomas had worked relentlessly to disprove President Andrew Jackson's 1835 observation, ". . . that they [the Native Americans] can not live in contact with a civilized community and prosper."[257] Thomas had always counseled his Cherokee brethren to "be sober[,] be industrious[,] and [be] friendly with each other and the whites."[258] Yet, an unnamed group of North Carolinians had bypassed the local government to appeal to the very elements of the federal government who had sponsored the removal of the Cherokee Nation from Georgia in the first place.

Faced with the resurgence of prejudiced behavior from a corner previously considered friendly, the Cherokee Agent carefully instructed his brethren within the Eastern Band, ". . . I don't want them to intertain [entertain] any unkind feeling towards the whites for petitioning for their removal solong as they do nothing more than to petition the government to do what they have no power to do no[.] [A]ttention should be paid to it . . . act in such manner as to give no cause of complaint."[259] With the rule of law and precedent on their side, William Thomas and the leadership of the Eastern Band held to the hope that their efforts at assimilation had been as warmly received as their more affluent neighbors and congressional officials had shown.

Overtly, William Thomas projected an air of confidence for his fellow brethren that an active demonstration of their adversary's flawed thinking would shame the dissenters into silence and abandonment of their rage-filled intentions. Although Thomas intellectually believed the truism of the proposed course and expected end, the blossoming Eastern Band altruist still could not understand the darker reservations of his adversaries.

"I regret to hear bad feelings seem to exist with some of the whites respecting them [the Cherokee]," Thomas wrote Felix Axeley [Axley] in a December 1839 letter. ". . . . I have advised them to be at peace with each other and their white neighbors and as yet I have not been informed of those unfortunate people having given any just cause of offense. If my advocating their rights has offended any of my friends however much I might under any other circumstances regret it[,] I have one consolation that I have faithfully discharged my duty to those people a [unreadable] discharge of which is worth more to me than the unjust approbation of the world and I had much rather be blamed for doing my duty than neglecting it and when entrusted with defending the rights of white or red man I hope I shall always be found faithful to my trust and am worthy of the confidence reposed in me without regard to consequences. The Indians are as much entitled to their rights as I am to mine they were born in the state have been raised in it and by the Supreme Court of the United States was denied the rights of foreigners in a decision made on the case between Georgia and the Cherokee Nation in 1831 and with North Carolina passed a law for their protection[,] which was giving the consent of the state for those people to remain in it."[260]

Lacking the asset of recently surveyed riches discovered beneath the modest soil of the Qualla Boundary, the ample pressure of an imposing state, or the attentions of legislative or executive governmental leaders, the lobbying efforts to remove the Eastern Band westward eventually dwindled to a trickle, then died when the minority realized the error of their ways. But, as with Tsali, the incident had once more illustrated the Eastern Band's vulnerability to criticism. Thomas and Chief Yonaguska's Cherokee had managed to dispel the unfocused and uneducated attack, but, with reports of rising levels of animosity among elements of the Cherokee Nation in the west, the signs forewarned of future attempts to spoil the Eastern Band's continued success.

By the closing months of 1839, William Thomas broke from the Cherokee Nation's and Eastern Band's well-established practice of reactionary politicking. Taking the initiative on himself, Thomas began using his cultivated Washington and North Carolinian legislative contacts to establish the Eastern Band as a federally recognized entity separate from the Cherokee Nation and implement a source of federally funded revenue for the advancement of the Eastern Band such as the United States was giving to the Cherokee Nation's leadership. Furthermore, he sought to firmly establish that no member of the Eastern Band would ever be removed from North Carolina without their express consent and to obtain the irrevocable right of his clients, as inhabitants of North Carolina, as citizens of the United States.

Thomas returned to Washington City and in a meeting with Van Buren's Secretary of War, Joel R. Poinsett, Thomas wrung from the secretary the promise that the North Carolina Cherokee "will not be tracked any more by troops. . . ."[261] Furthermore, the secretary admitted that "the Department was disposed to leave them to the freedom of their own choice and under the control of the state in which they resided . . ."[262] The North Carolinian then demonstrated the advancements his brethren had made in temperance, education, the acquiring of trades, and the cultivation of arable land for sellable produce. Thomas undoubtedly embellished a few points (as few of the Eastern Band's farms had yet to reach full self-sufficiency, let alone levels of sustainable economical mass production), but Poinsett was suitably impressed, and promised to write to the Eastern Band congratulating them on their marked transformation.[263]

William Thomas next moved to the Office of Indian Affairs and "applied for a separation of those [Cherokee] East from those West."[264] Commissioner Crawford took the request under advisement. Thomas was not satisfied with the answer, but before he could pursue the matter further, he received ill news. Chief Yonaguska of the Eastern Band had died.

While some might claim that sobriety had indeed saved his life, the eighty-year-old Cherokee Chief had been declining in health for years. When Chief Yonaguska felt the end was drawing near, he gathered the Eastern Band leadership under the roof of the town meeting hall. Brought into the room by attendants and placed on a nearby couch, he related to the assemblage his wishes that his Cherokee never leave "their own country"[265] and that, against all expectations,

William Holland Thomas, not the Chief's naturally born son, Flying Squirrel, would serve as the next leader of the Eastern Band of North Carolina Cherokee.

Chief Yonaguska then reportedly pulled a blanket tightly about himself, lay back on the couch, and expired.[266]

The old Chief's body was laid to rest beside Soco Creek with a small mound of stones to serve as a grave marker.

CHAPTER NINE

CHIEF THOMAS

While the news of his adopted father's demise deeply sad-
dened him, William Holland Thomas knew the Cherokee of
the Eastern Band were in the capable hands of Flying Squirrel (also
known as Ka'lahu', All-Bones, and Sawnook), while he was otherwise engaged.[267] It is unknown precisely when Thomas learned of
his elevation to the position of Chief of the Eastern Band of North
Carolina Cherokee, but, given the delicate nature of the work he was
conducting on behalf of the departed Chief, the man's opportunities
to leave the City of Washington for the lengthy journey home without penalty were decidedly limited.

William Thomas had not intended to stay very long in the nation's
capital. Acting as the Eastern Band's emissary, he had already wrung

from several Van Buren Administration officials the promises he and his clients needed to hear, but, as a businessman, legal expert, and now Native American leader, Thomas knew words were insufficient when compared with documentation. Thomas was resigned to the fact that he would not be leaving the Washington area until he held in his possession the signed documentation *his* Eastern Band required.

Thomas had chosen to visit the City of Washington at a peculiar time. While the spring weather was passable, the political climate was tempestuous at best. In his two consecutive terms in office, President Andrew Jackson had not only made enemies of the southern Cherokee but, through a series of legally dubious actions, had also managed to bypass a congressionally approved cabinet in favor of his own "kitchen cabinet," alienating his first Vice President (John C. Calhoun) and dividing members of his own Democratic Party with heavy-handed demonstrations (including the 1832 ordered presence of army soldiers to enforce South Carolina's summary compliance with federal tariff laws). In endorsing native New Yorker Martin Van Buren as his successor over Calhoun, Jackson had managed a *fait accompli*, setting north against south and Democrat against Democrat.

Van Buren's subsequent administration was little better. Shortly after he was sworn into office, the country suffered the first major depression in its history, the so-called Panic of 1837. As the economic situation worsened, President Van Buren tried to court southern Democrats back into the fold, advocating a stricter adherence to their preferred states' rights policy on slavery and openly opposing the abolition of the slave trade throughout the Washington area. The President, however, soon lost what little support he had gained when the man revealed that he was opposed to both the incorporation of the Texas territory into the Union and the expansion of slavery into developing western states.

Contrary to a cursory evaluation of the situation, however, William Thomas was in an advantageous position. Although not an aristocrat by birth or a legal professional by the standard of a formal education, Thomas was, as an established landowning and slave-trading southern

Democratic merchant, a member of the exact constituency the present administration wished to court for political favor in the forthcoming 1840 presidential election. He was a known Washington entity, bore some clout within the War Department for having aided Major General Scott during the Removal Program, and had a well-established history of providing clear issues for the Bureau of Indians Affairs review and approval.

While Thomas had immediately connected with Secretary of War Joel Poinsett, there was little beyond the application of pressure that the politician could do for him until the necessary paperwork was processed and presented for final approval. As spring weather entered full bloom, Thomas once more turned to Secretary Poinsett's subordinate Commissioner Crawford and his Bureau of Indian Affairs to expedite the businessman's claims, but upon arrival at the man's office, the North Carolinian found the Office of the Commissioner unoccupied. Instructed that T. Hartley Crawford would not return "before the middle of next month,"[268] Thomas again tried to return to Poinsett's office. Unfortunately, instead of finding the easily agreeable man with whom he had chatted before, he was informed that only Crawford could handle his Cherokee situation and file the necessary reports. If he wished to see his clients' claims fulfilled and his increasingly needed ten percent fee, Thomas would have to remain in Washington well into the summer.

While the pressing issues of family, finance, and leadership waiting for him at home weighed heavily on his thoughts, the prospect of returning home empty-handed and knowing that he would have to return again in the fall under a potentially less favorable political climate tipped the scales. Thomas remained in the warming city of Washington.

"I am in good health[,]" he wrote an inquisitive Tennessean colleague, "[have] some little money to spend[,] and [have] a tollerable [tolerable] stock of patience which has never been exhausted and I am in hopes will not be when attending to the business here [that] I have undertaken."[269]

Faced with his first abatement of Cherokee business since becoming the Eastern Band's Agent years ago and effectively stranded
in a modern city that served as a crossroads of the Atlantic coast,
William Thomas turned to his other business concerns at hand. He
sought bargains on tools, groceries, and other profit-making goods essential for his region's developing economic base, purchased them in
bulk, had them crated and sent as freight southward.[270]

The City of Washington's marketplaces and docks were a verita-
ble gold mine of sellable goods, but North Carolina's economy, hampered by consistently poor weather, was slow to recover from the
panic of the previous decade. With money continuing to remain scarce
at home[271] and little else to occupy his mind, William Thomas began
to fret over his store's dwindling profits.

Instead of reining in his own buying impulses, Thomas blamed
his falling solvency on debtor clients and potentially absent-minded
trading post staff. Firing off letter after letter, Thomas instructed his
employees to take care of his interests and keep accurate records of
every transaction. But as the situation continued to stagnate and his
profits continued to bottom out, he reached a point where he could no
longer continue his generosity to the few neighbors beyond the Qualla
Boundary to whom he had allowed a tab (claiming, "I had rather have
the goods than any debts which have to be collected by law"[272]).

Yet, in trying to keep his current projects afloat, Thomas did not
likewise want his own future business prospects damaged by poor
word of mouth. While the young businessman would infrequently
ask others to convey his best wishes to his mother and the Eastern
Band, William Thomas remained vulnerable to the potential ending of
his professional career as Felix Hampton Walker's had been, a failure.
Often writing that "[it] would afford me a pleasure to do any thing
[anything] you may want done in this place,"[273] Thomas grew increasingly determined in his business transactions to illustrate his
willingness to do others favors and follow up on others' loose ends in
the hope that they would keep him in mind for future potentially
income-generating projects.

As the weeks dragged on, Thomas periodically strolled into Craw-ford's Indian Affairs office to ascertain if the man had returned early from his undisclosed trip. Failing there, Thomas invariably began to stroll the city's streets in search of stimulation. On Sundays, he would occasionally attend church gatherings.[274] Weekdays, when the United States Congress was in session, the North Carolinian could often be found wandering the halls of the Capitol Building or listening to lec-tures held in the rotunda.* Yet, the man failed to be moved by the majesty of the democratic machinery over which his father had several times risked his life to secure, remarking to one business associate that "the other house [has] done nothing but squabble about the rights of five members from New Jersey to take their seats (whose seats are contested). . . ."[276]

When Crawford's brief absence of a few weeks grew longer still, William Holland Thomas filled the remainder of his time chasing the fairer sex.

"In the recess of Congress," he wrote Nicholas Woodfin, "this city is entirely uninteresting except . . . that gay and fashionable company of ladies which nearly every evening pass up [P]ennsylva-nia Avenue to the capital and the East garden . . . have not deserted this . . . place they seem engaged in their daily employment as usual. I have no doubt the gay and fashionable young gentlemen who have [unreadable] large fortunes and only want a help mate to spend them could be as well accomodated here as in any other market[.]"[277]

Long before the bachelor first entered the urban locale, the City of Washington had garnered a well-deserved reputation of provid-ing its gentlemen clientele with evenings of feminine entertainment throughout its numerous Red Light District establishments, but there as well the businessman failed to find anyone or anything to hold his attention. During a brief Fourth of July foray, he escorted two un-named women to the White House grounds to watch a pyrotechnic

---

* The few diaries which have survived Thomas's travels indicate that he favored preachers who stood against the abolitionist agenda of the north.[275]

display,[278] while on another occasion, the North Carolinian was smacked across the face for apparently ungentlemanly behavior when camped near a fishing hole with a young lady.[279]

William Thomas appeared to be largely dismissive of Washington's single women, claiming they were solely enamored by fashion, money, and the attainment of status.[280] Yet, Thomas's apparent disinterest actually belied a deep-seated well of insecurity. Writing a letter from his Washington quarters, Thomas explained to Captain Nimrod Jarrett of Franklin County, North Carolina, that, "all other Buncombe girls could do better than receve [receive] the addresses of an old bachelor like me—stated my difficulties in courting, a young girl might not love me if I did her[.] [O]ld maids scold and widows recollect the virtues of their past husbands and none of their vices. . . ."[281] It seemed that no matter how hard he pressed or how high he reached, the North Carolinian never felt himself accomplished enough to warrant the selfless affections of those who were not indebted to him.

When Commissioner T. Hartley Crawford finally returned to Washington days later, Thomas appeared at the man's doorstep once more. Given entrance and eager to expedite his situation, the businessman laid before Commissioner Crawford his recent North Carolina Cherokee Removal claims, the legal papers asking for a United States–recognized separation of Eastern Band affairs from those of the Cherokee Nation, and documentation outlining the authorized expansion of Thomas's power of attorney.[282]

"I am much pleased with Mr. Crawford," wrote Thomas to John Gillespie on July 1st, 1839. "[H]e is a very pleasant man to transact business with and[,] I believe[,] disposed to do right[.] [H]e seems to have none of [J]udge Kennedy's arstocratic [aristocratic] notions, . . . you have no doubt a more liberal construction would have been given to the treaty, and no sale of a reservation would have been regarded as a sale except such as would have been adjudged legal by the courts of the state in which the reservation . . ."[283]

While annoyed at the lost time, the businessman placed himself in sharp contrast to other more aggressive Cherokee agents and Native

American leaders with whom he knew Commissioner Crawford had dealt. As the two met in meeting after meeting, Thomas worked his warm, inoffensive, and pragmatic style on the old Jackson Administration appointee. Thomas's social graces were eventually returned in kind, but, for all his salesman skills, the North Carolinian would not budge from the rule of law or the bureaucratically tedious review practices of the War Department. No matter how genteel the atmosphere, William Thomas would still have to follow the legal motions of tracking claims and defending their representatives.

When the businessman judged the moment most opportune, Thomas jarred Commissioner Crawford and his superiors with a second request: an equal share of the War Department's removal funds. Whereas Major Ridge had agreed to the same proposal by Thomas years earlier in their discussions over the Treaty of New Echota, neither the federal government nor the now unchecked Principal Chief of the Cherokee Nation knew or acceded to the backroom deal. The Thomas–Ridge agreement appeared to have been nullified by the same bullets which had claimed the life of the Cherokee treaty signatory. As he knew Principal Chief Ross would never grant the seceded Eastern Band a single boon beyond readmittance to the Cherokee Nation, it was now the North Carolina Cherokee Chief's primary duty to convince the federal government of the benefit in giving the Eastern Band removal remuneration without forcing the group to actually sell their land and move westward.

Unbridled by the circumstances which had pressured Ridge to comply, the Washington politicians were less than enthusiastic with the North Carolinian's request. The Eastern Band, Thomas insisted, was never going to willingly rejoin the Cherokee Nation and would never seek removal to a western reservation as a group, but, as Principal Chief Ross's people had been compensated for the loss of their *ancestral* land and property, the Native Americans he represented were entitled to the same remuneration under the removal treaty.[284] He then placed before the Commissioner of Indian Affairs a formal request for $55,000 to be divided equally among his charges at

$55.33⅓ to be invested in an interest-bearing account, which would be used by now Chief Thomas and the Eastern Band leadership in their continued efforts to improve the living conditions and marketability of the Cherokee under their charge.[285]

Losing a share of the good graces recently fostered between them, T. Hartley Crawford balked at the new request. Given the history of division and geographic separation between the two Native American socio-political entities, the Van Buren Administration was willing to accede to the Eastern Band's request for a complete legal separation from the Cherokee Nation but, as to the second matter, denied Thomas's request as lacking merit. In the commissioner's own judgement, the Bureau of Indian Affairs was legally unable and morally unwilling to compensate Thomas's North Carolina Cherokee since the remaining applicants were unwilling to *actually remove.*

Upon receiving Commissioner Crawford's answer, William Thomas then brought the "per capita" request before Secretary Joel Poinsett. Banking on the man's seeming partiality towards the developing Eastern Band, Thomas explained to the man "his nation's" destitute position, his own growing indebtedness due largely to his time and efforts seeking justice for his Cherokee brethren as well as the securing of approximately fifty thousand acres of North Carolina real estate (largely the present confines of the Qualla Boundary) by means of $7,500 on loan from his own personal funds for the Eastern Band, . . . but Poinsett remained unmoved.[286] The government contended that situation, as the North Carolina Cherokee had actually left their ancestral lands years before the removal and had settled on *private* real estate (protected as such by North Carolina State law). As a result, unless Congress decided to change the parameters of the War Department's and Bureau of Indian Affairs' criteria of claimant evaluation, there was no legal reason to entertain Thomas's request.

Thomas began to court the sympathetic ears of Washington's congressional membership with an aim towards designing legislation to remedy the problem. William Thomas was dealt another blow. Having recently dealt with the disparate factions within the Cherokee Nation over the issue of removal, Commissioner Crawford had initially welcomed Thomas as a straight arrow, but his recent requests began to color Crawford's appraisal of the southern businessman.

Commissioner T. Hartley Crawford was a realist. Trained as a lawyer and legislator, the Pennsylvania-born 1838 political appointee had become largely inoculated against the appearing altruism on an Agent's or Native American leader's face (an occupational hazard apparently held by several of his subsequent office holders, including William Wilkens) or by the sweet-talk of those who, like Thomas, wished access to the Indian Affairs Removal Program funding. As a consummate Washington professional, the commissioner had likely heard of William Thomas's past altercation with breveted Brigadier General Wool, the businessman's pursuit of monies allegedly owed by the War Department to several private southern businessmen involved in supplying needed resources for the removal,[287] and the filing of the man's own business claims,[288] as well as the steadily increasing abundance of Thomas-submitted North Carolina Cherokee claimant documentation as either a valid series of warranted legal actions or the disgraceful machinations of a carefully crafted scam. Rather than chancing either the potential political pitfall of blind acquiescence or the fallout incurred by unactionable charges of fraudulent behavior against the private businessman, Commissioner Crawford subsequently ordered Thomas to supplement his claims with a comprehensive report.

William Holland Thomas's patience was waning, but little would be gained through further appeals. Upon receiving the request, a soured Thomas returned to his Washington quarters and, with due haste, began to prepare his response. He would not spend one day longer than absolutely necessary in the nation's capital. A few hours later, however, as Thomas pored over his collected books and papers, the man hit another snag. In his haste to submit the

North Carolina Cherokee claims, Thomas had left a number of documents (now deemed critical to the requested report) back at one
of his stores. Barely suppressing anger, the chagrined businessman
penned off a quick letter home, asking for his pertinent records, and
hastily returned to composing his report.

While Secretary Poinsett was unwilling to bypass the rule of law
for the North Carolinian, Thomas found in the man a solid supporter
of the Eastern Band. Shortly after receiving Commissioner Crawford's
assignment, the businessman was allowed a desk in the War Department and access to the executive agency's complement of resources
to assist in the completion of his report. Nearly every morning
Thomas would rise from bed, arrive at the proffered desk by nine
o'clock, and remain working at the post until approximately five in
the afternoon.[289] Likely breaking briefly for dinner, William Holland
Thomas would then return to his rented space and resume his litany
of researching and writing until the midnight hour, when he would
return to bed.[290] The businessman continued the lengthy records
collection and report-writing process from home for several months
more, but before the work could be completed, Thomas heard dis-
heartening news. The Cherokee Nation was sending a delegation to
Washington to demand the voiding of the allegedly illegally signed
Treaty of 1835 (as Principal Chief Ross himself had not been the
rightful signatory)[291] and, failing that, obtaining the totality of their
$200,000 in appropriated removal funds.[292]

While Thomas had found Major Ridge a reasonable man among
the Nation's past Washington delegations, the businessman knew
the dissenter would be marginalized by the heavy-handed actions
of his superior, Principal Chief John Ross and his growing number of
post-removal supporters. To complicate matters, Principal Chief
Ross refused to recognize the divide between the Eastern Band and
the Cherokee Nation, seeing the North Carolina Cherokee as little
more than an extension of his government. As a wrinkle in Principal
Chief Ross's belief that the removal had been an act of wholesale

government-orchestrated prejudice for the sake of a few thousand acres of land, the Cherokee leader had labored long and hard for the Eastern Band to be included in the Removal Program.

If William Thomas held any desire to depart for a brief summer visit home, the fleeting notion evaporated with news of the Principal Chief's imminent arrival. The businessman saw the Cherokee National leadership as foes as deadly as the vocal removal minority within his home state.[293] As a Caucasian agent of a collection of rebel Cherokee, Thomas was viewed with contempt by the group's majority. As a Cherokee Chief, however, the businessman would be characterized as an illegitimate pretender at best and an opportunistic parasite bent on ruining their North Carolina Cherokee brethren.

While recent events among the Bureau of Indian Affairs had held a negative connotation for the North Carolinian, Thomas also knew that no matter how little the Washington politicians thought of his actions, wedded with a proven track record in support of the Eastern Band's modernization, neither Principal Chief Ross nor his other delegates were sufficiently politically astute to intimidate the United States government's Bureau of Indian Affairs.[294] Similarly, with the State of Georgia having received that which it had long desired, Thomas now found, pursuing his own course of legislation with the Eastern Band, both Congress and the Van Buren (President Jackson's chosen successor) Administration were slow to revisit the decidedly humiliating events which had preceded the Cherokee Removal. As William Thomas had been called to task for his impetuousness, so too would Principal Chief John Ross, causing Thomas to gloat, "I calculate I shall be able to disappoint him so far as those East whose claims I have filed are concerned."[295]

In late July 1839, before the businessman could prove himself the superior legal and politically savvy strategist, word reached William Thomas and the Washington community that Cherokee leaders Major Ridge, his son John Ridge, Elias Boudinott, and Principal Chief John

Ross had been assassinated by unknown parties residing within the Arkansas territory.[296] Shortly thereafter, a second report arrived in Washington that only the Ridges had been killed.[297] Subsequent reports further muddied the situation, making it nearly impossible to judge the veracity of any report over the next, but as further unconflicting details arose, three points were becoming clear: (1) there had been either a power play or an act of retribution made against Cherokee Nation members (likely involving the Treaty of New Echota), (2) Major Ridge was dead, and (3) many of the gains Thomas and the Eastern Band had made since the removal were now placed in jeopardy.[298]

The sudden violent turn of events in the western territory shocked elements of the United States government. As relevant information dribbled into the nation's capital linking the apparent killings to the delegation's pending arrival, Commissioner Crawford ordered that "the agents west suspend the payment of all monies due from the United States until those difficulties are settled."[299]

In apprising his Cherokee clients in Cheoih of the situation, William Thomas stressed the gravity of the situation, writing: "The U[nited] S[tates] will demand the murderers of Ridge and Boudinott[,] will[,] if [they are] not given up[,] probably take them by force[.] No means will be furnished to any Cherokees to remove until that is settled. . . . Keep Temperate."[300] In filing a separation from the Cherokee Nation's legal status, however, William Thomas had sidestepped disaster for himself and the Eastern Band. By the time it was discovered that Cherokee Principal Chief John Ross was alive and en route to Washington,[301] Commissioner Crawford had already completed the review of several thousand Eastern Band claims and was now beginning to look over William Thomas's hastily written fifty-page report.

As Thomas began the lengthy appeals process regarding the granting of the $55.33⅓ to his Eastern Band Cherokee and started planning into which interest-bearing account he might place the sum, other problems began to surface for the businessman. Thomas had done little client screening when he had inherited a number of his filed claimants from his backcountry contemporaries seeking Washington representation for their clients. As a result, Thomas had initially dealt with the Cherokee personage of Betsy Woodward on claimant paperstock,[302] but as letters began to pour in from the woman asking where her money was, he began to see another reason as to why the client had been unloaded on his personage. After several attempts at correspondence, explaining to the woman the legal reasons for the delayed fulfillment of her claim to be paid for her move onto the western reservations in the Arkansas territory,[303] Thomas heard that Woodward was traveling to Washington to investigate the claim, herself.

According to Thomas, upon arriving at the Bureau of Indian Affairs, "Betsy went to see the Commissioner and informed him She was an Arkansaw Cherokee and come on to get her money. . . . She promised not to go back anymore until the business is Settled[.]"[304] William Thomas deftly maneuvered himself between the two and defused the situation, but the display of a female client unceremoniously bypassing her legal representation and going straight to the Commissioner of Indian Affairs had undoubtedly once more damaged Thomas's professional reputation with Commissioner Crawford.

His protracted stay in Washington may have saved Thomas from facing the dismantling of his prized Scotts Creek tanyard,[305] but, with money growing increasingly tight and creditors beginning to look for their funds, the businessman was left in the unenviable position of tracking down the apparently delinquent Reverend John Freeman Schermerhorn. Frustrated by his inability to escape Washington, Thomas sent his old associate letter after letter, first asking for a meeting, then, getting no reply, sending more inquiries as to the aging man's health and, later still, about the money Thomas had loaned him.[306] Weary of the silence and fearing the worst, William

Thomas finally resorted to writing the Utica Postmaster, asking if Schermerhorn had left the upstate New York city.[307]

Ready to give up hope of ever seeing either his money or his old colleague again, Thomas received word that the Postmaster had forwarded the letter to Schenectady, New York, where he believed Schermerhorn was then living.[308] Driven by the revelation, the businessman quickly penned a letter and dispatched it to the alleged Schenectady residence. It read:

Sir,

. . . I presume at least you have received my letter of the 1st of July which was directed to Schenectady and also by this time must have received my other letters directed to Utica,[.] [Y]ou are thereby informed of my situation and my delay here awaiting an answer from you. And if I am much longer detained by your neglect[,] I shall be under the necessity of charging you on our settlement with the losses I sustain[,] thereby which if you are unwilling to be answerable for I shall expect to be informed thereof by return mail, in case I am not and am delayed here much longer[,] I shall presume you are willing to allow me the amount of damages you have occasioned me to sustain, and will charge the same to your account. . . .

Little did I expect when I entered into an arrangement with you that the time would come when you would refuse to answer my communications, borrow my money[,] which I had reserved to pay my expenses[,] leave me in a strange city 700 miles from home without a dollar. I am not quite so poor[,] but if you would let me know you designed not to replace the money I loaned you [I] could have funds remitted me from home. I am sorry to have been compelled to say so much respecting one I had esteemed a friend and from whom I had a right to expect better treatment and would yet hope if I could with facts starring [staring] me in the face that I had been mistaken, I am not aware that I have given you any cause of offense or ever treated you improper. [I]f I have I have no knowledge of it[,] but on the contrary[,] when I last saw you in this city you met me as a friend[,] I treated you as such[,] and I

would yet rejoice to receive a satisfactory explanation would
enable me always to regard you in that light

yours and c. [et cetera][,]
WHT[309]

The letter conveyed William Thomas's exasperation over the
man's silence but also served as a seemingly suitable object upon
which he could justifiably vent his frustrations. Yet, precisely two
weeks later, the businessman was given ample reason to be embar-
rassed by his ill-timed words. Reverend Schermerhorn had received
his initial letter at his Schenectady home and explained his delay in
answering Thomas's letters and continuing their business discussions.[310] In realizing Reverend Schermerhorn might be able to intercede with Commissioner Crawford on his behalf, William Thomas
subsequently apologized for his rashness and continued to pump the
former Cherokee treaty-broker for useful information.[311] It is unclear
whether the monetary situation was ever resolved, but as the North
Carolinian continued to have trouble obtaining several of his Eastern
Band–awarded claims, it seemed not even the reverend's assistance
could hurry the Bureau of Indian Affairs.

As William Thomas continued to lose invested money and, on
occasion, shipments of goods sent home,[312] it seemed his time in
Washington might finally be coming to a close. In a series of decisions, the Bureau of Indian Affairs and the supervising War Department ruled in favor of a number of North Carolina Cherokee
claims,[313] that a number of North Carolina Cherokee were to be
awarded a "per capita allowance which will be set a part for their
benefit,"[314] and he also won the position of clarification that the
Eastern Band of Cherokee "would be permitted [to] remain in the
land of their fathers,"[315] but Chief Thomas's Cherokee would not
be entitled to his argued portion of the $55,000 Removal Program
budget.[316]

While the businessman was resigned to Commissioner Crawford's opinion that he would not receive any Removal Program funds

without appealing to Congress, William Thomas was relieved to find not only partial validation in the federal government's favorable assertions but also satisfaction in that his brethren-turned-followers would be allowed to remain within the State of North Carolina and that there was little Principal Chief John Ross could do to disrupt the established sovereignty of the Eastern Band within the southeast.[317]

As the new Chief prepared to deposit the hard-won "per capita" funds in the Railroad Bank of Georgia[318] and return to Western North Carolina, William Thomas met with one final snag. Commissioner Crawford would not allow the businessman to take the money, himself, from Washington and disperse it among his Cherokee clients as Thomas had initially believed and hence he would not receive his own ten percent remuneration, at least not directly. The man listened to the Indian Affairs commissioner as he explained that the written guidelines of the removal treaty specifically stated that any federal funds to be awarded to the Cherokee were to be handed *directly to the Cherokee*. William Thomas lobbied hard, but again the commissioner was bound by the rule of law.

After considerable thought, the two worked out a deal.

William Holland Thomas, Cherokee Agent, Eastern Band Chief, and private businessman, would now take on one more job, dispersing agent. Instructed to return to North Carolina, Thomas carried out another census of the Western North Carolina Cherokee, establishing names, locations of families, and a subset of entities through which the federal government could name and pay the appropriate parties.

In a matter of weeks, William Thomas appointed his new staffer and business partner James Wharey Terrell as his dispersing assistant. After making the rounds covering the entire countryside in a few weeks, William Thomas returned to Washington in 1840 and submitted the totals. Before turning for home once more, however, the businessman sought out the assistance of a congressional legal expert to act on his behalf when Congress reconvened and to handle the tracking of future claims that might arise. After several months of searching, William Thomas found a father and son team with the congressional influence and abilities he desired, Duff and Benjamin Green. Thomas explained the situation to the men, left with them the necessary documentation, and, after dropping his mother, Temperance, a note saying he would be home soon, departed the city of Washington as quickly as he could.

CHAPTER TEN

At Home in the Mountains

By the end of January 1840, the weary Eastern Band Agent had finally returned home. Now an experienced traveler, the North Carolinian had managed to slim his travel time between Haywood County and the nation's capital to the space of a week through a heavy reliance on a modern and antiquarian combination. Using steamship, rail, and a mounted horse or carriage,[319] he arrived at his mother's house in Stekoa Fields and lay down to rest. The duties of his chosen occupation had apparently begun to wear on the businessman.

At the age of thirty-five, William Holland Thomas already seemed to have accomplished a number of his early desires. Through his business dealings in sundries, land, and slavery, he had become known as a reliable backcountry provider of goods and services. As a legal expert, he had come to be regarded as a reliable and methodical representative for many of his Caucasian and Native American neighbors' legal concerns, and as an Agent of the Eastern Band he had brought about moderate security and stability for his Cherokee brethren. Furthermore, the businessman's continued efforts also ensured that his widowed mother's home would be kept well stocked and maintain a high level of repair.[320] With each successful transaction, he grew in influence and power.

Yet, his life as a successful merchant and ally of the North Carolina Cherokee had caused Thomas to spend increasing amounts of time on the open road or in distant cities to plot, plan, and strategize ways to meet both his needs and those of clients against defendants, competitors, and procedurally bound bureaucrats in an economically viable number of hours. Try as he might, however, the juggling act of business solvency, responsibility, and leadership had recently begun to destabilize more and more as his time in Washington had grown unacceptably long.

During his prolonged absence, William Holland Thomas had, in part, managed to mitigate the cries of his store's local creditors, authorizing his staffers to draw upon their reserves to dispense with as many store debts as they could.[321] In doing so, the businessman had gambled that he would soon draw from a wellspring of awarded Washington legal fees and the man had, indeed, been saved by the partial Indian Affairs claimant awards as well as the favorable granting of the title of dispersing agent.[322]

Still, the man's positive local appearance was only part of Thomas's concern. Having expanded his business to encompass several moderately yielding trading sectors on both sides of the Appalachian Mountains, Thomas also required the complacent support of his recently acquired contacts and creditors in the shipping and packaging business for the supplies increasingly being sold by his stores, support which could not be guaranteed by defaulted loans.[323]

The businessman had planned to visit his product traffickers in Charleston, South Carolina, to settle several debts of appreciating value on a circuitous route home,[324] but his lengthy exacting ordeal in Washington had made that goal physically unattainable. After as brief a rest as he could fiscally allow, William Thomas pulled himself onto a saddled horse with a portion of his accrued profits and a pistol, traveled to the southern port city, discharged his debts, and made for home once more, secure in the knowledge that he had staved off a potentially ruinous situation.

Upon returning to Haywood County, William Thomas finally reintroduced himself into the daily operations of his business with the management of shipments, inventory-checking, and conducting personal evaluations of his staff's effectiveness. Knowing the time would soon come again when he would be required to consult Duff Green and his federal contacts on the continued initiative to obtain "just" compensation[325] for the Eastern Band choosing to remain in North Carolina, Thomas sought out the services of someone who could act as a store manager on a day-to-day basis but could also, as the need arose, bring a learned and experienced understanding of the world to whatever endeavors the businessman needed him to follow to their beneficial conclusion in Thomas's periodic absences. The businessman found his trusted right-hand man in James Wharey Terrell.

At the age of twenty-three, James Terrell was a more youthful and substantially darker mirror image of William Thomas. Born on December 31, 1829, in Western North Carolina's Rutherford County, Terrell had been brought to Haywood County to be raised by his grandfather.[326] Eventually recruited by Thomas, Terrell proved himself to be a man of many talents and a dedicated worker. In the course of a few years' service, the tall, lanky Terrell had risen from the role of a simple store and tanyard clerk to become Thomas's store enterprise supervisor and book manager, a secondary Indian Affairs dispersing agent for the North Carolina Cherokee's federally sanctioned removal funds, a Quallatown post office manager, a quasi land broker (working on behalf of Chief Thomas's Eastern Band interests when land around Quallatown became available for sale and inclusion within the confines of the Qualla Boundary), and a part-time teacher to the Eastern Band.[327] As the man further grew into his position and married, Thomas played with his own personal resources to allow the man, with his new wife, to live "rent free" with "a garden of at least half an acre to cutivate [cultivate] also to be rent free, also ten cords of fire wood, and[,] at the end of the year[,] three hundred dollars deducting said Terrells support and account for store goods and . . . to keep a milk cow in his pasture."[328] By the outbreak of the War of the Rebellion, the relationship between the two men had grown so close that William Thomas asked James Terrell to bring his skills into military service to become Colonel Thomas's second-in-command.

Thomas also fostered a sense of shared productivity and comradery with the remainder of his staff. "My long absence furnishes you with a fare opperternity [opportunity] of trying your skill in the management of a mercantile establishment," he once wrote to staffers Allen Fisher and H. P. King.[329] Rising beyond the standards Felix Hampton Walker had once granted him, Thomas frequently rewarded his employees' dedication with promotions, greater responsibilities, high contractually stipulated salaries, and, occasionally, offers of partnership in the enterprise he was building. In the space of just a few years, for example, Johnson King went from being a Quallatown store clerk to the manager of the Murphy store and eventually managed to bring his brother, H. P. King, into the Thomas business.

Furthermore, Thomas's letters and diaries illustrate his dedicated nature to his subordinates. While away on business, Thomas counseled staffer James H. Bryson that he "should go to school and become well acquainted with calculating interest and etc. [et cetera]."[330] When news reached Thomas of the birth of Allen Fisher's (his Scotts Creek staffer's) second child, Thomas sent the man his congratulations and advised him to take good care of his wife.[331] Even with one of his less reliable staffers, H. P. King, William Thomas recognized the man's skills and renewed the younger King's contract "to allow such additional compensation as your qualifications justify."[332]

Yet, the businessman's sense of dedication to his employees also seemed to end with the grave. In December 1845, Johnson W. King, one of Thomas's most valued partners and staffers, suddenly died. Sensing an opportunity in the vacancy, William Thomas dubiously maneuvered Samuel R. Mount, the son of his periodic Washington rooming house landlord, into his mercantile operations with the promise of a promotion after four years' satisfactory service.[333] In facilitating the rapid transfer of responsibility, Thomas chose to avoid reconciling the now deceased King's long owed back-salary.[334] As a result, King's widow was forced to sue the businessman several times throughout the 1840s in the pursuit of adequate compensation.*[335]

With his affairs in order, William Holland Thomas turned once more to the affairs of his Cherokee brethren. Given the initially warm reception he had received in Secretary of War Joel Poinsett's office, the new Chief of the Eastern Band was encouraged to continue with his plans to modernize the North Carolina Cherokee. On one of his business trips north, Thomas secured the educational services of Marylander George T. Mason to teach the Eastern Band how to produce brooms for sale.[336] On other trips, Thomas secured a quantity of exotic seeds capable of growing in the Western North Carolina climate, hoping to market the products to supplement the Eastern Band's meager income.[337] Similarly, after several poachers attempted to hack and steal timber from the Quallatown area for profit (sometimes with success), Thomas decried subsequent attempts with bold threats while simultaneously encouraging his Cherokee brethren to take advantage of the raw material themselves.[338] Yet, each attempt failed to turn the quick profits upon which Thomas had been banking.

* The extent to which the woman was able to recover her husband's owed salary from William Holland Thomas is unknown.

Furthermore, when silk and sugar were being encouraged by the North Carolina legislature in the late 1840s, William Thomas seized the initiative, but this time, he added his own twist to the exportable idea. Thomas spared no expense in attempting to get his latest and grandest moneymaking scheme running profitably. He bought the necessary supplies,[339] swiftly gained state-sanction for the creation of The Cherokee Company (which Thomas claimed would oversee the production of Western North Carolina's sugar and silk production assets), garnered a 12,000-acre allotment of land (conveniently located within Haywood County), and even procured an engraved seal of the company from a Washington store.[340] For all his vision and planning, however, Thomas's grand scale venture returned negligible earnings and the leased land eventually reverted back to the state.[341]

Chief Thomas continued to try every available scheme, asset, and marketable position to stimulate economic growth for his inherited followers, but his economic failures were mounting. The gravity of the Eastern Band situation deepened as rumors spread of a forced removal of the Catawba (a less advanced and disassociated group of Native Americans who lived several miles south of Quallatown) from North Carolina.[342] Thomas's modernization and public relation efforts had managed to stave off the seemingly impending fate of the Cherokee's ancient enemy for the Cherokee, but the implied threat had risen once more.

The Cherokee Chief had to succeed. Having exhausted every conventional alternative, the businessman turned to a decidedly unconventional approach.

In his many travels, Thomas had experienced a far greater number of vistas and locales than most Western North Carolina men of his generation or his father's generation. While some of his store-supplied goods were grown locally, others were brought by regional waterways as well as mountain trails. Where the coastal cities and towns had benefitted for centuries from their ready access to the Atlantic Ocean and nearby river tributaries,[343] inland territories were beginning to steadily grow to rival their coastal neighbors through the application of a long-standing militarily engineered convenience, manually constructed highways.

As William Thomas had traveled through Washington's, Philadelphia's, Charleston's, and New York's various inland properties over the years, the cost-effectiveness of dirt roads over wilderness, wooden roads over dirt, and cobblestones over wooden planks had an appreciation with the speed at which one might travel with wagon-laden goods to their destination. Since the 1830s William Thomas had interminably lobbied local friends and political leaders for support in the erection of a highway through Haywood County and across the mountains into Georgia. Although the matter met with some local favor, the businessman failed time and again to win either the favor or the fiscal assets of the coastal leadership to make the dream of his Ocanaluftee Turnpike happen.[344]

By 1850, more than half of the state continued to remain dependent on foot and horse-drawn wagons to get their goods to market.[345] Wooden roads cost money, time, and a labor force with which to make such lengthy projects not only happen but also endure. While convict labor was used when possible,[346] such resources were limited and prone to the engendered hazards of uprising, murder, and escape. As a result many North Carolina communities, including Fayetteville, built their own network of wooden-planked roads, but the results of their efforts were short-lived, as use and weathering reduced the fashioned surfaces to pulp in the space of a few years.[347]

Slow to act, the 1850 North Carolina legislature finally began to charter companies for the express purpose of road construction, but due to a lack of funds (and suspected personal inclination on the part of the vote casters) all white males between the ages of eighteen and forty-five from the surrounding area were compelled to construct the roadways themselves (free blacks and male slaves between sixteen and fifty years of age were also required to assist in achieving the project's goal but were instead relegated to serving the direct orders of the state-appointed overseer).[348] Those who refused work and could not supply a slave as substitute labor were reportedly subjected to a fine of a dollar a day.[349] Over time, subsequent roadways were built to Charlotte, Concord, Wilmington, and Asheville.[350]

Rather than wait for the coastal leadership to rise to the occasion, William Thomas moved on his own. Figuring in 1839 that the creation of an Ocanaluftee Turnpike would not only increase his own business but also promote Haywood County and the Qualla Boundary for development, the businessman had made several trips over the months and years to the seat of North Carolina's government, Raleigh.[351] In securing the permission for the creation of such a road network, Thomas returned home and instituted the planning and operation of the Western North Carolina turnpike. Although it is unclear as to how the roadway was slated to be built, within a year's time he had already appointed local resident Robert Collins as the turnpike's toll collector and ordered the network be kept well repaired.[352]

In light of the roadway's addition to Western North Carolina, William Thomas turned once more to the aggressive acquisition of land for himself and his Cherokee,[353] but before the man could further enrich his parcel assets and, conversely, deplete his recently amassed fiscal solvency, the businessman's attention was once more called to Washington to attend to the affairs of the Eastern Band.

With the renewed threat of removal of the Catawbas in 1840, North Carolina governor J. M. Morehead had resisted the idea of allowing the Catawbas residence within North Carolina and had begun making intimations of a political nature that he saw the North Carolina Cherokee as equally deleterious to the southern state.[354] In concert with the political protestations, William Thomas and his Washington associates had introduced into the United States Senate a document describing the history, treaties, and advancements of the Eastern Band over their western counterparts in the hope that Congress might first, formally legitimize the sovereignty of the Eastern

Band as a lawfully existing segment of the State of North Carolina and, second, intercede on their behalf in the Indian Affairs dispute over the issue of compensation.[355] However, as Thomas had learned in prior visits to the nation's capital, Washington leaders were reluctant to move swiftly on any issue that failed to obtain immediate profit for themselves or their constituents.

While William Thomas continued forwarding the necessary documentation to the appropriate federal authorities[356] and the documentation needed to fuel Duff and Benjamin Green's continued attempts to cajole their federal contacts to favorably review the Eastern Band's request for "a fair compensation,"[357] the Cherokee Chief began to pursue other previously unexplored avenues in the search of Eastern Band legitimacy. In December 1846, Thomas timed the drafting and submission of a memorial for consideration by the state legislature to granting the Eastern Cherokee–recognized land rights to George Hayes in Raleigh, North Carolina, just as a bill was about to be passed in favor of granting a similar boon to the Eastern Band surviving family members of renowned Cherokee warrior Junaluska (Junaluska had been instrumental in turning the tide against the Creek at the 1814 Battle of Horseshoe Bend and had been rewarded for his actions years later by President Andrew Jackson with the threat of forced removal). William Thomas also continued to show interest in investing the pending federal compensatory claims in North Carolina banks,[358] but neither gambit proved to attract political supporters until 1845, when Whig Governor William Graham showed a degree of favor to Thomas, asking that the state's request to expedite the North Carolina Cherokee claims be sent to Washington.[359]

Hoping to gain further traction, William Thomas once more returned to Washington. For his troubles, the businessman not only lost some money and a "memo book" to a thief along the way,[360] but he was also beginning to tire of daily life in the nation's capital. In the 1830s, Thomas had discussed the removal situation with Jackson and Van Buren Administration officials to little end. On March 4th,

1841, the businessman had braved pouring rain to witness the three-and-a-half-hour inaugural of William Henry Harrison, but, after the President died a month later from apparent pneumonia, William Thomas continued to see little progress in the Eastern Band situation well through much of the Tyler Administration. Suddenly, in late 1844, the Greens began to report progress. With the rise in interest over the Mexican War and the resurgence in the sectional crisis, Thomas and his associates moved into action. Hoping to catch the favoritism of southern politicians and a sufficient number of placatory northerners, the legal minds once more placed the Eastern Band's compensatory situation under the noses of the appropriate officials and waited.

As William Thomas's efforts were about to reach fruition, however, in stepped Principal Chief John Ross of the Cherokee Nation. As Thomas had previously suspected, the stark Cherokee politician had made little headway with his attempts at gaining a greater share of the appropriated claimant money. Bereft of the mollifying influence of Major Ridge, Chief Ross had become an overwhelming presence in Washington. While he was an appropriate contrast to the North Carolinian in almost every way, the Cherokee Nation's presence alarmed the Chief of the Eastern Band. Principal Chief Ross's presence had hindered Thomas's previous attempts to gain his Cherokee client's requested removal and compensatory claims and, as expected, Duff Green informed William Thomas, on December 13th, 1844, that the long worked for bill had been placed before Congress for consideration,[361] as Principal Chief Ross made his move, demanding a new treaty be made that would address all concerns of his Cherokee Nation (including the distant satellite of the Cherokee Nation who called themselves the Eastern Band of North Carolina Cherokee). As a result, once more Thomas's federal efforts stalled.

With his progress momentarily arrested, the North Carolinian's adversaries now moved to neutralize Thomas as a principal negotiator and, if possible, separate him from his Cherokee brethren. Soon several emissaries of the Principal Chief (most notably Thomas

Hindman) began whispering discrediting words into the ears of their official contacts at Indian Affairs about William Thomas. Starting with his business practices as a Cherokee Agent, they alleged Thomas had frequently perpetrated fraud in filing dubious census report information over the past several years and was even now engaged in the misappropriation of those funds the governmental had recently placed in the dispersing agent's care. Next, they attacked his private business ventures, alleging evidence of serial malfeasances had been uncovered years earlier in Thomas's brief altercation with breveted Brigadier General Wool. Finally, as William Thomas was becoming aware of the slanderous accusations, his adversaries also began claiming that Thomas was taking Eastern Band money, buying land, and assigning the sum to his name for his own purposes.* As a result of the caustic accusations and fear of administrative impropriety/complicity with suspected legal activities, the Bureau of Indian Affairs promptly rescinded the suspect's responsibilities as a North Carolina dispersing agent in favor of Hindman (James Terrell's powers as dispersing agent remained intact for years to come).[362]

As the emissary of Principal Chief John Ross took to ministering to the fiduciary concerns of the Eastern Band, Thomas also began to hear word that other Cherokee agents were similarly looking to lure away members of the Eastern Band with promises of prompt monetary returns and enticements to remove west.[363] While a few Cherokee did sign themselves over to the new agents, the preponderance of the Eastern Band remained largely loyal to their Chief and longstanding friend. After several failed attempts to gain the favor of the Eastern Band, Thomas Hindman gave up on Principal Chief Ross's Cherokee National recruitment and was subsequently fired by the Bureau of Indian Affairs and in 1851 replaced by A. M. Mitchell as dispersing agent.[364]

Still, William Thomas would not allow such allegations as had

---

* Although these claims were technically true, as Native Americans could not hold land, Thomas remained vigilant in keeping his Eastern Band holdings separate from acquired Thomas family property.

been made about his character to continue unchallenged. Enlisting the aid of the United States Army, William Thomas tracked down Major General Winfield Scott and breveted Brigadier General John E. Wool.[365] Both men furnished Thomas with testimonies regarding the man's wronged state and genuine good intentions towards the Eastern Band of North Carolina Cherokee as evidenced in both the removal and the Tsali incident. Not wishing to have either the Eastern Band or himself suffer further injury over the issue of land and monetary tribal assets, at the next opportunity William Thomas presented his Eastern Band leadership with a $20,000 bond against the land secured in his name for the Qualla Boundary.

While Principal Chief John Ross had, indeed, won a reprieve with his motions and machinations, William Thomas, Duff Green, and the United States had managed to work out a reasonable deal with the Cherokee Nation by the conclusion of the 1848–1849 electoral session. The Eastern Band would receive their $53.33⅓ compensatory claim per head with interest for having lost their ancestral land, regardless of whether or not they were inclined to remove. When William Thomas self-effacingly turned to arguing that a lump sum payment would serve to benefit the federal government, the Eastern Band, and, by association as claim filer, himself, the North Carolina businessman won an improbable fight against his Cherokee National counterpart and managed to successfully wear down the United States government.

As part of the Washington treaty settlement, William Thomas was forced to pay lip service to the Cherokee Nation and the Bureau of Indian Affairs in allowing a governmental representative to travel with the Chief of the Eastern Band to every Cherokee point of habitation within the State of North Carolina, offering each collective the proposition of sending a delegation westward to better assess the possibility of their rejoining the Cherokee Nation. Thomas had thought little of the idea, but the federal official had persisted. At each town, the governmental representative raised the question and, to William Thomas's pleasure, at each town, the motion was rejected.

His task completed with grudging satisfaction, the federal official departed for Washington as quickly as he could, leaving behind the Chief of the Eastern Band and his now federally protected Cherokee brethren.

CHAPTER ELEVEN

STATE SENATOR

Fresh from his Washington victory, William Holland Thomas returned home with a renewed sense of purpose. Free of the danger of a forced removal by federal troops or a mandatory inclusion of the Eastern Band within the ranks of the atrophying Cherokee Nation, he began to expand his interests beyond the realm of bartering, hard currency, and legal documentation into the arena of North Carolina politics.

While Thomas had long been counted as a member of the North Carolina Democratic Party and had often encouraged his Cherokee brethren to support Democratic platforms,* the backcountry politician had held little initial interest in the real day-to-day realm of North

---

* It is unclear if the North Carolina Cherokee actually held or utilized their right to vote.

Carolina organized state politics. He had come to know a number of regional leaders through his merchant activities and had even met with a fair share of state representatives over the years due to his activities as the Cherokee Agent of the Eastern Band, but the sudden rise to dominance of the state's Whig Party in the 1830s (against the federalist machinations of the Jackson Administration) and the subsequent tabling of nearly every one of Thomas's requests for Western North Carolina improvements had pragmatically precluded his ascent to state office.

In 1840, however, the North Carolina Democratic Party was in a dire need of candidates. Hoping to prevent a complete Whig sweep of state governance, party officials approached the apparent Washington insider and Western North Carolina entrepreneur about the prospect of serving his party in the State Senate. William Thomas graciously accepted the offer but before he could complete the candidacy process was once more called away to Washington on Eastern Band business.

As the deadline for filing neared, Thomas managed to extricate himself from the nation's capital for a brief trip to announce his candidacy in Asheville, North Carolina, and thereupon promptly returned to Washington. Along his way back south, however, the Democratic Party's designs on the businessman met with a sudden, almost tragic, end as the train carrying the potential candidate suddenly ran off its tracks several miles from Thomas's destination. Although William Thomas had escaped injury by jumping free of the train before its derailment and had assisted in righting the vehicle back onto the tracks along with his fellow passengers, he arrived far too late in Asheville to register as an electable candidate for that year.[366]

Over the next several years, Thomas watched the Whigs ride a platform of public education, legislative reform, urbanization, and intrastate improvements to a series of electoral and legislative landslide victories. Declining to enter the 1846 elections to pursue Eastern Band and personal affairs, he studied his potential adversaries and prepared for the day he would next oblige the Democratic Party to upset the Whig's abolitionist-tainted control of Western North Carolina.

With the arrival of the 1848 electoral season, William Thomas finally formally moved against Haywood County's Whig elements. As a member in good standing of the North Carolina militia despite his interstate business affairs[367] he demonstrated his commitment to the defense of North Carolina and adherence to duty. As a business-man who had funded the construction of the Ocanaluftee Turnpike with $2,400 of his own funds[368] Thomas stood in sharp contrast to the state's Whig contingent, who had seemingly placed a higher level of importance on improving the state's coastal and southern re-gions than making good on promised Western North Carolina in-roads. On the subject of state reform, Thomas advocated the relief of long-standing land debts his neighbors owed the coastal authority for land purchased immediately prior to the sudden economic downturn of the late 1830s and also put forward the issue of creating a state road from the state capital at Raleigh across the Appalachian Mountains into Georgia, a limitation on congressional salaries, im-proved educational initiatives, and a self-sustaining prison made possible by convict labor.[369]

Cloaked in the raiments of his Whig adversaries and held in the light of his recent series of victories in Washington, William Hol-land Thomas won over the voting populace of Haywood, Macon, Cherokee, and Jackson counties (landowning Caucasian males) in 1848 and was subsequently elected to the Fiftieth State Senatorial District seat in North Carolinas's Raleigh-based General Assembly.

Thomas, however, was not alone in his victory over the Whig Party. Due, in part, to the growing nationalistic fervor surrounding the Polk Administration's Mexican War policies, the eventual mollifying effects of the Compromise of 1850 on the more centrist elements within the nation's abolitionist movement, and the Executive Branch's support of the sale of public lands to benefit the state's depleted cof-fers, the North Carolina Democratic Party was once more on the rise. Wishing to guard against a reversal of fortune in the next election, the Democratic leadership placed its new electees where they might gain the most exposure and curry party favor with the now vulnerable block of Whig supporters in the state's western region. Taking his past experiences into account, party officials awarded William Thomas appointments to the state's Committee on Internal Improvements (holding jurisdiction over North Carolina's fledgling system of railroads and roadways)[370] and the Committee on Cherokee Lands and Banks and Currency (holding legislative control over all Cherokee territorial interests within the state).[371]

As the first Democrat to hold the biannually elected Fiftieth Senatorial District seat in eight years,[372] State Senator Thomas took to his duties with great enthusiasm. Shortly after taking office, he sought to fulfill his campaign promise to defaulting Western North Carolina landowners, submitting a bill to the General Assembly in hopes of alleviating the debt of former Cherokee lands the state had released over a decade prior as a result of the federal Removal Program.[373] Utilizing his position on the state's Internal Improvements committee, he also pushed for the creation of additional mountain infrastructure similar to his planked Oconaluftee Turnpike, and the state-sponsored maintenance of existing roadways.

On the issue of education, he lobbied against over a century of coastal political hegemony, arguing that the state must "place within the reach of the poorest boy in the country the means of obtaining an English education."[374] Defending against detractors who claimed that such schools were unnecessary, the state senator drew from his own home-tutored past, saying, ". . . while an education may, like the mechanic and fine arts, be obtained without teachers, by much loss of time and long continued exertions, I am, nevertheless, well satisfied of the great utility of schools and colleges. A general system of education would cause the farmers, mechanics and merchants to be duly represented in the halls of legislation. . . ."[375]

Hoping to further ensure both his reelection and the continuance of Democratic Party electoral dominance, State Senator William Thomas also pressed for the implementation of two rather radical ideas, a flat tax and the allowance for universal Caucasian male suffrage. Unlike the "green" politician's other points of contention,

Thomas had failed to consider the economic and electoral ramifications of his positions, and the radical initiatives died a slow, quiet death. Still, with a little assistance from his party associates, in time state newspapers like the *North Carolina Standard* began to report favorably on the senator from Haywood County's actions.[376]

William Thomas also worked tirelessly to make reality a dream he had inherited from his old political colleague John C. Calhoun (one of the architects of the Compromise of 1850). When Thomas first began to expand his small operation into a franchise of stores scattered about the Mountain region, he rapidly came to realize the limitations travel time imposed on his business plans (especially as evidenced in the months following his Welch-Love agreement to work both the Scotts Creek store and his own outpost at then Indiantown).

In 1836 the man heard about an expedition led by certain influential southern political figures (including William Sloan and John C. Calhoun) to ascertain the feasability of cutting through the Blue Ridge Mountains' mineral deposits[377] to lay down the requisite number of rails to link with Georgia proper. Sensing the venture as a means by which he might ingratiate himself with members of the Washington leadership circle (undoubtedly thinking he might one day be in a position to return to his rural pathfinding skills with a little future legal influence of their own), Thomas quickly offered his services, but as the group traveled along the North Carolina border with Tennessee and Virginia, the young businessman became enamored with his colleague's vision of the swift and steady steam-drawn means of travel across the murky outback.

"Colonel Thomas was so forcibly impressed with the views and opinions of Mr. Calhoun," one fellow traveler later chronicled, "that on an interview with him some years after . . . he declared his intention, if his life was spared, to devote his best energies to the consummation of this great project."[378]

While the state legislature had chartered North Carolina's first railroad in 1833, the coastal leadership's first steps towards a transportation revolution had been, at best, haphazard and, at worst, counterproductive. Time and again plans were drafted by officials, areas were surveyed by scouting parties, and companies were liberally chartered by the legislature, but when the moment came for the actual implementation of the agreed upon plans, the money seemed to evaporate into thin air as it had with numerous similar previous turnpike initiatives.

In 1856, however, the state legislature finally subsumed to the modernizing influences of the Industrial Revolution in allowing the necessary finances (valued at three million dollars in capital stock, of which one third would have to be acquired independently of the State of North Carolina)[379] for the completion of a northeast-to-southwest-running route from Goldsboro to Charlotte, North Carolina.[380]

At a length of 223 miles of track, however, the new line fell far short of William Thomas's shared dream with John C. Calhoun. Using his authority on the Internal Improvements committee, the state senator pushed his colleagues to overcome the "limited division of western North Carolina."[381] Instead, State Senator Thomas offered his colleagues his years of backcountry experience, showing that Western North Carolina was an ill-used and largely overlooked wellspring of raw materials and resort potential[382] and an underutilized asset as a central location for interstate commerce with Georgia, Tennessee, South Carolina, and Virginia. As proof of his claims, William Thomas needed to offer no further evidence than his own now well established business history. Realizing the weight and potential merits of the man's argument, the State Senate conceded the point and, by late 1850, they had approved the ambitious creation of a Tennessee River Railroad Company—managed line to run from Charlotte to Cincinnati, Ohio.[383]

In the following months, the state senator returned to his metaphorical as well as literal roots, hiking about the Western North Carolina mountain ranges in search of better pathways, supervising the project's construction workers,[384] and ensuring the proper supplies were being utilized. With the entire project tallied at $15,000 per mile

across seventy-one chartered miles, however, Thomas's dream was far
from his own private venture. Unlike with his merchant's trade,
William Holland Thomas was not only responsible to his constituents,
and the taxpayers of North Carolina, but he was also beholden to the
whims of more influential North Carolina politicos like Whig Party
member and United States congressional representative Zebulon
Vance.

Like William Thomas's father, Zebulon Vance's grandfather,
Colonel David Vance, had served with distinction in the American
Revolution and had helped settle Buncombe County after the war,
but there the similarities between the two men end. Where William
and Temperance Thomas had struggled long and hard after the untimely death of Richard Thomas, Zebulon Vance enjoyed every
creature comfort his landowning and politically influential father
could provide. Rather than working the soil of the backcountry, the
young Vance had been provided with a formal education in the clas-
sics and the legal profession.[385] Whereas William Thomas had been
inaugurated by popular acclamation into the position of Chief of the
Eastern Band and had come to be well regarded as an influential
player in Washington politics, Zebulon Vance had failed to place in
his first election at twenty-four years of age.

With his father's influence, in 1858 Zebulon Vance won a seat in
the United States House of Representatives (to which he was also
later reelected in 1860). A power broker by nature, the Whig saw
some promise in State Senator Thomas's railroad initiative, but, contrary to the original project designs, the man was inclined to have the
railway run from north to south. Sharing his vision with others, State
Senator William Thomas soon found his pet project co-opted by a
statesman of superior influence and abilities.

In a matter of months, the Tennessee River Railroad Company
had been merged with several others within North Carolina and
across neighboring states to become a monstrous multistate-funded
project under the umbrella of the Blue Ridge Company.[386] State

Senator Thomas was willing to work with the new revision and made several trips to secure the requisite number of private partners,* but other participants were not as optimistic. With the addition of greater state involvement and less monetary investment, private funders grew wary of the project's continued feasability and began to pull their financing from the project. In response, the four states involved in the project (largely North and South Carolina) balked at the prospect of being left with the project's full cost, and refused to allocate further funds to the project until the situation stabilized.

State Senator Thomas tried to save the situation by linking the initiative to the issue of equal taxation. Far from saving the situation, the act only brought Zebulon Vance's ire. "Bill Thomas," Robert Brank Vance wrote his brother, "will scare off hundreds out west by making them believe it will Kill off the R.R. So goes the World."[388] Failing that, the representative of Haywood County then tried to bring the disparate parties together in Western North Carolina at a party hastily orchestrated with his Cherokee brethren supplying the day's entertainment, but nothing materialized. In the end, after only fifteen miles of track had been laid,[389] the project ran out of funds and died, leaving William Thomas with bitter memories of what might have been and the dubius moniker "The Father of the Western North Carolina Railroad."[390]

During his time on the railroad project, however, the state senator found something else of immeasurable value, Sarah Jane Burney Love.

William Thomas had been deeply involved with the rather large and prosperous Love family of Western North Carolina since the opening of his first store and acceptance of the Eastern Band advocacy position.[391] Like his father, the Loves had provided at least two fighters of their own in the 1770s struggle against the British Empire and had helped settle Haywood County, and, like Zebulon Vance's father, the Loves had gone on to service in the state's General Assembly,

---

* Two were located in New York City.[387]

but beyond his 1830s business dealings (including the purchasing of James R. Love Sr.'s share of the Scotts Creek store), William Thomas apparently little noticed any of the man's eight children until Sarah (or "Sallie," as Thomas would refer to her later)[392] reached a socially acceptable age.[393]

Whenever the businessman would stop by James R. Love's in White Sulphur Springs for a visit or a night's rest before continuing on his travels, there would be Sallie ready to greet him early every morning.[394] Having been friends with the family prior to the girl's birth on October 26th 1832, and having endured years of scurrilous remarks from friends about his continued pursuit of the bachelor's life over the years, William Holland Thomas found it initially difficult to pursue the hand of his friend and business associate's daughter, twenty-nine years his junior.

Somehow, the two allowed themselves to show public affection for each other and, on occasion, could be found sitting together in the family parlor with her younger sister Mary Josephine Love and her beloved, an attorney.[395] Due to her father's own business interactions with Thomas, there was little ambiguity in the affairs of business and statecraft about which the suitor needed to qualify for his beloved. Yet, during their courtship, William Thomas felt a pressing need for his prospective wife to understand and assist in his position as Chief of the Eastern Band of North Carolina Cherokee.

He explained:

> I look on them as a proper field for the practice of some of those Christian virtues, which you possess. Your . . . examples and communications . . . may do much good among the small remnant of the poeple who are now passing away, who were once the owners of the whole country, and whole hearts were inclined to protect an orphan boy when he went among them.
>
> I presume that it will be with you as it will be with me, your Friends will be my friends, be them rich or poor, and mine will be thine even the poor oppressed Indians. I look forward to the time when we will ride through their settlement on our way

to our mountain home when you will witness the affection of those people for their "so called chief."[396]

Sarah Love accepted his offer and soon became Sarah Thomas by right of North Carolina contract law[397] and family ceremony (held at the Loves' White Sulphur Springs homestead), on June 30th, 1857.[398] William Thomas then brought his bride home to Stekoa Fields. Seemingly in seclusion at the Thomas homestead while William Thomas was away on business in Washington or Raleigh (as the General Assembly met on a biannual basis), Sarah tended to her husband's farming affairs and kept an eye on his stock of slave labor.[399] She would also write often to her husband to keep him apprised of affairs occurring in Haywood County and on occasion would also take trips back to her father's house above Waynesville.

When away on business, William Thomas often bought his youthful love gifts to make the solitude of Stekoa Fields more tolerable. Knowing of her family's predilection towards musical study and instrumental play, Thomas spent countless hours prowling Washington's plethora of shops in search of sheet music to complement his wife's collection.[400] At one point, likely feeling guilty about the disparity of the accommodations between the husband at work and the wife sequestered at home, William Thomas penned a quick letter to Sallie, writing:

My Dear wife
[Y]our letter of the 30th ultimo has just arrived[.] I had been walking to the Post office daily, impatient to hear from home.
I have instructed Mr Terrell to supply what may be needed for the family,[.] [As] I am unable to give any instructions with regard to work on the basement story, you will have to bear with a few days longer,[.]
It is quite gratifying to me to be informed that "all the family are well", you can scarcely imagine the great anxiety I have to be at hand. But at the same time I am tird [tired][.] I am here by causes over which it is impossible for me to exercise

much control. In a previous communication I informed you of
the progress of my business here. . . . This question is too important to admit of my leaving until I get their decision in writing. That being done it will be easy to effect the balance. In
addition to this detention J[.] L[.] Williams who owes me about
one thousand dollars is expecting to recive [receive] a large fee
if he recives [receives] it while I am here he will pay me, which
would be of much advantage. I will under these circumstances
be compelled to bear with impatience a few days longer. But
unless prevented by accident[,] you may still look for me home
in this month, to take at furthest a Newyers [New Year's] dinner with my wife mother and friends. At furthest this is but seventeen days,[.] [W]hen I get home[,] I will have to take you
visiting[,] for I know that you must be tired of home[,] having
been confined there so long. I keep sending your music to you
by mail. I send [sent] you the other day ["]the old arm chair["]
and ["]Willie we have missed you.["]

I have another debt in this city which I may be able to convert in to [into] some musical interestment [entertainment] to
keep you company at any time when I am absent, and to amuse
me and my friends when they come to see me. . . .

I have been kindly treated since here by all old friends,
but I have mingled but little in society[.] I am generally in my
room writing when not at the office. I sometimes have regret-
ted that you did not come with me, but then you would have
been exposed to cold, in travelling, which would have been un-
amiable Don[']t forget to take care of your health. [M]y own
health was never better in my life. . . . [R]emember me to
mother[,] the family and enquiring friend.[illegible] for my
own Sarah[,] may the same Providence that [illegible] her
Willie in the wilderness[,] continue his protection to both in future wherever they may be.

Your own[,] Willie[401]

William Thomas also pursued a series of long nagging questions
regarding the legal status of his Eastern Band members. Were they
or were they not citizens of the United States and, as a right conse-
crated by the bloody American Revolution now less than a hundred

years past, not also entitled to exercise their legal status as taxpay-ers* to elect public officials?

Shortly after the removal and 1839 death of Major Ridge, William Thomas had suggested that his Cherokee brethren become citizens of the State of North Carolina.[402] When he was elected to the level of state senator, the Caucasian Cherokee Chief began applying the pressure of his office to make public his position[403] and, in January of 1845, he submitted a resolution to the General Assembly to pressure Congress to resolve the situation with the Eastern Band, but the United States Congress was not forthcoming.[404]

Next, Senator Thomas took the issue directly to his governmen-tal colleagues. He quickly won support from North Carolina Gover-nor Bragg, who placed the matter before the legislature, . . . there too the Cherokee Chief found disappointment.[405] Desiring to leave the past firmly planted behind them and pressed to take up issues grow-ing from the rising sectional crisis over "state versus federal" legal supremacy, the General Assembly was unwilling to affirm the East-ern Band any powers or privileges beyond their already codified abil-ity to hold land and pay taxes.

In 1859, William Holland Thomas was finally able to place the matter before the North Carolina Judiciary Committee.[406] The re-port† outlined the Eastern Band's treaty history with the United States, land acquisition record, federal awards, entitlements, and legal representation and implied that North Carolina was required to con-fer upon the Eastern Band the full entitlement of citizenship as the federal government had in the past decade moved to rectify the East-ern Band's situation. The report was an odd maneuver for the West-ern North Carolinian senator, who had long held himself to the Democratic standard of states' rights, made all the more bizarre by the opening statement that the reporter was "Embracing historical facts of the Tribe The Cherokees are supposed to be a part of the Ten

---

* Thomas had been paying their taxes out of his own pocket for decades.
    † The report was formally submitted by a William A. Holston but actually written by Thomas.

lost tribes of Israel."[407] In deference to William Thomas's years of service, the document was quietly put aside and the issue was tabled.

By 1859, it seemed little had changed since Thomas had taken office, but with the rising tide of abolitionism throughout the country, North Carolina's political, economic, and social landscape was about to change with Thomas at its center.

CHAPTER TWELVE

THE SECESSION CRISIS

I n one of his 1850 stays in Washington (probably on Eastern Band business), William Holland Thomas had spent several hours listening to a great orator rail against slavery, claiming, "I owe it to myself, I owe it to truth, I owe it to the subject to say that no earthly power could induce me to vote for a specific measure for the introduction of slavery were it had not before existed. . . ."[408] Thomas had watched from the gallery as the distinguished gentlemen of the 1850 United States Congress argued over the central issue of the Compromise of 1850, the continued extension of slavery into the new territorial acquisitions of the United States of America. Lacking the large tracts of arable land by which slavery could have been economically utilized (although at a declining detriment), North Carolina and her slave state contemporaries "were linked to the ruling class by ties of kinship, aspirations for slave ownership, or mutual dislike of Yankees and other outsiders. A caste system as well as a form of labor, slavery elevated all whites to the ruling caste and thereby reduced the potential for class conflict. However poor and illiterate some whites may have been, they were still white."[409]

Still, for William Thomas, the slave trade held a deeper attraction. A trader and slave master nearly his entire adult life, Thomas played the institution for short-term profits and long-term insurance. Unlike most, the North Carolinian's buying and selling of slaves (largely on short term loans or as a demand-oriented supplier) actually reaped short term profits.

For years, Thomas had supplemented his income through the procurement of slaves[410] and the loaning of slave labor to neighbors[411] and public works projects,[412] as well as to meet tribal needs (a policy first enacted by his predecessor, Chief Yonaguska, from whom William Thomas had inherited the slave Cudjo)[413] and deal with matters pertaining to the continued running of his stores.[414] He attended anti-abolitionist lectures and sermons.[415] He had used his stock of slaves as a form of currency in the acquisition of James R. Love's share of the Scotts Creek store (for which Thomas paid three slaves and $1,400 in cash). He had entrusted his slaves to deliver large sums of money[416] and allowed one to hold his own store account[417] and would even trust one of his personal slaves with his back in the coming War of The Rebellion.[418] Far from the stereotypic slaver, Thomas viewed slavery as just another expedient tool of his entrepreneurial ventures. It was far removed from having any moral implications.

As a slave trader and slave owner, William Holland Thomas was decidedly against the abolitionist tendencies towards which the North had been moving since the onset of the Second Great Awakening and the urban-based Industrial Revolution around the time of his birth. Yet, the man did not view Senator Clay's position on the Compromise of 1850 as a matter of slavery versus abolitionist rhetoric. Taken with his elder colleague John C. Calhoun's Nullification

Crisis* of decades past and the Cherokee Removal Program, the issue, which seemed to increasingly occupy much of the state senator's time, was rather a question of the limitation of federal powers and each state's rights of self-governance.

There had been calls in the General Assembly for North Carolina's secession from the Union as early as November 23rd, 1850, but William Thomas and the majority of his colleagues had voted the motion down.[419] Given his personal experience with the United States Congress and Department of War on behalf of the Cherokee, as far as the state senator was concerned, there was little point in antagonizing the abolitionists and the rising tide of Radical Republicans when there was nothing to be gained.

Yet, as the debate changed with the nomination of Abraham Lincoln to the candidacy for the Office of the President of the United States, State Senator Thomas's perceptions began to undergo a metamorphosis in terms of rhetoric. With threats of secession coming from the surrounding states should the Republicans demonstrate their contingent's northern electoral prowess (as the North had already outdistanced the southern states in population growth)[420] and the threat of the unilateral ending of the slave trade, the Western North Carolina businessman began to see the situation fostered by "the black republican party"[421] as a "crusade against the South."[422]

By 1860, the issue of secession had been reintroduced on the floor of the General Assembly. State Senator Thomas ignored his colleagues who had insisted that the ascent of Lincoln to the White House would warrant the continuance of the American Revolution that the north had given up for the security of federalism. Instead, Thomas offered his colleagues the means to directly address the situation. Summoning the calm evenness that he had displayed in his

* On November 24th, 1832, Senator John C. Calhoun and several other southern leaders attempted to curtail the increasingly frequent use of federal governmental power on behalf of the urban north through the nullification of the tariffs of 1828 and 1832. President Andrew Jackson replied with the threat of force, but Senator Henry Clay was able to broker a deal, which momentarily forestalled an American civil war.

early arguments with the agents of the federal government and Cherokee Nation, the state senator proposed a series of resolutions upon which the General Assembly would vote to make their disapproval of Abraham Lincoln and the policies of Radical Republicanism publicly known in a series of legally binding public documents.

A few of William Thomas's General Assembly colleagues mistook the man's political stance, dispassionate demeanor, and decidedly unspectacular suggestions of understanding and constructive dialogue as reflections of the covert actions and venomous nature of a closet federalist and vigorously attacked the party Democrat. In response Senator J. G. Ramsey publicly bated the senator, calling him a "tame submissionist"[423] who held "many fears of the little man in Springfield, Ill[inois] . . . ,"[424] but William Thomas stood firm.

In the mind of the self-taught attorney, the South's only redeemable course of action remained through the channels of lawful due process.

Instead of responding to the calls of his accusers, Senator Thomas invoked General George Washington, presenting him as the reluctant hero of the American Revolution who had stood before the injustice of the tyrant King George III and when the British had come with their redcoats had moved to defeat them.[425] Sensing that the argument had not sufficiently mollified the Assembly's contingent of detractors, William Thomas then moved on to attack the cause of abolitionism and the radical work of abolitionist Hinton Rowan Helper.

Helper's *The Impending Crisis of the South*, printed in 1854, had dealt a resounding blow to the anti-abolitionist leaning of the southern states and North Carolina in particular. A North Carolina–born and raised citizen, the author had examined in minute detail the wide disparity of income, trade, population, social ramifications, and mechanized orientation surrounding the issue of slavery and compared the data for every state in the Union.[426] Although he conjectured on the depravity and morally bankrupt nature of slavery, the man had dealt a more serious blow to North Carolina's leadership in allowing the entire literate world to witness its deleterious state of economic affairs. While there was little to no comparison with its northern neighbors in shipping supplies, income, and population, the disparity with the remainder of the southern states was far greater than the North Carolina leadership was willing to admit.

In his work, Helper also intricately examined the means by which North Carolina could reverse itself from its long-standing economic malaise, arguing for an increased emphasis on industrialization and mechanization, greater infrastructural improvements, and the more widespread availability of education.

William Thomas had long addressed these points of contention with the General Assembly and the United States government on behalf of his Cherokee clients and Eastern Band members, but, time and again, his calls for support had gone unanswered by an uninvolved federal government and an indifferent North Carolina coastal authority. Indeed, when he had run for the State Senate he had campaigned successfully on a similar platform but upon arriving in Raleigh again found himself faced with severely limited gains and the grossly misplaced priorities of others.

Had the issue of slavery not remained at the core of Hinton Rowan Helper's argument, William Thomas would have found in the author a kindred North Carolina intellect and possible friend of the Eastern Band, but the friendship was not to be. When the Republicans began introducing legislation allegedly written by Helper and were seen waving copies of *The Impending Crisis of the South* in the tempestuous electioneering of 1860,[427] Senator Thomas and his colleagues relentless attacked the man's political leanings and protestations of a declining North Carolina.[428]

Still, Senator Thomas failed to secure the confidence of his colleagues.

After Governor John Willis Ellis was replaced by Zebulon Vance in 1861, William Thomas's standing in the General Assembly began to noticeably shrink. Neither man had forgotten what the other had done in the railroad controversy a few years prior. As Governor Vance found "That a Majority of old N.C. [North Carolina] is in favor of secession I believe That Nearly all the democrats is for it,"[429] William Thomas found his calm, cool, and dispassionate advice to the General Assembly ironically coming back to haunt him.

William Thomas sorely wanted to leave Raleigh to be with his expectant wife, but again his duty demanded that he remain in the state capital and see the crisis through to its conclusion. Eventually, the vote was called for the convening of a meeting of elected delegates to discuss the State of North Carolina's position on secession and Senator Thomas was found at opposition once more with the controlling interests of his state.

"The crisis here is rapidly approaching its denouncement," wrote Zebulon Vance to a confidant. "The Administration is literally dropping to 'smash.' The timidity, vacillation and corruption of the President, the recent discovery of the astounding and enormous frauds and defalcations, and the known and acknowledged complicity of the Executive with all the plans and schemes of disunion, make every honest man damn the day that placed Buchanan in office."[430]

Yet, for State Senator William Thomas, the situation continued to grow bleaker. The anti-secessionists narrowly averted the state's Secessionist Convention (46,672 to 47,323 votes cast),[431] but their success would be short-lived. Thomas had been beaten into submission. Soon others would follow and eventually another vote on the matter would be called. With the threat of treasonous accusations, it was only a matter of time before Thomas's reserved compatriots would fold.

No other conclusions could be made.

North Carolina would eventually be going to war against the United States of America.

CHAPTER THIRTEEN

A WAR OF REBELLION

Since his tête-à-tête with the General Assembly's ardent secessionists, the state senator demonstrated greater care with his
legislative associates and their public anti-Unionist passions. As his
years as legal counsel to the Eastern Band had proven, quiet and
deliberate moves seemed to suit the methodical and deliberate
Western North Carolinian.

In the years leading up to the secessionist crisis, William Holland
Thomas's entrepreneurial and managerial experiences had been
perceived as a boon to the Democratic Party. Yet, as party leader
William W. Holden publicly lauded the man as "one of the truest
men to party organization"[432] and claimed that "no member in the
Assembly is more successful than he is in schemes for the benefit of

his constituents,"[433] North Carolina's other factions were already savagely taking Thomas to task for his political naïveté. With the rising tide of resentment against the federal government joined with the inherently fluid nature of political moods and social rhetoric in the prewar state capital, William Thomas was left in a situation far different from anything he had previously encountered.

"I have the honor to represent a portion of the State which is a grazing country," he said in an 1851 speech before the General Assembly, "where slave labor yields but small profits; yet my constituents will unite in sustaining and defending an interest in which any portion of the State is interested. And if the time should come, that it becomes necessary for North Carolina to take a stand in favor of preserving the compromises of the Constitution of the United States, and is forced to the alternative of deciding between dishonor and political degradation and maintaining her political rights as secured by the Constitution of the United States, I am in favor of our doing as our ancestors did—pledge our *lives, fortunes,* and *sacred honor* to preserve the rights and liberties of the Old North State and defend her to the last, and fight the last battles in the Mountain passes of my native portion of the State. . . ."[434]

By 1859, however, Thomas's supportive words were rendered moot by the machinations of his enemies. In the weeks that followed J. G. Ramsey's personal attack on the North Carolinian, William Thomas had learned through bitter experience that his political enemies preferred sharp rhetoric over refutable facts and clustered together in packs to effectively neutralize their shared opposers rather than debate matters one-on-one. In pursuing a proactive course for his western constituents and occasionally retaliating against his adversaries' charges, legally minded Thomas simultaneously came to learn that making the "right choice" was not always the "best choice," as men he had unknowingly spurned in his attempts at erecting serviceable roadways and rail lines (including the increasingly influential Zebulon Vance) began to move behind the scenes to marginalize Thomas's influence. It was little wonder that in the past century the state's coastal leadership had accomplished little for their state's inland citizenry. Rather than risk alienation, public humiliation, and electoral defeat, in the late 1860s the ill-practiced public speaker and novice politician followed the pattern of other southern initial opposers to secession and resigned himself to the wishes of his party's majority.

Where North Carolina's dissident elements had been marginally inconvenienced by the 1860 failure to gain approval for the convocation of a secessionist convention (a political formality similar to the First Continental Congress prior to the issuance of a declaration of separation from the governmental union), their leadership contemporaries among the neighboring southern states shrewdly maneuvered themselves to take advantage of an increasingly alarming series of events to further public acceptance of their desire to form a new confederated southern government.

In 1859 the savage guerrilla actions of abolitionist preacher John Brown at Harpers Ferry offset Hinton Helper's rational statistical argument against slavery and bolstered southern fears (albeit speciously) of potentially bloody slave uprisings. The following year former United States major general John E. Wool, now stationed in New York, elevated tension levels further when he threatened to "raise 200,000 men at short notice" to hold the south within the Union by force if the south moved to secede.[435] Furthermore, in the fall of 1860 a northern-supported collection of anti-slavery/federalist elements were elected to congressional and executive offices. If the southern anti-secessionists were looking for signs of hope in the final hours of the Buchanan Administration, they were similarly left wanting as Congress raised the rates of trade duties with the Morrill Tariff Act (a rated high last seen in the 1840s), threatening to the south's struggling economic base and key export crop, cotton.

As the weeks passed in the state capital and the political debate and in-fighting grew more bitter, William Thomas saw his "watch and wait" associates fall before the alarmists. It was only a matter of time before the southern states would break away from the Union. Rather than spend his remaining weeks and months waiting for Acting Governor Henry T. Clark (Governor John W. Ellis had suddenly died in office on July 7th, 1861), the state senator followed the example of other politicians and returned home to spend as much time as possible with Temperance, his Sarah, and their young children, William Holland Thomas Jr. (reportedly affectionately referred to as the "Little Indian Chief" and "Junaluska"[436] in his father's writings)[437] and James Robert Thomas, born at White Sulphur Springs on December 16th, 1858, and December 16th, 1860, respectively.[438] Once home, however, William Thomas again became consumed by his duties, trying to control the damage done to his political reputation with the drafting, printing, and distribution of fliers to clarify his anti-federalist stance for more influential supporters and conferring on the western region's next move with the local leaders.[439]

Apart from William Thomas's side slave trading and the intrinsically human psychological drive to feel superior to another, the State of North Carolina actually stood to lose little economically from a federally enforced relinquishment of their slave stock. As a result, Hinton Rowan Helper's argument found some merit with Thomas's southern Appalachian community (as well as a small cluster of Unionists across the mountains in Eastern Tennessee). Yet, the state senator and his North Carolina cronies were also realists. Bordered by the pro-slavery states of Virginia, South Carolina, Tennessee (with slavery largely supported by the state's western occupants), and Georgia, the leadership knew that if their neighbors seceded, North Carolina had two choices: either abandon their platform of states' rights and join the Union (which engendered the risk of an internal uprising as well as an invasion/occupation by the combined might of their southern neighbors) or follow the standard of states' rights into secession from the Union and work within the new system of confederated states to effect some benefit.

Though steeped in the rhetoric of a reignited Patriot cause and a continuance of the long unresolved issues of the American Revolution (in which northerners and their southern sympathizers were viewed as Tories and President Abraham Lincoln as the reincarnation of British King George III) and on politically opposite sides, North Carolina's leadership's seemingly shifting sympathies were far from the proscribed "noble reasons" offered in decades of postwar/pro-Confederate literature. Men like William Thomas and the rising star of the Democratic Party, Zebulon Vance, began to see the crisis as inherently advantageous to the business interests of their constituents and, more important, themselves.

Were the southern and border states to make good on their threat of secession, Thomas and Vance knew North Carolina would be at the geographic center of the new nation, but there the two men's shared dreams diverged. While Thomas saw the illegality of seceding without immediate cause, he also envisioned the right post-crisis investments of his seceded state easily leading to a new renaissance of economic stimulation for Western North Carolina brought about by cross-country and international commerce. Similarly, Zebulon Vance held glorious dreams for his home state, desiring a strong northerly lying central government,[440] free of "vacillation and corruption of the President . . . astounding and enormous frauds and defalcations,"[441] for the new southern confederation (in which he undoubtedly dreamed of eventually playing a leading role).[442]

Like most dreamers, they initially believed that they only needed to wait for their rewards to come to them. Despite the state's avaricious desires, however, North Carolina's reluctance to take the initiative had left the matter of secession to be decided by their less blind neighbors. While the anti-abolitionists fanned the flames of war with anti-federalist and anti-abolitionist propaganda, the leaders of the secessionist movement (mostly centered around the affluent Virginian and South Carolinian aristocracy) believed that the Union would not risk a war if the southern states seceded with the nation's border states (Maryland, Delaware, Kentucky, and Missouri) in a peaceful parting. If not, there would be war.

On December 20th, 1860, South Carolina began the final round of political brinkmanship when they publicly removed themselves from the Union. Mississippi, Florida, and Alabama followed shortly thereafter (January 9th, January 10th, and January 11th, 1861, respectively). Next, Georgia and Virginia declared their independence (on January 19th and April 17th, 1861, respectively). By the close of April 1861, the southern states of North Carolina and Tennessee stood undecided.

With the border states of Missouri, Kentucky, Maryland, and Delaware hanging in the balance, State Senator William Thomas was recalled to Raleigh. On May 1st, 1861, the North Carolina General Assembly was called into emergency session to once more revisit the issues surrounding the crisis, but this time the situation was different. When news reached the capital of the April 12th, 1861, firing of secessionist artillery on South Carolina's federal-held Fort Sumter, matters of personal philosophy and personal loyalties were put aside in favor of practicality and security. As Tennessee's western secessionist populace began to rise up against their largely Unionist eastern mountain neighbors and force their state's secession (May 7th, 1861), Acting Governor of North Carolina Clark called for the May 13th election of 120 delegates to represent the interests of North Carolina's counties in a May 20th secessionist convention.[443]

Having campaigned long and hard over the previous months, in the following weeks William Thomas had managed to orchestrate a brief reversal of fortune. Elected as Jackson County's convention delegate to preside over the official secession of North Carolina from the United States of America on May 20th, 1861, Thomas was quickly tapped to sit on committees by his party leadership, eager to dually utilize the man's well-demonstrated managerial talents while simultaneously keeping the apparently much-loved Western North Carolina representative from the trouble that had plagued him earlier.

Over the next few months, William Thomas argued for the authorization of public schools and the appointment of Justices of the Peace as well as institution of new, more representative state elections and the creation and placement of defensive forces throughout the countryside, but, by early 1862, the Haywood County–born convention delegate was once more growing wise to the machinations of his now Confederate contemporaries. On May 22nd, 1861, a hundred gun salute and a flock of citizens had gleefully celebrated North Carolina's secession.[444] Similar sentiments were shared again later in June, with news of the Confederate victory at the First Battle of Manassas, but, in the months that followed, the elation seemed to evaporate with the arrival of a fleet of Union ships ordered to blockade the southern coastline and the onset of the Union Army's Peninsula Campaign to retake the seditious states.

With few sources of state income to draw upon, a few political rivals were beginning to blame William Thomas for failing to provide North Carolina's defensive militias with the proper means to repulse the invaders. Furthermore, as the weeks dragged on and the Union began to reveal their tactical plans, it was becoming plain to most North Carolinians that unless the Confederacy's military could either turn back or stalemate their Union counterparts, North Carolina was going to eventually become a battlefield.

Weary of being placed in dubious positions by his political contemporaries, William Thomas began to use his newfound power and influence towards the betterment of his Western North Carolina neighbors. As a backwoods merchant and a schooled student of Cherokee history, he knew about the inherent vulnerability of his home region to over-mountain raids. If the south's new war for independence continued to unfold the way Thomas was watching, Western North Carolina would likely come under attack from Unionist raids or even full scale over-mountain assaults (likely launched from the contested region of Eastern Tennessee). With the region's recent loss of the Haywood Rangers (captained by Sarah Thomas's first cousin, James R. Love II) in a reallocation of military assets in favor of defending Raleigh from nearby Camp Lee before being eventually sent on the offensive northward, the region was at the enemy's mercy.[445]

Drawing on the defensive precedents made by the ancient Cherokee at the Soco Gap, North Carolina Patriot colonel John Sevier's 1780–1781 campaign against Chief Yonaguska's mountain settlement, and his own father's southern campaign against British major Patrick Ferguson's 1780 forces at Kings Mountain, William Thomas used his considerable mercantile talent and appropriative influence to push for the creation of a defensive militia force.

By the onset of summer in 1861, William Thomas had managed to gain enough support to orchestrate the enlistment of two hundred Cherokee volunteers under the banner of the Junaluska Zouaves, but the Western North Carolinians' idea also had unforeseen consequences. Thomas had tapped Cherokee brethren out of the need for able-bodied men and as a preemptive demonstration of their loyalty to their new government, but whereas the North Carolina leadership had coolly endorsed the idea, the regional newspapers began covering the story of the volunteers in textually unflattering, racially stark warnings, cautioning the "Northern barbarians, with A. Blinkun at their head," to fear for their Yankee scalps as the Cherokee were standing post.[446] However incorporative the remarks were of the Eastern Band, parts of North Carolina remained largely untouched by Chief Thomas's public relations efforts and Delegate Thomas's political ministrations. William Holland Thomas and his Cherokee brethren would have to do something to change the minds of North Carolina's non-regional populace or all three might suffer the loss of a lifetime's worth of progress.

CHAPTER FOURTEEN

DEFENDING WESTERN NORTH CAROLINA

By early 1862, William Holland Thomas was growing weary of his political wartime position. In his three sessions with the seceded North Carolina government, he found his constituents' positions being consistently marginalized again and again in favor of the more immediate short-term concerns of the state's Lower Piedmont and coastal counties. When he continued to push his western agenda with political influence garnered over the years, Thomas found his ranks of friends thinning and his own legislative prowess reduced to the advocacy of largely expedient committee actions. It was becoming readily apparent that the Western North Carolinian politico's power was waning, and if the man's fortune did not soon change, his profits, his constituents, his clients, his brethren, and he would shrink into insignificance.

Following established habit when confronted with a situation of diminishing returns, Thomas looked hard for the prospect lying just beyond his borders that, if carefully cultivated, would bear the fruit of his salvation. Consequently, his eyes settled on the armed conflict already raging throughout the country.

Like many fence-sitting southerners, as secessionist talk gave way to secessionist action Thomas had come to embrace the seemingly seditious actions of his more eager colleagues out of political necessity and the promise of a revitalized postwar Western North Carolina as the geographic center (and, by default, a key economic hub) of the new Confederate States of America.[447] Since they now were in political decline and personal danger from a Union conquest of the state, his and his constituents' last best hope for postwar prosperity lay in the success of the ill-equipped and mismanaged hodge-podge of militia volunteers, farmers, and federally trained military careerists of the Confederate Army.

In the first few months of the conflict, the War of the Rebellion seemed to be proceeding apace for the State of North Carolina. While the Confederate States of America had failed to induce the border states into the southern fold as initially hoped, the rebellion had succeeded in seizing a surplus of federally stocked fortifications and had thus managed to gain enough initial battlefield victories to drive their ill-organized enemies to distraction and, some prayed, to capitulation. Yet, as the Confederate military began to capitalize on their good fortune (largely in the State of Virginia), a few hurried Union messages and a handful of ably executed defensive orders not only had managed to preserve the marginal defensive integrity of the United States but also had managed to set in motion a military machine to exact serious material and psychological losses on the main conduit of rebel troops and supplies to the Virginian theater of combat, North Carolina.

Instead of a brief, bloody conflict fought in the northern locales for honor, integrity, and the supremacy of states' rights followed by the issuance of a bitter federalist capitulation, North Carolinian leaders and their constituents awoke to find their reviled enemy bearing down on key back roads, bridges, and coastal positions with violent intent. On August 29th, 1861, North Carolina suffered unexpected losses in men, supplies, and security in the loss of Hatteras. On February 7th, 1862, the Union Army threatened the body of the state with invasion in the amphibious landing and occupation of Roanoke Island and simultaneously neutralized North Carolina's meager naval forces moored at Cobbs Point. Finally, as if to punctuate the gravity of the situation, a few days later, on February 19th, 1862, federal troops carried out the razing of Winston.

In 1862 the consequences of their secessionist decision had been brought home to the Tar Heel State, but, as William Thomas rapidly discovered, North Carolina's leaders were unable to rise to the occasion. Rather than choose a few key defensive points, the state had diffused its military reserves to canvass as many of their sprawling assets as they could manage. Acting opposite to the standard military convention of marshaling one's reserves to either contain or disrupt the enemy's operations, the now fright-filled politicians first drew a blanket of security around the state capital, then set about criticizing Thomas and others for failing to sufficiently support their defensive preparations. Contrary to his adversaries' hopes, however, William Thomas fought the instinct to rage against his opponents and endured the baseless accusations so that he might effectively later turn the tables on his detractors and rise to new prominence through his newest idea, Eastern Band military service.

Earlier, Thomas had successfully argued for the creation of a backcountry militia force comprised of native Cherokee to monitor and defend Western North Carolina's mountain passes and was authorized to raise the 200-man contingent in May 1861 dubbed the Junaluska Zouaves. In one motion, Thomas had managed to preempt his less accepting colleagues' potential motions against the Eastern Band and shore up his own political career after the humiliation he endured during the secessionist crisis and also had set the stage for him to petition the new Confederate government for the relocation funds the United States Congress had previously promised the Eastern Band and him but, as of yet, had failed to provide.[448]

As the conflict widened into total war, however, William Thomas saw newfound potential in his previously political move. As reports began to circulate of the bloody onslaught taking place in Virginia,* the vocal anti-secessionist actions of some East Tennesseans and the rise of militant factions to the north (in the nearby northerly outback territory of future breakaway state West Virginia), it seemed to be only a matter of time before his new Western North Carolina's defenders would be removed from the Mountain region under state order and, like Sallie Thomas's cousin James R. Love II's Haywood Rangers, be forced to take up coastal defensive positions beside other previously politically appropriated regional security forces.

Rather than allow others to file paperwork ordering his enlisted brethren to reallocate for frontline service and leave the entire Upper Piedmont and Mountain regions exposed to privation and attack, Thomas worked to manipulate the staggering short-sightedness of his own state's leadership to the advantage of the Eastern Band and himself. Capitalizing on North Carolina's established commitment to protect the state's Cherokee populace during the removal period and the previously secured endorsement of the state's former congressional representative, Thomas Bragg, for the Cherokee's explicit inclusion in the rolls as state citizens,[449] Thomas positioned the Eastern Band of North Carolina Cherokee as an indispensable asset to the war effort and Confederate postwar prosperity.

While North Carolina leaders like Zebulon Vance likened the ill-advised defense of Hatteras to "the Spartan Martyrs of Thermopylae,"[450] William Thomas cobbled his own meager counterinsurgent and tactical operations force from willing neighbors and Cherokee brethren. Melding his business-savvy skills to his political

---

* Antietam and the Wilderness.

connections, William Thomas then pitched the idea of a mountain-based interdiction force to build and man defensive positions against Tennessee and Virginia (as, at the war's onset, North Carolina's border with Georgia was comparatively free of subversive elements).[451] Before his political detractors could link the Junaluska Zouaves to the Thomas defense plan and publicly counter the move, the formerly accused anti-secessionist then wedded his proposal to Confederate President Jefferson Davis's own recent advocation for similarly scaled semi-autonomous forces to counter potential Unionist subversive actions.[452]

George Hayes, an old Thomas friend turned bitter political nemesis, killed the official bill for the creation of his unit in the House,[453] but President Davis's continued interest kept the notion alive while William Thomas gathered a popular consensus and political allies.

The proposal had several meritorious points, which continued to increase with daily growing relevance as the Mountain region began to destabilize with old rivalries rising anew, settling old scores under the guise of Unionist or Confederate ideology. It seemed on the verge of tacit acceptance (including the implicit detail of granting the Eastern Band Chief military command of the contingent), but, in the spring of 1862,[454] Thomas's carefully crafted pitch to muster a company of the Eastern Band of Cherokee and Western North Carolina neighbors into Confederate service was nearly upended when Confederate Army major Washington Morgan (also known as George Washington Morgan, A'gans'ta, and Ogonstoka) entered Western North Carolina and began recruiting Cherokee for active service in the defense of East Tennessee from Unionist aggression.

While Major Morgan held little distinction with the Eastern Band as an emissary of the Confederate Tennessee and Mountain Theater Commander, Major General Edmund Kirby Smith, the Confederate major was, however, a mixed blood Cherokee warrior whose father had reportedly commanded ranks of Cherokee warriors beside their Eastern Band brother Junaluska at the Battle of Horseshoe Bend.[455] Upon hearing Major Morgan's own call to action, a few members of the Eastern Band were moved to volunteer their services as warriors for the Confederacy.[456]

Before a formal pact could be made between the prospective Cherokee volunteers and the Confederacy, however, Thomas interjected himself into the dialogue.[457] In a sudden about-face, the Chief of the Eastern Band answered the Confederate officer's enlistment pitch with a persuasive argument against not only Major Morgan's call for volunteers but also any suggested Eastern Band involvement in the conflict. Speaking in direct opposition to his political efforts of the past several months, Chief Thomas, in the presence of Major Morgan, asked his Cherokee brethren to put aside the notion of involving themselves in a war that *he claimed* was not theirs and to, instead, look to the care of their Western North Carolina homes and families.[458]

The assembled members of the Eastern Band were doubtlessly puzzled by the sudden reversal but, having learned over the years to trust their adopted brother's instincts in such matters, nevertheless acceded to their Chief's wishes. In adherence to the council of their elders the few Cherokee warriors who had expressed interest in the Confederate Army promptly rescinded their offers of military service, forcing the Confederate officer to leave empty-handed and somewhat bewildered.[459]

With his prospective plan to reinvigorate his faltering triple-fold career once more unhindered, a few weeks after Major Morgan's departure, the businessman publicly revealed his support of the southern military to the Eastern Band. On April 9th, 1862, the rebel Chief was inducted into military service and granted the rank of captain in the Confederate States of America and promptly assumed command of his own company of roughly one hundred and ten Western North Carolina residents and Cherokee[460] (likely pulled from the Junaluska Zouaves and other regional volunteers).[461] The Eastern Band responded in celebration of their now active opposition to the United States with the wearing of traditional ancestral ornamentation (including feathers and paints) and convened a war dance at the Qualla townhall on Soco Creek (the dance was also repeated at various intervals throughout the rebellion).[462]

Yet, just as soon as Captain Thomas had assumed command and started to enact his plans, he found his situation far less autonomous than he had anticipated. Without a fixed post recognized and validated by either the Confederate theater command staff or the firm endorsement of state leaders, Captain Thomas continued to remain at the relative mercy of partisanship back east. In organizing the raising of a supplemental company of Confederate volunteers and showing his latest defensive plans for a Western North Carolina (centering around the mountain gaps and the Ocanaluftee River on the Tennessee border) to key South Carolina officials in a bid for legitimacy,[463] however, the captain had attracted the attention of the southern high command.

Rationalizing that any element of surrender would fall under the command of the returning Confederate major George Washington Morgan, Captain Thomas brokered a shrewd business deal to protect Western North Carolina, in Confederate service across the mountains in East Tennessee. In return for the surrendering of his second company of Western North Carolina defenders to an assigned post within the hierarchy of the Confederate Army, the supervisory leadership promised his original company of Eastern Band members and Western North Carolina volunteers (signed on for three years of service each) would continue to defend the Mountain region against attack for the duration of the war.[464] In the end, serving on the frontlines of a prospective incursion into Western North Carolina through Virginia and East Tennessee seemed more palpable than fighting malaria and fever and fending off sniping attacks from North Carolina politicians.

Captain Thomas then transferred to the head of his soon-to-be-detached Western North Carolina company. With orders issued making Thomas's store bookkeeper and claim assistant James Terrell and relative Matthew Love first lieutenants and promoting several able volunteers, including Astoogatogeh,[465] William S. Terrell, and three other local enlistees, to the rank of second lieutenant,[466] by the time Major Morgan took command, Captain Thomas had organized his command into an efficient group of 100 Cherokee warriors and twelve backwoodsmen.[467] According to a Confederate major, they were "as fine a body of men as ever went into the service."[468]

Far from coastal service or following Thomas's brother-in-law's orders to bolster General Joseph E. Johnston's Virginian ranks, on April 15th, 1862, the volunteer Confederates of the North Carolina Battalion of Indians and Highlanders were conducted away from their homes and led on a circuitous course over the Appalachian Mountains and towards the Confederate-held East Tennessee city of Knoxville. Along the way, as southern partisans had during the American Revolutionary War, the recently activated element encouraged passersby to join the rebel cause. Marching over the next several days, often through inclement weather, across the landscape of North Carolina, Captain Thomas and his men furthered their recruitment efforts with the ordered dispatching of runners ahead of the column with messages to announce their approach to such regional locales as Cheoch, Sandtown, and Valleytown.[469]

When the Confederate volunteers moved into Sweetwater, however, the feeling of comradery and judicious decision-making began to erode and fall away. As the company arrived at the railroad depot, Major Morgan promptly detached three of the company's Caucasian enlistees with orders to drive the contingent's supplies by wagon to Knoxville, Tennessee, unaccompanied, and then abruptly ordered Captain Thomas to accompany him the remainder of the way to Knoxville separate from their own men.[470]

Leaving Lieutenant James Terrell in the unenviable position of securing freight transport and overseeing the military training of his remaining hundred-odd subordinates, Captain Thomas boarded the train. With the accommodations little different from the several other rail lines the former businessman had taken over the years, the North Carolinian took the initiative and, turning on his well-practiced charm, over the next several hours detailed for the major his own perspective on the war and the defense of the southern states and his own recent ruminations on the potential asset in creating a counterinsurgent force to combat the recent rise in Unionist raiding parties and saboteurs. In conclusion, Captain Thomas recommended that his men be promptly rejoined at Knoxville, augmented with support troops, and equipped by August 1ˢᵗ, 1862.

Major Washington Morgan was receptive to the captain's ideas, but the conversation concluded with no promises, no rewards, and no resolution for the man's informal proposal. Instead, when Lieutenant Terrell and the company arrived at Knoxville, the company was conducted outside the city to wait beside other new units for their allotted supplies and the issuance of assignments.

East Tennessee was a peculiar rallying point for the rebel chief and men. In the years before the American Revolution, Cherokee warriors had assaulted the city.[471] Thereafter, the sparsely populated region grew at a pace similar to Western North Carolina, but, unlike the distinguished businessman's home, Tennessee embraced the technology of telegraph, railroad, and roadways. With the 1858 completion of the East Tennessee and Virginia Railroad, the region had finally become a central transportation hub, ferrying goods from the expanding western frontier to feed the increasing demands of the burgeoning urban East Coast populace.

Yet, the expansion had come at a heavy price. East Tennessean farmers who had long anticipated the advent of regional railways as a swift and reliable means to send greater yields of fresh produce to market without fear of spoilage found themselves supplanted by western territorial farmers. With little advanced industrial capacity, the region was unable to successfully compete with more-established factory centers. Furthermore, when the secessionist crisis bloomed in the 1850s, Tennesseans also found themselves fearing not only federal occupation (as a sizable sector of the state's eastern populace supported the Union) but also the potential of an uprising from one fourth of her populace in a slave rebellion.[472]

The state was a powder keg ready to erupt.

As they marched in double columns down Gay Street towards their campsite, the predominantly Cherokee contingent attracted the attention of young children and passersby. Pressing onward, the crowds continued to thicken with quizzical spectators as the Cherokee progressed through the city. When the contingent reached Main Street, the force was ordered to halt before a reportedly impassable crowd of onlookers,[473] but instead of attacking the foreigners as others might have, the crowd marveled at the group of exotic strangers volunteering to defend the city of Knoxville and East Tennessee from her populace's more seditious Unionist sympathizers, a reaction Captain William Thomas had worked and waited his entire life for, such a display of affection from his fellow North Carolinians.

Receiving the warm, inquisitive sentiments from the crowd, Captain Thomas's company of mixed Cherokee and Caucasian solders returned the spectators' interest benignly and patiently waited for the spectacle to dissipate. When the crowd finally thinned to a fordable size, the contingent resumed their march and took up a stationary position with other Confederate volunteers waiting on the outskirts of the Confederate-held city. In honor of Major Morgan, the company then bestowed his Cherokee name upon their East Tennessee rallying point and bedded down at "Camp Ogonstoka."[474]

Since the firing on Fort Sumter earlier in the previous year, the city of Knoxville had played a key role in the region's reformation as a Confederate stronghold. As the secessionist talk of college students, legal experts, and slave holders was augmented by the rallying cries of influential East Tennessee businessmen (vying for imagined greater profits under a confederation of independent states),[475] many within the Confederacy's command structure recognized Knoxville as an exploitable regional hub through which they might transport men and supplies from uncontested southern regions to the war zone, a matter made even more pressing by Admiral David G. Farragut's April 25th, 1862, taking of New Orleans and the subsequent seizure of control of the Mississippi River.

Within a matter of weeks of the war's onset, the Tennessean city had become encircled by a rapidly increasing number of volunteers for the southern cause. Unlike William Thomas, who had the foresight and means to equip his colleagues with the essentials of outback living, most Confederate volunteers enlisting at Knoxville were forced to endure lengthy periods of quartermasters furnishing them with the leanest tools of warfare, rifles and ammunition. After waiting for several months to be issued their rifles (and hence their action orders), a number of volunteers requisitioned the local armory's only unclaimed ordnance, 400 dusty flintlocks.[476]

Once the men had made camp, Captain William Thomas and Lieutenant James Terrell fell back into the regimented familiarity of providing for a large populace of dependents. Instead of filing claims and keeping store inventories for civilians, however, the two men began to manage the paperwork and procurement of the necessities of survival for their soldier subordinates. On May 6th, 1862, Captain Thomas signed a requisition for a tent.[477] Later, he followed the missive, asking for a gross of cartridge boxes, waist belts, canteens, rifle caps, shoe pouches, packing boxes, powder horns, and rifle powder.[478] As the supplies were delivered, both North Carolinians' administrative efforts and the daily increasing readiness of her troops now were almost indistinguishable from their theater counterparts.

When time allowed, Captain Thomas also resumed his long neglected business of encouraging local interest in the Eastern Band of North Carolina Cherokee. Given their city reception, the Cherokee Chief did not have to work as hard to project an inviting atmosphere for the East Tennesseans as he had in North Carolina. In direct polar opposition to his public relations efforts at publicly modernizing the Eastern Band, the annual Green Corn Dance and other occasions of public Cherokee heritage celebration, the elite of East Tennessee apparently needed no invitation to visit the encampment, as the elite of Knoxville society cast them as "the wonder of all the city."[479]

The North Carolina company further intrigued city residents when they conducted Christian services at the nearby First Presbyterian Church.[480] Led by their preacher, Unaguskie, Captain Thomas and his company reportedly enchanted on-lookers with full services, complete with prayer, hymnals, sermon, and song in native

Cherokee.[481] In their spare time at the encampment, the Cherokee occasionally entertained crowds, demonstrating their competitive ballplay sport in which players (traditionally men—naked except for a small cloth around their waists) chased after a ball with their long, curved sticks.[482]

As the captain and his men entertained their Knoxville contemporaries, however, plans for the North Carolina element were being plotted by the region's Confederate theater commanders. Officially sanctioned as part of the Confederate Army's Department of East Tennessee, Captain Thomas and his men were placed under the command of intrepid Confederate colonel John C. Vaughn.

Within two weeks of making camp outside of Knoxville, the company was ordered to march once more through the adoring crowds on city streets and make, with all due haste, for a strategic eastern-lying transportation hub: Strawberry Plains.

CHAPTER FIFTEEN

THE THOMAS LEGION

L eaving the busy Confederate-held city of Knoxville, Captain
William Holland Thomas's company first marched northwest
along the East Tennessee and Virginia Railroad to Camp Kirby
Smith at Clinton, Tennessee,[483] then proceeded on a southeasterly
course across the sprawling green fields and rolling hills of East Tennessee to their base of operations, a railroad hub several miles away
called Strawberry Plains. When the North Carolina soldiers finally
reached their destination, the soldiers, now placed under the local
command of Colonel John C. Vaughn, began setting up fixed positions
and camp facilities. If the region's pro-Unionist disposition and the
strategic importance of the surrounding territory were any indication,
these soldiers would soon be sorely needed.

Beyond the concerns of political ideology and the economic benefits of the regional railway network (made even more important with
the May 1st, 1862, loss of both New Orleans and Confederate control
of the Mississippi River), the State of Tennessee held deep importance for both the Union and Confederate military. As a centerpiece
of the western secessionist government, East Tennessee had become
a staging area for the southern military in the west, capable of striking
deep into Virginia, Kentucky, and points north. Yet, the region east of
Knoxville was also an inviting southern military target for those same
reasons and a few others. By degrading the Confederacy's military
presence through either clandestine operations (primarily efforts at
sabotage, subversion, and espionage) or an invasion launched against
East Tennessee, the Union could seriously limit the effectiveness of
Virginia's ability to make war, threaten the political center of the Confederacy with a similar prospective move against Richmond, and, in
forcing Tennessee's neighbors (Georgia, Alabama, Mississippi, and
Arkansas) to take the defensive, introduce a potentially catastrophic
element into the southern rebellion, fear of imminent destruction.
For each warring faction, total victory could only be achieved by riding through East Tennessee.

With the threat of invasion rising as Union major general John
Frémont (a former Georgian turned Californian governor) began to
move against Confederate forces throughout the mountain theater
(most notably those of Confederate general Thomas "Stonewall"
Jackson), East Tennessee–based commanders focused on fortifying
their porous borders. Flanked by the Cumberland Mountains to the
north and north west and the Appalachians lying to the east and
northeast, in 1861 Confederate general William Churchwell managed the deforestation and fortifying of the likeliest source of a
northern attack, the mountainous border confluence of Kentucky,
Virginia, and East Tennessee called the Cumberland Gap. As a secondary measure of security Confederate major general Edmund
Kirby Smith placed similar regional elements (including Captain
William Thomas's North Carolina company) within striking distance

of the Gap and its smaller Cumberland Mountain breaks (including the pass called Bull's Gap), as well as the tracks, depots, and bridges of the East Tennessee and Virginia Railroad.

Still, threats of northern incursions ran behind Captain William Thomas's more immediate concerns. In early May 1862, shortly before the North Carolina contingent's arrival at Strawberry Plains, tensions between East Tennessee's Unionists and Confederates reached new heights when several hundred Unionist protestors gathered at Strawberry Plains for a rally. The gathering suddenly turned violent when the group of protestors began pelting a nearby train of Confederate soldiers with rocks. Obliging the Unionists, the Confederate soldiers picked up their weapons, leveled them at the protestors, and fired.*[484] The altercation illustrated not only the necessity of keeping order at Strawberry Plains but also how well the men needed to integrate themselves with their new surroundings. Although the majority of Captain William Holland Thomas's subordinates had gained their wilderness experience on the other side of the Smoky Mountains, the contingent rapidly translated their survivalist skills into functional military assets. Within a few weeks of their arrival at Strawberry Plains, Captain Thomas, apparently bolstered by new additions, followed standard military practice and divided the North Carolina contingent into two halves,[485] creating one company for active duty and offensive operations and a second company to serve in a stand-down position to guard base camp, respond to emergencies, and discourage future local factional conflicts. As a result, during their initial months on patrol, the North Carolinian element reportedly managed to drive off several Unionist guerrillas and rescued a Confederate picket force trapped in the Cumberland Mountains.[486]

Yet, the North Carolinians were effectively neutralized for a short time by at least one enemy. Within a few weeks of their arrival at Strawberry Plains a number of the Eastern Band volunteers began to

* Luckily, no one was killed in the exchange.

rage with fever. The illness, which was later diagnosed as measles and followed hard upon by mumps, managed to reach epidemic proportions throughout the camp.[487] Relying on traditional Cherokee remedies, the North Carolinian contingent was unable to effectively respond when the Confederate defenses at the Cumberland Gap were abandoned in June 1862 to the forces of United States brigadier general George W. Morgan. Encumbered by illness and apprised by headquarters that "a plan is being secretly formed to burn the bridges at Loudon and Strawberry Plains" and that "Federal soldiers dressed in citizen's clothes have been seen concerning [consorting] with Union tories . . . are busy in collecting their friends about those bridges to burn them,"[488] Captain Thomas and his men were unable to join General Kirby Smith's drive into Kentucky later that August to cut the United States brigadier general's supply lines and successfully drive him from the Cumberland Gap. Dejected, the North Carolinians were, instead, relegated to the function of bridge-keepers and watchmen, waiting for the enemy to appear. The threat did not materialize.

Rather than continue to sleep under the open sky, Captain Thomas fell back on an old vice he had acquired during his past business travels, moving into the creature comforts of a rooming house. Based out of the house owned by the Stringfield family, he renewed his campaign for command of a battalion, writing Tennessee governor Clark his ideas for a counterinsurgency force staffed by regional volunteers that, once amassed, would in turn be used as a home guard for the Confederate state.[489] Given the recent issuance of the Confederate Conscript law, the idea met with little reaction from the Tennessean politico, but the idea did germinate in the mind of Mrs. Stringfield's stepson, William W. Stringfield.

Born in Nashville, Tennessee, but raised in Knoxville by descendants of transplanted North Carolinians, the young Stringfield had enlisted in the Confederate Army with the opening shots of the war.[490] He served initially as a private in the Tennessee Cavalry, but in 1862 logistical demands soon necessitated the educated man's elevation in rank and transfer to a Knoxville-based administrative post.[491] By the

time Captain Thomas had arrived at Strawberry Plains, Captain Stringfield had become disenchanted by the mundane life of East Tennessee's paperwork bureaucracy and began to petition his superiors for
a more active duty assignment. Rather than being granted a combat
position, however, the young Tennessean soon found himself relegated to the other end of the thankless bureaucratic war-machine,
army recruitment.[492]

Sharing the same house between their respective assignments,
Captains Thomas and Stringfield rapidly developed a working relationship and casual friendship. In time, as the North Carolinian realized the young man might be able to make his military desires a
reality, Captain Thomas came to adopt a fatherly stance with Captain
Stringfield, listening and giving advice to the young man on how
best to use the connections he had to make the best of *their* shared
situations. Following the same patterned affectionate, helpful, and
reserved demeanor he had utilized with hundreds of business associates in the past, the North Carolinian soon managed to secure not
only the young man's confidence but also his administrative support
in seeing to the North Carolina element's needs, and most important, when on the road, the active seeking of recruits for a Thomas-
led regiment.

Yet, the North Carolina businessman had learned from past experience not to trust one source with ensuring his future prosperity.
In early July, Captain William Thomas left Strawberry Plains in the
care of his subordinates and set off for the Confederate capital of
Richmond, Virginia. After a short jaunt on the Tennessee and Virginia Railroad his men had been tasked to defend, Captain Thomas
shed the trappings of military protocol for the expediency of politicking and self-promotion. Failing to secure support for a proposed
modification to the Confederate Conscription Act that would ease
the officer's military duties, Captain William Thomas was instead rewarded for his time with the addition of a Cherokee company and
four Caucasian companies to his command.[493] The man had received
a modicum of what he had desired (the command of a Confederate

battalion), but his time at Richmond was also beginning to show the North Carolinian was falling out of practice with the fine art of deal-making.

While the North Carolinian and his men were otherwise engaged, Union forces were on the move in the west. Rallying behind their recent victories at Fort Donaldson, Shiloh, and New Orleans, the federal forces started applying pressure on the Confederate theater forces of Major General Simon B. Buckner, General Braxton Bragg, Major General Kirby Smith, and others. The Confederates responded to the new threat by dividing their forces into several segments that the invaders would have to deal with individually before attempting to lay definitive claim to the region, but, in doing so, the Confederates had also unknowingly left themselves open for a palpable strike. In the late spring of 1862, Union major general Ormsby Mitchel saw an opening and ordered his adjutant Brigadier General James Negley to take Chattanooga. Although the Tennessee city was naturally buffered by the winding Chattanooga River and guarded by a mass of earthwork defenses, Confederate commanders were alarmed by how rapidly and, seemingly, effortlessly the Union Army was bringing their forces forward and placing their artillery batteries within reach of the seceded city.

Unable to remove the threat themselves, the Confederate city called for assistance. Upon arriving at the embattled field, Captain Thomas and forty of his men were deployed as scouts to obtain actionable intelligence on the enemy. Working his way towards the Union Army's position, the North Carolinian spotted a solitary Union soldier, took him prisoner, and conducted the man back to the Confederate lines. While the captured federalist likely failed to produce any actionable intelligence, the Eastern Band members among Captain Thomas's command were galvanized by the capture, promising that "each of them must take one to be even . . ."[494] When Major General Kirby Smith arrived at the besieged city, Captain Thomas and his men were readying themselves to unseat the enemy from their position in their first fixed military engagement. As Captain

Thomas marched towards the battlefield, however, Brigadier General Negley began to withdraw his forces.

Momentarily deprived of the chance to prove the character of his men in battle, the captain was ordered to return to Strawberry Plains and resume his prior duties. The contingent, however, would not have to wait long for their chance to see action. On September 15th, 1862, a contingent of Captain Thomas's men was patrolling the Kentucky-Tennessee border of the Baptist Gap when they were ambushed by a group of federalists. Responding to the sudden attack with the learned audacity of a superior military and merchant partner, First Lieutenant William Terrell ordered his men to charge the enemy. In the ensuing melee the North Carolina Cherokee of the Eastern Band were dealt their first wartime blow with the death of Junaluska's grandson, Second Lieutenant Astoogatogeh. Instead of reeling from the blow, however, the unit rose up and exacted vengeance upon the Union forces. By the time the battle had ended, the group of Confederates had left several of the ambushers dead and taken a handful of scalps as bloody trophies.[495]

When Captain Thomas learned of the incident, however, the North Carolinian ordered his brethren to give up the scalps. Fearing that both his and Chief Yonaguska's work was about to be undone by a few ill-conceived words spoken to the Eastern Band members by one Knoxville woman (calling on the group to return with bloody scalps of Union soldiers)[496] and the blood red obscured sight of combat vengeance, Captain Thomas returned the scalps to the Union with their apologies. The participants in the counterattack were admonished for their conduct, but, in later years, retired Confederate officer James Terrell conceded that scalping was "the only thing [about] which Thomas could not control them."[497]

In the following weeks, the Confederate high command paid little attention to the incident. Far from their penalizing the Strawberry Plains commander or his troops for the inappropriate actions, on September 27th, 1862, William Holland Thomas was elevated to the rank of colonel.[498] Aided by the footwork of Captain Stringfield in securing additional volunteers on a somewhat unorthodox trip to Western North Carolina, Colonel Thomas was next granted his long desired prize, an augmented command.

Although administratively renamed the "Regiment of Indians and Highlanders Legion of North Carolina,"[499] the contingent not only retained the elements of the colonel's previous command but also expanded its tactical capabilities with the additions of skilled sappers, masons, miners,[500] craftsmen, gunsmiths, and gunpowder workers as well as seasoned infantry, cavalry, and artillery specialists. Once his contingent was filled with regional talent, Colonel Thomas next, returning to his roots, secured the transfer of both his now battle-hardened in-law, Lieutenant Colonel James R. Love II, and his command, the Sixteenth North Carolina Infantry Division[501] (Lieutenant Colonel Love had already served several months under the Virginia command of the already legendary Confederate generals "Stonewall Jackson" and Robert Edward Lee but had also experienced Confederate incompetence under Confederate general Joseph Johnston at the May 1862 near victory turned disaster called the Battle of the Seven Pines). To ensure the administrative efficiency of the contingent of seven companies, James Terrell was raised in rank to captain and was elected to the position of assistant quartermaster, and, in response to the young Tennessean's assistance, William Stringfield was transferred into the new contingent and raised in rank to major. In October 1862, the command, already being referred to in certain circles as "the Thomas Legion," continued to take shape with the attachment of Confederate major William Walker's four infantry and three cavalry units. By war's end, Colonel William Thomas's command would reach a size of at least 1,770 officers and men.[502]

With his desired military assets now in place, Colonel Thomas was eager to show the Confederacy what his command could do, but, as the region of East Tennessee continued to remain a breeding ground for raiders and Unionist sympathizers, the legion was forced to remain encamped at Strawberry Plains. Well into the fall, the mixed command continued to post guards at the nearby bridge and conducted frequent patrols in the area, but, as time went by without an attack, the Confederates' senses grew dull with boredom.

On a quiet evening in November 1862, the situation changed dramatically. About eight men from the Thomas Legion were standing post on the bridge at Strawberry Plains when orders came for several of the men to withdraw. The post's artillery pieces had been withdrawn earlier that morning by the recruiting officer, leaving only Cavalryman James Keelin and another to guard the bridge.[503] At midnight on November 8th a party of forty Union raiders suddenly appeared before the stunned sentries and made for the bridge with all deliberate speed.[504]

Keelin's associate fled into the night, leaving him alone to fight the insurgents. Thinking quickly, the Confederate dove under the bridge, took up a firing position against one of the embankments, and waited for the torch-wielding enemies to come into range. Next, Keelin picked the nearest Unionist as his first target and waited for him to come into range. With a single shot, he dropped the man in his tracks. In the returning hail of enemy fire, the young sentry was wounded by several shots to the head, side, and left arm. Still, Keelin refused to surrender. With negligible time to reload, the soldier dropped his rifle, pulled his long silver "Arkansas Toothpick" from its sheath, and waited for the onrushing enemy to climb up the embankment.

James Keelin slew two of the raiders, coming at him nearly in single file, and wounded six more with his knife before losing his own hand. Bleeding all over, Keelin continued to fight against the enemy en masse when suddenly the Unionist leader Bill Pickens reportedly called out, "Let me up there, boys, I'll fix the d——n rebel," and rushed Keelin.[505] In landing two cuts on Pickens, the Confederate soldier forced the enemy leader to reconsider the situation.

Believing a Confederate contingent to be encamped nearby and now likely alerted to their presence, the raider leader ordered his men to withdraw with their wounded, leaving the sorely wounded member of the Thomas Legion to watch over the once more secured bridge and the bodies of three dead Unionists until help finally arrived.

As the minor skirmishes and violent demonstrations which had characterized the first months of the western theater war drew more and more closely in resemblance to the bloody fighting taking place in Kentucky, Louisiana, and Virginia, Colonel William Thomas continued to regularly demonstrate his men's commitment to the southern cause. Better than he had likely expected, the North Carolinian unit not only had acquitted itself well in its series of initial trials but also had earned a reputation for reliability as a quick response force for East Tennessee and stalwart defender of the gateway to the south. With continued success on the battlefield, it seemed only a matter of time before Colonel William Holland Thomas and his men were to be rewarded for their efforts.

CHAPTER SIXTEEN

THE FALL OF EAST TENNESSEE

A s the rebellion entered its second year, Colonel William Holland Thomas's command was steadily becoming one of the East Tennessee theater's most heavily utilized auxiliary units.

"From September, 1862, to June, 1863, there was .... much unpleasant nature to be done by men of similar characters," wrote Major William Stringfield. "Enforcing conscription—disarming the people— the impressment of property, forcing magistrates and civil authorities to take an oath of allegiance to the Confederacy, was disagreeable work [for the Thomas Legion]. Much hard work was [also] done in building block houses and stockades on the entire railroad line, 250 miles."[506]

While some of the colonel's more eager subordinates might have considered the tasks handed down by the Confederate military hierarchy to be thankless work beneath their skills, Colonel Thomas had worked hard to maneuver his command into the support position. In fulfilling their assigned duties promptly and without question, the contingent was rewarded with amenities lacking in most Confederate *and* Union combat forces, including decent equipment, adequate food, and reasonable living accommodations. Moreover, in return for fulfilling the theater's necessary war services, the Thomas Legion was granted relative safety from the war's northern killing fields (including Shiloh, Antietam, Fredericksburg, and Chancellorsville) and the demonstrated admiration of the Confederate citizens they protected with their daily presence.

Yet, the prosperity and relative safety also engendered a problem for the man who had come to thrive on attention and influence. Colonel Thomas and his men would neither gain the recognition of their contemporaries (including Colonel and later Brigadier General Stand Watie's contingents of Cherokee Nationals hazarding Union positions throughout the western end of the Confederate States of America)[507] nor reap the unquantifiable benefits of rising beyond the level of local heroes. In order to make good on his promises of prosperity to his Eastern Band charges and his voting constituents in North Carolina and enhance his own postwar business standing with a reputation of military prestige *without* jeopardizing the Thomas Legion's integrity or repositioning to a frontline position, Colonel Thomas would once more need to call on his creativity, vision, and salesmanship to steer his complement once more through the precarious waters of politics to achieve success.

After some concerted thought, in late 1862 Colonel William Thomas offered the city fathers of Knoxville the use of his men as a quasi national guard.[508] Failing there, Colonel Thomas next turned to his old political contacts in the hope of currying local favor on both sides of the mountain with a reversion to the Confederacy's conscription statutes (a high profile cause affecting the southern middle class at the exclusion of the elite). Yet, there as well, the North Carolinian's intentions were swallowed by the quagmire of politics.

With little recourse, Colonel Thomas widened his focus to include a larger audience, grander ideas, and, consequently, an increased possibility of the situation moving beyond his control. Renewing his call for regional security, the North Carolinian next launched a series of proposals at a wider number of regional authorities, arguing that his command could handle the greater responsibilities of renovating theater infrastructure, [509] fortifying a proposed over-mountain highway into Western North Carolina with legion soldiers,[510] establishing a transport depot at Strawberry Plains, and potentially reactivating Kentucky's Goose Creek Salt Works (a vital utility which aided in the preserving of the Confederacy's sundries until it was neutralized by Union forces in the previous year).[511]

His assertions were met with dubious silence.

Attempting one final gambit, Colonel Thomas tried to enlist the assistance of an old political adversary, North Carolina governor Zebulon Vance. In the aftermath of the failed North Carolina railroad project, an awkward silence had fallen between the two men.

Gambling that the passage of time and the present crisis might encourage the governor to overlook their past disagreements in favor of now shared interests, Colonel Thomas wrote:

> In the progress of the war men and circumstances change. . . . I find myself at the head of a Regiment or Legion of Indians and mountaineers, entrusted with duties in East Tennessee and Kentucky. And your duties relate principally to the defense of North Carolina permit me to submit for our consideration a few facts believed to be connected with the public services and the defenses of the State.
>
> 1.st [First,] Would it not be advisable to make an arrangement to have able[-]bodied negro men belonging to the counties in reach of the enemy employed by the State and transferred from their present positions to work on the extension of the

Railroad. They could, I presume, be employed for the cost on
ensurance [insurance] and food and raiment. By this[,] two ob-
jects would be gained. 1st [First,] every negro would be a saving
of $1,000, to the owner,[.] 2d [Second] Every able[-]bodied ne-
gro kept out of the hands of the enemy would lessen the number
of troops we have to raise in defense, equal to a saving of[,] at
least[,] $1,000 per year. Thus if North Carolina employed ten
thousand negroes on the road where a small force could keep
them in subjection, $10,000,000 would be saved to the owners,
and 10,000 men less would defend our cause.

One consideration now animates us all. What will ensure
success[.] [N]ot what would be most agreeable to us. The Legislature appropriated two millions of dollars to defend Eastern
North Carolina and the Western frontiers. Both are now in danger. The western Counties are in danger of being over run
[overrun] by deserters and renegades who by the hundred
[hundreds] are taking shelter in the [S]moky [M]ountains. The
men between 35 and 40 west of the Blue Ridge should be furnished with the arms and ammunition, and required to aid in
guarding their homes[.] And the Confederate should be required to place Military compys [companies] at every trap in
the Smoky [M]ountains from Ashe to Cherokee [County]. As
long as we can hold the Country encircled by the Blue Ridge
and Cumberland [M]ountains and their outside slopes[,] we
have the heart of the south, which commands the surrounding
Plains. The loss of this country larger than England or France is
the loss of the Southern Confederacy and we sink under a
despotism. . . ."[512]

On the surface, the two men shared a backcountry kinship,* but
there the similarities between the two men ended. Born into a powerful Buncombe County political family,[513] Zebulon Vance had been
granted all the benefits of a classical education, a leisurely adolescence, and the acceptance of a legal apprenticeship with a presti-
gious firm (made successful, in part, through the assistance of North

---

* Vance had been born in nearby Buncombe County.

Carolina Whig governor David L. Swain).[514] With few tangible goals,[515] Zebulon Vance indulged his political curiosity, used his family's connections, and struck up a political career. Unlike Thomas's withering public service experience, the subtly persuasive Zebulon Vance used his influential family and friends as both skillfully crafted shield and sword. Entering public service at twenty-four (nearly twenty years younger than Thomas), Vance rapidly moved through a series of highly visible Buncombe-backed positions, including prosecuting attorney, state senator, and congressman, and with the secessionist crisis had managed to secure the governorship of the State of North Carolina.[516] Far from kindred powers, Zebulon Vance was now far beyond the Confederate soldier's stature, vision, and abilities.

THE RECEIPT OF THE LETTER could not have been more mistimed. The North Carolina leader, already steeped in a steadily escalating issuance of conscription requests, supply requisitions, military movement orders, increased yields in agrarian products and refinery, and the rapid degradation of the state's nascent infrastructure (due to both overuse and lack of ability to furnish maintenance),[517] was now drowning in bureaucratic paperwork, undesirably mixing the confiscation of essential men, materials, and tools with the perpetual series of a politician's unending commitment to constituency accessions, political deals, and nepotism found in every political office.

Slow to modernize, the State of North Carolina had only a modest supply of essential supplies (including cotton, fish, and other crops),[518] accessible natural resources (including the metals copper and iron and the minerals gold, anthracite coal, and graphite as well as sulphur and the phosphates needed to produce gunpowder),[519] and refined goods (including clothing and lumber)[520] with which they might care for their own peacetime populace. After the firing on Fort Sumter, the call was answered for additional supplies to raise their army. The region strained under the new demand but continued to meet the Confederacy's needs. With demands now exceeding their resources and manufacturing abilities, as the conflict extended past the initial weeks and months promised by leading secessionists, and other southern resources were bypassed or given sanction to contribute a lesser level of resource, however, the state's dissenters were beginning to wonder how much life, liberty, and property they might need to surrender to the Confederate cause.

Beyond meager stores, local politics, and the personal enmity Governor Vance held for the politician turned soldier, Colonel Thomas's plans also failed to consider several national security issues. When word first reached the Confederate high command of North Carolina's hastily gathered together meager supplies to support such an undertaking, Richmond would have increased their demands and effectively rerouted the Thomas Legion's reserves. As a second complication, the Union forces waiting nearby to launch operations into the state once Union forces had made sufficient headway in the north and/or the Deep South, Colonel Thomas's notion of stolid mountain defenders would have seemed largely tactically unwise, militarily inefficient (as the majority of the bordering seceded states of Tennessee, Virginia, and Georgia continued to remain firmly in Confederate hands), and politically naive (as the power of the state remained firmly in the grips of the eastern-based aristocracy). With allusions being made towards waging a scorched earth policy against the rising expectations of invasion,[521] Colonel Thomas's reasoning was neither militarily feasible nor politically expedient.

WHILE EASILY DISMISSED AS an ill-timed missive carrying ill-conceived advice in peace time, Colonel Thomas's letter also engendered the more subtle reminder for Governor Zebulon Vance that William Thomas was an irritant. While the businessman held little ill will towards the newly elected governor, Governor Zebulon Vance remembered then Senator Thomas's lack of political acumen, his unwillingness to bend on the issue of a state railroad, and his long-standing opposition to secession. In attempting to curry favor with the governor, the state senator turned confederate soldier was now demonstrating his short-sightedness regarding the war effort, and the apparent placement of his own interests, thinly veiled by assertions of security, above the strategic integrity of the Confederacy. Colonel Thomas would have to be watched.

Before the Confederate soldier could deal with the situation, Colonel Thomas and several of his men were handed a special assignment. Ironically, as Colonel Thomas had predicted, a contingent of fifty Unionist insurgents had, indeed, swooped down through North Carolina's western-lying mountain trails to raid Madison County and set fire to several buildings and were plundering large quantities of salt from the state's meager stockpile.[522] Temporarily relieved of his East Tennessee responsibilities, Colonel Thomas and 200 of his men were ordered to assist General William G. M. Davis in neutralizing the threat.[523]

Contrary to the hopes of the southern confederacy, President Lincoln's Administration had neither faltered nor fallen to the anticipated rising of outraged border and northern region state's rights constituents. Instead, the much maligned Republican (nominated by his party as a compromised concession to the south's views on slavery over such radicals as Senators William H. Seward and Salmon P. Chase) had risen to the occasion, bringing focus to his party, security and contiguous integrity to the remaining states, a tranquilizing element to the remaining national populace, and clarity to the conflicted Union military.

Conversely, in weathering the Confederacy's increasing number of hard-fought battlefield victories (including Fort Sumter, Manassas, Richmond, and Chattanooga), the United States actually galvanized the southern Unionist minority into lashing out at their rebel county and state neighbors. Until late 1862, however, few measures had been initiated to neutralize the new threat. Left unchecked, the fifth columnists and Unionist insurgents, now called "Tories,"[524] grew emboldened. In a matter of months, parties of like-minded Unionist supporters (and, as with Goldman Bryson, a few deeply bitter southerners desiring to take their revenge on regional Confederate power brokers) were gathering into large guerrilla factions for increasing numbers of raids against strategic targets and offering reprisals for the terror they felt had been inflicted upon them in prior years.[525] When scores of Confederate Army deserters began drifting into the Western North Carolina mountains from the north and east hoping to find refuge from persecution, as many Cherokee had years earlier, the self-stylized American revolutionaries[526] of the south decided the disharmony and dissension had reached an untenable level.

Sent back across the Appalachian Mountain Range, Colonel Thomas divided his accompanying elements into semi-autonomous groups and dispatched them to patrol several known trouble spots throughout the state's western counties. While the North Carolinian had hoped to capture their target, as the weeks unfolded the element of the Thomas Legion came to be deployed with increasing frequency as pickets and hounds to steer the Confederate Army's prey away from more tempting downland targets and, hopefully, into the main Confederate expeditionary line.

In a few months, the raiders and southern fifth columnists evaporated back into the wilderness, but in sweeping through the Mountain region the detached legion element also apprehended several deserters from the Confederate Army in Warm Springs and Madison County. The undue burden of conscription continued to resonate deeply with Colonel Thomas and his state's political contemporaries, but the incessant misappropriation of professionally talented individuals from needed assignments to reinforce inefficient fighting positions appeared to be an even greater waste.

In questioning the men, Colonel Thomas found the deserters in the possession of desirable skills (several of the deserters were skilled sappers, miners, carpenters, blacksmiths, gunsmiths, and support personnel). Rather than remand the errant soldiers and conscientious objectors for punishment, confinement, or another position on another firing line, Colonel William Thomas shrewdly offered the men the opportunity to serve under his command and *without question*, unarmed, as the Thomas Legion's professional craftsmen, and within a few hours the colonel's ranks were swelling with new recruits.

With the deserters' promise won and their mission now concluded, the colonel's ill fortune appeared to be changing once more, but, as Colonel William Thomas led the augmented legion back into East Tennessee, he was greeted by a troubling development. General Kirby Smith had been moved to a new command. As Colonel Thomas drew closer, matters worsened when it was learned that the new administration was attaching the Thomas Legion to a brigade under the control of a reportedly xenophobic military bureaucrat by the name of General Alfred E. "Mudwall" Jackson,[527] whose entire brigade-sized command would, according to orders, consist solely of the Thomas Legion's assets.[528] Colonel William Thomas would retain his rank, but in effect, the Thomas Legion was now General Jackson's private army to command.

Over the next several months, the Thomas Legion was moved through a series of posts (including East Tennessee's Gatlinburg and Clark's Creek) and continued to provide the region with security, but the change had shaken the command more than any previous combat loss. As each day passed, the North Carolinian's appreciation of General Jackson steadily lessened as the man began reorganizing the legion to suit his style.

When General Jackson ordered the deserters and conscientious objectors Colonel Thomas had found in North Carolina to once more take up arms, the colonel reached his limit of permissiveness. Realizing the order's implementation would likely mean the disintegration of the Thomas Legion, Colonel Thomas came forward and explained the bargain he had made with the group of professional craftsmen. The general, however, refused to rescind the order, and consequently, shortly thereafter, nearly a hundred of the recently acquired men once more deserted their posts.[529]

On August 15th, 1863, as the Union Army began to close in on the State of Tennessee from the south, west, and north, the two senior officers fought one final time. After a heated argument, General

Alfred "Mudwall" Jackson ordered the colonel placed under arrest, charged with disobedience of orders, and conveyed to Knoxville for formal court-martial proceedings.[530] Colonel William Holland Thomas's career in the Confederate Army appeared to be coming to a disgraceful end, but, as the prisoner was being transferred to the capital, the Confederate lines faltered and broke. Before reinforcements could arrive, the Union Army interceded themselves between General Alfred Jackson's wishes and the fate of his subordinate.

After securing the port of New Orleans in May 1863 and securing valuable intelligence from Union colonel William P. Sanders and a contingent of over a thousand men in their June 19th, 1863, raid on the city of Knoxville (the force had actually dismounted near the Confederate city's armory, reconnoitered the area, remounted, and skirmished with a few southern units before withdrawing with barely a handful of casualties), Major General Ambrose E. Burnside crossed the Kentucky border into Tennessee and drove his army towards Knoxville with all deliberate speed. The Confederates, unable to effectively hold their positions against the onrushing enemy, evacuated the city of Knoxville and prepared to retake the region with the assistance of Lieutenant General James Longstreet's forces. On September 1st, Burnside seized Knoxville, but before the Confederates could spring their hastily fabricated trap, their efforts were undone by the surrender of the Cumberland Gap, September 9th.

With their theater headquarters captured, their lines of communication degrading before the enemy advance, and the threat of a second Union advance through the northern Cumberland Gap, the Confederate Army of East Tennessee was forced into flight. As they needed every commander they could find, the charges against Colonel William Thomas were quickly dropped and he was returned to his command at Strawberry Plains. Upon his arrival, however, the North Carolinian found that General "Mudwall" Jackson had had Thomas's wife's cousin James Robert Love II elevated to the rank of colonel and placed in charge of the Thomas Legion's infantry complement[531] and was ordering the majority of the command into the northern country with the intention of bolstering the Confederacy's Virginia lines, causing one soldier to recollect, "[t]hose were gloomy days to those of [us] who left our homes and loved ones at the mercy of the enemy."[532] Major General Burnside's forces now bearing down on the level fields of Strawberry Plains, Colonel William Thomas was ordered by Major General Simon Buckner to gather the remaining complement of his original force (consisting largely of two companies of North Carolina Cherokee whom General Jackson distrusted and roughly a hundred infantry)[533] and pull back to the East Tennessean roots of the Appalachian Mountains.

By the fall of night on the 2nd of September, Colonel Thomas and his men had departed Strawberry Plains for the final time.[534] On September 6th, Major William Stringfield was placed in charge of 200 men and a battalion of cavalry, reconnoitered the surrounding area, and made for Jonesboro. Reinforced by General "Mudwall" Jackson, Colonel Love, and the remaining elements of the Thomas Legion, the group attacked elements of the Union Army's 100th Ohio attempting to establish a forward position at nearby Telford's Depot, hoping to buy time for Lieutenant General Longstreet's forces to rescue the region from near certain Union domination. In the engagement, Colonel Love's command killed twenty, wounded thirty, captured 314 prisoners, and secured nearly 400 separate small arms (including the ubiquitous Enfield Rifle) at a loss of only six killed in action and fifteen wounded.[535] The Confederates fell back to Carters Depot and fortified the position to wait for the relief Lieutenant General James Longstreet might bring them, but ten days later, as the Cumberland Gap defenses collapsed, several Union regiments appeared before the band and forced the inferior men into a fighting retreat. As Lieutenant General Longstreet's reinforcements were nowhere in sight, the Confederates' heroic action had only delayed the inevitable.

As East Tennessee fell about the ears of his former subordinates, Colonel Thomas's command steadily made for the eastern-rising peaks of the Smokies. Unintentionally guarded for a time by General "Mudwall" Jackson and the shattered elements of the legion still under his command, the group of North Carolina Cherokee and mountaineers rapidly crossed the East Tennessee countryside without incident, but as the group reached the vicinity of Sevierville around September 7th they were interdicted by several Union elements.[536] Colonel Thomas and his men were forced to fight their way through the enemy but quickly resumed their retreat up into the East Tennessean side of the Smokies. Safe for the moment, the group then began carrying out the colonel's original plan for the region, blocking and blockading every mountain road leading into North Carolina.[537]

Once his command post had been established, Colonel Thomas began writing anew, this time for a reversion of his original command to defend Western North Carolina and now South Carolina and Georgia from invasion, but again the North Carolinian's efforts were ill-timed.[538] Although the nearby Cumberland Gap was now in enemy hands, the defense of Western North Carolina remained tertiary in importance to halting the retreat of General Robert E. Lee (who had been losing ground since the Confederate defeat at Gettysburg) and arresting the joined advance of Union brigadier generals Ambrose Burnside and William Tecumseh Sherman deep into the heart of the Confederacy from the east and the north.

CHAPTER SEVENTEEN

COUNTERINSURGENCE

With the Smoky Mountains at their backs, the newly reinstated Confederate colonel and the surviving remnants of the Thomas Legion watched East Tennessee fall into anarchy and his own postwar prospects fade before their eyes.

Since the onset of the secessionist crisis, the Confederate military had invested political capital and manpower heavily to hold the divided western territory. Offering the economic carrot of greater postwar prosperity under the Confederacy and the stick of sudden violent army reciprocity with the other, the East Tennessee theater remained firmly under the control of southern authorities. By 1863, however, southern military commanders were forced to switch tactics from strategic maneuvers aimed at overwhelming the enemy to assistance to theater-stationed men and supplies.

As East Tennessee forces continued to lose large quantities of troops and supplies to the Confederacy's hasty attempts to neutralize the enemy force rising from the seized Mississippi River, while simultaneously underwriting Generals Johnston's, Jackson's, and Lee's do-or-die campaign against the northern lines, in-country Unionists, and fifth columnists, they began to plan for inevitable attempted Union conquests of the region. Finally, when General Burnside's men marched into Knoxville and seized the capital almost uncontested, the Confederates found themselves surrounded by an untrusting and, in some cases, hostile populace trying to delay the retreating Confederates until the might of the Union Army could arrive.

With few available resources, the theater's new Confederate high command won the approval of President Davis to initiate a daring plan, calling for reinforcements from the north and the Deep South to crush the Union Army as they attempted to consolidate their new prize, the city of Knoxville.[539] While Colonel William Holland Thomas was being arrested and conducted westward, the southern leaders were preparing to pull back and await the onrushing enemy, . . . but, at the critical moment, the plan went awry. Without warning, parties of fifth columnists suddenly rose up throughout the region and almost simultaneously attacked Confederate depots and transfer points with uncharacteristic audacity. Next, on September 9th, 1863, the Cumberland Gap, through which Confederate Army reinforcements were anticipated to pour into the region, was seized by elements of the Union Army. Finally, the last chance of a Confederate-held Tennessee evaporated when the rescuing forces of Lieutenant General James Longstreet, riding at flank speed, fell upon heavy enemy resistance far short of their objective. With their commander still suffering from recent family losses* and hampered by bitter in-fighting with his theater superior, General Braxton

* Including his daughter, Mary Anne, and sons, James and Gus, to scarlet fever.

Bragg, the southern general was unable to turn back the rising Union tide. Tennessee was now beyond recovery.

Deprived of Colonel William Thomas's experience, the Thomas Legion was swept along with the increasingly chaotic state of theater operations. "A trap for Burnside's army . . . proved to be a double[-] triggered trap for us," reported the legion's Major Stringfield. "The Federal Authorities were fully alive to the importance of grasping from us and holding this section, so fertile for all, and so loyal to them, being urged thereto by the highest consideration of honor, duty and interest."[540]

Now relatively safe and secure, Colonel Thomas established a base of operations near Gatlinburg and resurrected his old mountain defense plan. In hope that he might yet be able to save Western North Carolina from the fate of its neighbor, Colonel Thomas and his men next moved to obstruct or blockade every mountain road leading into the State of North Carolina.[541] In spare moments, Colonel Thomas also began appealing for a reversion of his original command, but once again the North Carolinian's efforts were ill-timed.[542] Before siege preparations were completed or a response could be received, Colonel Thomas's de facto defensive end of the Thomas Legion was once more relieved of semi-autonomous status and placed under the command of the East Tennessee Confederacy, under Brigadier General John Crawford Vaughn.[543]

Again, Colonel Thomas was unable to contest the loss of his freedom. At first glance, the situation appeared to mirror the antithetical relationship Colonel Thomas held with his last superior, but as the North Carolina colonel started receiving orders similar to the period prior to General Jackson's assumption of command (including orders to round up as many deserters and supplies as he could muster),[544] Colonel Thomas came to appreciate the breadth, size, and disposition of his new commanding officer's task force. Similarly unlike General Jackson, Brigadier General Vaughn was a proven fighter with a sizable command. Accountable to Lieutenant General Longstreet, the ranking East Tennessee leader cared far more about

arresting the Union advance than the managerial or hierarchical structure of his auxiliary forces. If he had to stay within the confines of the
dwindling East Tennessee theater command structure, this was a
man with whom the North Carolina colonel thought he could work.

By midfall, 1863, Union troops and insurgent elements began to
exploit the Cumberland Gap and Appalachians with increasing frequency.[545] Soon word reached Confederate authorities of a resurgence in Unionist activities in the Mountain region. When a party of
southern-born Union volunteers began to raid the countryside between Monroe and Polk counties in Tennessee and Cherokee County
across the mountains in Western North Carolina, Brigadier General
Vaughn called for action. When intelligence was ascertained impli-
cating that Haywood County–born Goldman Bryson might be involved, Colonel Thomas's men (including the recently reunited
company of Lieutenant Colonel Walker's cavalry battalion) were
once more called upon to act as scouts to assist in the tracking and recovery of Bryson's company of raiders.

On October 27th, Brigadier General Vaughn's detachment of cavalry and Cherokee Confederates followed the Union insurgent's trail
across the mountains into Cherokee County, North Carolina. Catch-
ing up with the enemy at Evan's Mill on Beaver Dam Creek, General
Vaughn ordered the Confederate soldiers to close with their quarry.
When two of the enemy were killed in the ensuing action, the seventeen surviving members of Captain Bryson's band promptly surrendered.[546] As Brigadier General Vaughn ordered their summary
execution as a lesson for future raiders, however, it was revealed that
their leader had somehow managed to escape once more into the
wilderness.

On the following day, Lieutenant C. H. Taylor of the Thomas
Legion departed Murphy County, North Carolina, with nineteen
men to hunt down the fugitive leader.[547] Finding Captain Bryson's
trail, the company of North Carolinians and Eastern Band Cherokee
rapidly gave pursuit across the mountains. Coming within sight of
their quarry and a traveling companion approximately twenty-five

miles outside of Murphy, the young lieutenant immediately sighted his target, discharged his weapon, and dropped the insurgent leader to the ground. They rapidly closed with the two men and subdued the traveling companion.[548]

Confirming the now dead man was Captain Bryson, the detachment of Thomas Legionnaires hurriedly searched the man's belongings for actionable intelligence. Amid a ream of papers they discovered that the men had been carrying, the Confederates found Special Field Orders from Union Army Headquarters at Knoxville, confirming Brigadier General Vaughn's suspicions of Captain Bryson's Mountain region posting "for the purpose of recruiting."[549] The documents were promptly bundled together and dispatched to East Tennessee Theater Command, but the Thomas Legion's Cherokee remained concerned that their feat would fail to be recognized. Seizing the initiative, the group tore off the Union soldier's bloody bullet-riddled uniform and carried the cloth from town to town in public proclamation of the insurgent's violent demise.[550]

With the fall of the west, the enemy momentarily slowed their advance towards the Appalachians. Remaining in the vicinity of Gatlinburg, Colonel Thomas's Legion element continued to run patrols and foraging operations for their superiors as ordered. Taking advantage of the area's lack of strategic military assets (such as railroads, fortifications, and major supply junctions) as well as all of their financial spare time between assignments, the Colonel returned once more to the full strength of his own military projects, which included the attempted construction of a formal roadway linking East Tennessee with Western North Carolina, but as East Tennessee began to solidify under the reimposed leadership of the north, plans were being made for the consolidation of the entirety of the state.

After Colonel Thomas led a December raid on nearby Sevierville* to rescue several Eastern Band Cherokee soldiers who had

---

* Ironically, the site was named after the American Revolutionary Era subjugator of Chief Yonaguska's Cherokee tribe.

been captured in the wake of the Knoxville disaster and made off with a sizable supply of Union rifles,[551] the Union Army dispatched the Fifteenth Pennsylvania Volunteer Cavalry under Colonel William J. Palmer to pacify the region.[552] Originally mustered out of Carlisle Barracks, the Pennsylvanian cavalry regiment had been formed under General Robert Anderson and, called the Anderson Cavalry, quickly distinguished itself as a rapid response and intelligence-gathering unit.[553]

Shortly after dawn on December 10th, Colonel William J. Palmer and his 150-strong Anderson Cavalry contingent approached the southern outskirts of Gatlinburg just as a second contingent of 50 other Anderson Cavalrymen was approaching from the north.[554] Locating the encampment of Colonel Thomas and his legion atop a steep wooded ridge, Colonel William Palmer ordered his men to dismount, deploy skirmishers, and proceed to the location on foot.

Almost immediately, the Union contingent's movements were detected by the pickets Colonel Thomas had posted. As sporadic fire filled the air, the Anderson Cavalry attempted to rapidly envelop the enemy from both directions, but the Thomas Legion offered stiff resistance. After approximately one hour of constant fire, Colonel William Palmer managed to push Colonel Thomas's men up the ridge and beyond the confines of the camp.

Still, the Thomas Legion was loath to give ground without exacting a costly penalty.

"It was impracticable to prevent the rebels on retreating from taking up this mountain where we could not reach them," explained Colonel William Palmer, "and where they continued firing from behind the thick cover for several hours. They finally retreated, scattering over the ridges to the Great Smoky Mountains."[555]

Once the surprised Colonel Thomas had withdrawn his forces safely up the mountain, Colonel Palmer began to inventory his spoils, including a single prisoner, sixteen horses, eighteen muskets, two boxes of ammunition, bushels of salt, meal, dried fruit, blankets, clothes, and Colonel Thomas's hat.[556]

The captured equipment was stockpiled and the camp destroyed. Colonel Palmer ordered his men to scour the area for Confederate casualties and stragglers, but none were found.

The wily Confederate colonel and Cherokee Chief had escaped with his entire complement.

"I very much regret that we were not more successful," admitted Colonel William Palmer. "We rode all night over a foot path that many of the citizens considered impracticable; and while I cannot see that we could have done better under the circumstances than we did, yet I can now see from my knowledge of the ground (which was entirely unknown to us before) how I might have captured most of the party by making certain dispositions before reaching Gatlinburg."[557] At the price of two wounded officers and a sergeant, the exercise had been a tactical blunder for the Union Army.[558]

The ambush had, indeed, been a surprise, but, rather than showing elation at the escape of himself and his men without a single reported casualty, Colonel William Thomas's mood darkened.[559] While many among the Confederacy had viewed East Tennesseans as loathsome, taciturn enemies,[560] Colonel Thomas and his men had until only recently received the warmest of praise. Yet, the ambush had been made possible by intelligence passed from a group of discontented Gatlinburg residents to the Union Army.[561] And the town of his youth, Waynesville, North Carolina, had recently been hit by raiders.[562]

The United States of America was placing a bounty of $5,000 for his assassination on the open market.[563]

His own debts were mounting.

Rumors of Union orders to execute captured Confederate Native Americans were beginning to circulate.[564]

Once more they were on the run.

For the retreating Confederate colonel and Cherokee Chief, life was becoming an unending gauntlet of disappointment and pain.

While the Confederate military seemed to be propelled by a closed circle of self-interested urban gentry, every private business venture or political initiative he seemed to foster failed to find acceptance from the mountain community or political quarter. As the great Confederate Armies of the North were resoundingly turned back from their last hope of a quick and decisive victory to begin their slow, steady, and bloody retreat, the best Colonel Thomas could hope to achieve by continuing the secessionist fight was a measure of pride at a hard-won stalemate and, the worst, the demise of everything and everyone around him.

Realizing he had no other choice, Colonel William Thomas resolved himself to continue the fight with the Union to the bitter end. During a brief two-week stay at Quallatown for Christmas and New Year's, the aging North Carolinian reacquainted himself with Sarah, their children, and his adopted brethren. In his spare leisure moments, as the snow began to fall on the bitterest winter in North Carolina memory,[565] he resumed his role as Cherokee agent, settling local matters. Like many North Carolinians, the Eastern Band had suffered greatly with the loss of their stock of able-bodied men and with the fickle mountain weather. With starvation rampant, Colonel Thomas was once again forced to supply his Cherokee brethren with his store's reserves of clothing and sundries.[566] Although the allotment was a generous gesture, he soon realized the short-sightedness of the gesture should the community fail to recover immediately (a near impossibility). Unable to find an exploitable source of renewable revenue, Colonel Thomas continued to submit claims for Eastern Band subsistence (this time to the Confederate capital of Richmond) through Assistant Quartermaster James Terrell[567] and began petitioning his old political, business, and social colleagues for support.

There were also wartime moments from whence Colonel William Holland Thomas could draw pride. In the cold winter of 1864, Confederate soldiers passing through and stationed in the area were amazed at the resilience and discipline of the common Confederate Cherokee soldier (one man reportedly marveled at a member of the Eastern Band who had stood watch for approximately fourteen hours in the middle of a fierce snowstorm).[568] Their loyalty was also without question. Confederate Eastern Band members, promising to murder Colonel William Thomas in exchange for their freedom, were released from their Union prison cells at Knoxville,[569] found their way home and promptly renounced their agreement in favor of Colonel Thomas's continued support.[570] Forty other men who had served under him in the Thomas Legion were petitioning Governor Zebulon Vance to allow them to transfer back under Colonel Thomas's command.[571] Colonel Thomas's ranks were once more growing with agreements from captured deserters.[572] Mirroring the ancient spirits of Cherokee warriors said to occasionally wander across the bald spots of the Blue Ridge Mountains as glowing spots of lights, he became certain that the men would remain unwavering at his side throughout the conflict.

By the time the North Carolinian received orders to link up with Brigadier General Robert Vance[573] en route from Asheville to launch over-mountain operations into East Tennessee in early January 1864, Colonel William Thomas had regained some of his pallor. Upon joining his 150 Confederate Cherokee with Brigadier General Vance's main body, the commanding officer revealed his intention to cross the Smoky Mountains, split the force into an offensive and defensive team, then hunt down, capture, and return with their captured Union supply convoy. Knowing the increasing number of enemy patrols on the other side of his mountain home, Colonel Thomas raised objections to the dangerous and, in his view, ill-conceived plan, but the brigadier general, recovering from a bout of typhoid fever,[574] remained unswayed.

On January 12th, 1864, the massive Confederate contingent of 100 infantry, 375 cavalry, and an artillery unit emerged from the Cherokee foot-worn Ocanaluftee Gap path.[575] Driving into the besieged countryside of East Tennessee once more, Brigadier General Robert Vance detached 180 cavalrymen from the expedition force. Ordering Colonel Thomas and Lieutenant Colonel James Love Henry*[576] to move on towards Gatlinburg and await word, the

---

* A descendant of Western North Carolina pioneer Robert Love and American Revolutionary–turned Judge John Henry.

brigadier general then rode off with the contingent towards Sevierville in search of their objective.[577]

The next day Brigadier General Vance caught sight of their objective, a seventeen-wagon Union supply convoy.[578] Rapidly closing the distance, the Confederates fell upon the Union detail and secured the captured convey in a matter of minutes. Dispatching a courier with orders for Lieutenant Colonel James L. Henry and his command to add their strength to his, the general turned the seventeen captured wagons about and made for the relative safety of the Confederacy.[579]

On the following day, the brigadier general ordered his men to fall out at Schultz's Mill on the banks of Cosby Creek and await their summoned escort. Shortly after noontime, a contingent of mounted men were sighted riding hard upon the makeshift Confederate camp. As the men closed with the raiding party at breakneck speed, the Confederates realized they had failed to secure the parameter with a line of pickets and, even worse, the contingent bearing down upon them was not the expected reinforcements but a counterinsurgent force under the command of the Union's Anderson Cavalry leader, Colonel William B. Palmer.

Chaos ensued as Brigadier General Robert Vance's men abandoned their posts, threw down their weapons, and fled in terror before the hooffalls of Union colonel Palmer's pursuing 200-strong cavalry element.[580] In practiced precision, the man who had dogged Colonel Thomas the month before deployed his complement into four columns and moved to surround Brigadier General Vance. Over the next several minutes, staggered shots were fired and returned, but the defensive fire was no match for the Union element's military precision. Outflanked, outnumbered, his forces in disarray, and two of his complement already dead, the North Carolina brigadier general was given little choice but to surrender his captured prize, his command, and himself into the custody of the Union Army.[581]

Yet, as Colonel Palmer called for additional forces to canvass the area for supporting Confederate units and as the last members of the Confederate raiding force were flushed from their hiding places, one question lingered: Where were Brigadier General Robert Vance's ordered reinforcements?

CHAPTER EIGHTEEN

"Bloody Hands to Hospitable Graves"

Instead of advancing towards Brigadier General Robert Vance's stated objective, Lieutenant Colonel James Love Henry had judged the situation far too precarious and the potential rewards far too few to risk his reserve of infantry and artillery. Abandoning his superior to the onrushing enemy, the lieutenant colonel fell back to Gatlinburg, where he joined forces with Colonel William Holland Thomas.

Hoping to allay a political reprisal for the loss of his superior officer, Colonel Thomas wrote Governor Vance, explaining precisely how the man's brother had been captured, while simultaneously asking that the errant elements of the Thomas Legion once more be reconstituted under his command.[582] Governor Zebulon Vance was enraged. When the Confederate commander of the Army of Tennessee, Brigadier General Joseph E. Johnston, learned of Lieutenant Colonel Henry's disobedience of orders, Colonel Thomas's subsequent failure to order the adjutant to follow the issued instructions, *and* the abject failure of one of the largest Confederate overmountain operations of the war,[583] North Carolina Governor Vance's burning political ill-will towards Colonel Thomas merged with the now besieged Confederate military's necessity of finding fault, administering justice, and expediting the war against the oncoming horde of northerners.[584] In short order, Colonel Thomas and his disobedient relative by marriage were arrested and formal court-martial proceedings were scheduled to be held on February 23rd, 1864, in Asheville, North Carolina.[585]

As Thomas once again faced the loss of his command, a dishonorable discharge, financial ruin, and potential imprisonment, a cloud of depression began to descend on the aging North Carolinian. Whether a result of the dissembling East Tennessee Confederate command structure before the advancing might of Union general William T. Sherman, the paltry state of Western North Carolina's defenses, the vague circumstances of his arrest, or the man's own political connections, the Confederate colonel retained command of his surviving group of legionnaires. Once he was admonished with a verbal reprimand,[586] the charges were soon dropped and Colonel William Thomas was returned to duty. "If I live through the war," the colonel wrote his wife, "I shall have done enough to be satisfied to spend the remainder of my life in retirement surrounded by my family and friends."[587]

Rather than lighten at the turn of events, the North Carolinian's mood soured further when news reached him that, on the night of January 3rd, a group of Unionists had murdered his Thomas Legion comrade Lieutenant Colonel William Walker, at the threshold of the man's Cherokee County, North Carolina, home.[588] It fell further still after February 2nd when the Union's Fourteenth Illinois Cavalry raided Quallatown, killing several Confederate soldiers and capturing several members of the Eastern Band (who, subsequently, defected to the ranks of the Union) in direct reprisal for Brigadier General Vance's failed over-mountain expedition.[589] In February, Union forces drove their point home again, ambushing Colonel Thomas's encampment of 300 men at the mouth of North Carolina's Deep Creek.[590] According to Dr. W. L. Hilliard (the husband of Sarah's sister, Margaret),[591] the colonel appeared to be "laboring under some peculiar mental excitement—that his mind was a little out of balance."[592]

With the transfer and loss of Brigadier General Vance, Confederate colonel John B. Palmer (formerly of the Fifty-eighth North Carolina Regiment) took over as field commander of the District of Western North Carolina at Asheville.[593] Having already made several forays into enemy-held territory (including timely assistance to Lieutenant General Longstreet),[594] Colonel Palmer was a popular choice as the theater successor to the governor's brother (an opinion further reenforced by the colonel's assistance in the destruction of the East Tennessee railroad[595] and rescue of General Vaughn at Bull's Gap[596]). Ironically, however, just as the course of the war began to reintegrate members of the Thomas Legion once more, Colonel William Holland Thomas ran afoul of his new superior.[597]

It is evident that this district," wrote Colonel John B. Palmer for an October 28th, 1864, report, "as I have always urged, affords an admirable base from which to operate against and threaten the enemy in East Tennessee. Thomas's legion, as at present organized, is of but little if any use, either for local defense or aggressive movements."[598]

When it was learned that Colonel Thomas was continuing to recruit deserters from other Confederate units and incorporate them into his own re-forming Thomas Legion, Colonel John Palmer had enough reason to remove the untidy end from his command. In September 1864 Colonel William Holland Thomas was once more the subject of a court-martial for insubordination, but this time he also faced the charges of harboring deserters during a period from 1863 to 1864, conduct unbecoming of an officer, and incompetence.[599]

While the beleaguered colonel was preparing to defend himself, his situation was further muddied by a few of the enemies he had made over the course of his life. The *Henderson Times* renewed their venomous criticism of the man,[600] and other North Carolinians began to claim they had "just been robbed by some of Thomas pets (deserters) of about three thousands dollars worth of goods."[601] Yet, the colonel's chief detractor remained Governor Zebulon Vance. Moving through back channels to sever the North Carolinian from his command once and for all, Vance characterized the North Carolinian as "worse than useless, he is a positive injury to that country [Western North Carolina]. His command is a favorite resort for deserters, numbers of them I learn are on his rolls, who do no service, he is disobedient of orders, and invariably avoids the enemy when he advances."[602]

Sent to Greenesboro, North Carolina, for trial, Colonel William Thomas was promptly found guilty. Finally understanding the forces now arrayed against him, the convicted man appealed the decision to the most powerful voice in the south and a personal nemesis of Governor Vance, President Jefferson Davis, at Richmond. Moreover, in the Confederate capital Colonel Thomas filled his ample time requesting sundries for his legion,[603] launching initiatives aimed at tempering Confederate zeal against dejected North Carolina Unionists (whom the colonel saw as playing a vital role in the postwar period),[604] and securing the necessary Confederate congressional concessions to provide "payment of the interest on the removal and substance fund due the Cherokee Indians in North Carolina."[605]

By November 1864, Confederate president Jefferson Davis had reviewed Colonel Thomas's court-martial appeal and, much to the chagrin of his growing number of Confederate adversaries, promptly overturned the decision. Before returning to Quallatown, at the request of President Davis, the Secretary of War penned off a document affirming: "Authority is hereby given to Col. William H. Thomas of Thomas Legion to recruit companies of the Legion within the enemies line in east Tennessee and the adjacent counties of North Carolina west of the Blue Ridge where the conscript law cannot be enforced, and after filling up such companies in the region indicated to be made part of the Legion. [T]he Indians and persons not liable to service belonging to the Legion may at the expiration of their time be reenlisted for the war with the usual allowance of bounty. . . ."[606]

Understanding the recalcitrant nature of North Carolina governor Zebulon Vance and his minions (having spent the past several years arguing over politics, representation, supplies, force allocations, and munitions),[607] President Jefferson Davis wanted the message declared clearly and unequivocally that *he* had seen the lengthy string of theater-detrimental reorganizations and the court-martial charges levied against Colonel Thomas as disingenuous and destructive to the Confederate cause. Furthermore, unwilling to offer their shared adversaries another opportunity to remove his old colleague, the Secretary determined that

> Col[.] Thomas is authorized to employ one of his companies as Engineers, or Sappers and Miners and such companies as may be necessary as Sharp Shooters and as Mounted Riflemen. The Legion will be entitled to the services of quarter master and commisary of [if] they shall be requisite. Companies belonging to the Legion will not be detached from Col. Thomas command except in emergency and then only temporarily.
>
> By Command of the Secretary of War.
> Samuel W. Melton[608]

Returning home vindicated from Richmond, Colonel William Holland Thomas found that Colonel Palmer had been replaced by Brigadier General James G. Martin[609] and that his young military protégé from East Tennessee, Major William Stringfield, had assumed temporary command of the re-forming Thomas Legion's mountain defenses. Although the young man had performed his duties admirably, the colonel was confronted with a series of fundamental administrative problems: His men were no longer being paid,[610] they were rapidly running out of supplies and ammunition,[611] and the Eastern Band had already reached the point of starvation.[612] Fearing desertion, the now abysmally indebted North Carolina businessman turned soldier once more opened his coffers and his storehouses to meet the needs of his subordinates and his community. For ammunition, however, Colonel Thomas was forced to draw on an old Eastern Band secret, the old Smoky Mountain Alum Cave.

While tracking a bear in his youth, Chief Yonaguska once reportedly stumbled upon the Smoky Mountain cave near Indian Gap.[613] Reasoning the cave with its abundance of epsom salts, alum, nitrates, magnesia, and copper would be a valuable asset should the conventional war become a guerrilla action of indeterminate length, Colonel Thomas had previously stationed sentries to guard the site from explosive-savvy Unionists. Now in dire need of an additional munitions reservoir, Colonel Thomas dispatched his team contingent of miners to begin extracting the elements necessary for the fashioning of gunpowder.[614]

In early March, Union colonel G. W. Kirk marched into Haywood County with approximately two hundred infantry and four hundred cavalry, looking for federally inclined citizens to assist them in hunting down the last remnants of the mountain-based Confederate Army units.[615] Rejected by the local populace, the Union soldiers reportedly began confiscating as many horses as they could find[616] and killed those who resisted their will.[617] Returning from the north, Colonel James R. Love spotted the Union force and drove the enemy across the Balsam Mountains to the Soco Gap (named "Ambush Place" in remembrance of the Cherokee Nation's ancient victory over the Shawnee).[618] On March 6th, a second Confederate contingent met the invading Union force at the Soco Gap and drove them across the mountains into Tennessee.[619] The conflict had occurred on the very doorstep of the Eastern Band.

By the end of March 1865, the main Confederate lines buckled, then broke before the might of the Union Army's strategy of encirclement. As Confederate president Jefferson Davis fled the burning Confederate capital of Richmond, Virginia, in early April, Colonel William Holland Thomas was almost paradoxically once more coming into his own. On April 1st, Colonel Thomas and Colonel James R. Love reunited the final elements of the Thomas Legion in the mountain gap above Waynesville, and with Thomas's legion once more at his disposal (reportedly including 400 Cherokee) and ably stocked,[620] the men were finally ready to bring the invading Union Army "with bloody hands to hospitable graves."[621]

On April 9th Confederate general Robert E. Lee surrendered at the Appomattox Courthouse in Virginia, yet on the morning of April 13th Union major general William Tecumseh Sherman, entering the city of Raleigh, North Carolina, was shocked to find that "people here had not heard of the surrender of Lee . . ."[622]

To counter the oncoming Union forces, Colonel Thomas and Colonel Love joined with Brigadier General Martin at Asheville. The Confederates then traveled to Waynesville, where on April 25th Brigadier General Martin sent a small unit of men under a flag of truce through nearby Balsam Gap to Knoxville, requesting his terms for surrender. The men were thrown into the city's jail.

A few days later, Brigadier General Martin's company narrowly managed to escape the Union seizure of Waynesville. Instead of fleeing into the mountains, however, Colonels Thomas and Love turned the Thomas Legion about and waited for the Union Army to secure the area and continue on its course. On May 6th near the White Sulphur Springs Love homestead, twenty-three-year-old Lieutenant Robert T. Conley of the Thomas Legion and his company of sharpshooters opened fire on the Union Army's 2nd North Carolina Regiment.[623] In the engagement only a single Union soldier fell to the ground dead,*[624] but the action had served its purpose. When Union colonel William C. Bartlett next raised his head, he found Waynesville surrounded by the entire Thomas Legion.

Throughout the night the Cherokee of the Thomas Legion chanted and danced around their mountaintop campfires in full view of their encircled quarry. On the dawning of May 7th, Brigadier

---

* Reportedly, the last reported casualty of the war east of the Mississippi.

General James G. Martin, Colonel James R. Love, and Colonel William Holland Thomas walked into Waynesville under a flag of truce. Proceeding towards the town's Battle House Resort Hotel and flanked by twenty armed and garbed Cherokee warriors of the Eastern Band,[625] Colonel Thomas and his Confederate compatriots presented themselves to Union colonel Bartlett.

As terms were discussed, Colonel Thomas, bare-chested, painted and feathered in the raiments of a Cherokee Chief (as befitting his station), threatened the Union colonel with the loss of his scalp if he did not immediately surrender his forces to the Confederacy.[626]

The Union colonel admitted that he was at the Thomas Legion's mercy, but further bloodshed would not solve the Confederate contingent's primary problem. They were an army deprived of a country.

With Union reinforcements anticipated, the adversaries brokered an equitable deal. The Confederates would officially surrender to the Union colonel, but each man would be allowed to retain his weaponry *and*, in exchange for their promising to order their men to disband and return home, the Union contingent would march out of Waynesville and never return. The Confederacy was no more.

On May 9th, 1865, Colonel William Holland Thomas and the Thomas Legion stood down from duty and went home.

They were the last Confederate regiment to disband east of the Mississippi.

CHAPTER NINETEEN

RUMINATIONS AND RECRIMINATIONS

Returning home to Stekoa Fields in 1865, the defeated colonel of the Army of the Confederate States of America now saw few virtues in having followed the party line. In the space of a few short years, Colonel William Holland Thomas had been stymied by his political contemporaries, ridiculed by the press, relegated to hunting down undesirables in remote regions, forced to dodge enemy fire, targeted for assassination, subjected to multiple court-martial proceedings, lost many papers and a war journal during the rebellion,[627] and compelled to surrender his aspirations in both the Confederacy and the United States of America.[628]

In light of the Confederate Army's disintegration, the occupation of the State of North Carolina by Union forces, the subsequent assassination of President Lincoln (the most vocal advocate of mercy for the southern states), and the branding of every Confederate leader as a traitor, William Thomas's political future appeared negligible. But the War of the Rebellion had also cost the North Carolinian far more in money, time, labor, and resources. His thirty-two slaves were now free.[629] His stock was sorely depleted. His franchise of stores was mired by heavy debts to several parties, and the economy made finery almost impossible to move. His reserves of liquid assets had evaporated, and his health was failing. When the secessionist crisis erupted into the War of the Rebellion, William Thomas had been fighting for his political survival. Now the aging businessman was fighting for the survival of his family and loyal Eastern Band brethren.

In the fall of 1865, Colonel Thomas started to regain his foothold in the Western North Carolina business world. While liquidating his more dispensable assets to temporarily generate capital,[630] he brokered several deals to keep his franchise solvent and rekindle his prospects. In October, he tore down the Thomas Legion's hastily constructed wartime barricades at Indian Gap in preparation for the creation of his long dreamt of over-mountain mercantile turnpike.[631] Next, concentrating on his lifelong power base, the colonel reopened his meager repair shop[632] and entered into a contract with his long-time business associate and wartime comrade, James Terrell, to return his prized Quallatown tannery to operational status.[633] Finally, the aging merchant moved to hire on as many of his old slave hands as might stay on to work for him at salaries commensurate with his prewar staff and their duties.[634]

Just when it seemed as if he might be able to outdistance the shadows cast by his wartime troubles, however, the businessman was forced to deal with another price of involving Quallatown and his Eastern Band of North Carolina Cherokee in the War of the Rebellion, disease. In the months after the Cherokee Chief's return a steady stream of captured-then-released Cherokee soldiers began pouring back into Quallatown, bringing bitter memories, war stories, and the negative aspect of the cultural influences to which they had been exposed, but as the weeks passed, it became apparent that the Cherokee warriors had also brought an uncommon illness with them. One returning soldier suddenly grew sick and died; then a score more who had attended the man's funeral likewise fell ill and began to die. When Colonel Thomas arrived and inspected the afflicted, he noticed many of the ill were covered in bumpy rashes that were turning into white seeping pustules.[635] The disease was Small Pox.[636]

Racing home, Colonel Thomas bundled off Sarah and their children to stay with relatives in Waynesville, then hurriedly penned off a request to Dr. John Mingus for an ounce of asafetida (a homeopathic remedy made from castor oil, garlic, and camphor and worn about the neck) and a quantity of whisky to fortify himself against the disease.[637] He then set about tracking down the nearest available doctor willing to vaccinate the remainder of the Eastern Band. He found one in Sevier County, Tennessee.

As the days progressed and still greater numbers of Eastern Band members continued to fall ill and die from the disease,[638] the infection reached epidemic proportions. When the doctor arrived, Colonel Thomas made certain every one of the afflicted was treated and saw that every remaining healthy member of Chief Yonaguska's people was vaccinated, but the efforts were far too little or far too late. With the infection now running rampant throughout the mountain town, a number of Eastern Band members abandoned their Chief's modern medicine in favor of more traditional ancestral remedies.[639] When those too failed, a few delved still deeper into the practices of the distant past, embracing "the heroic aboriginal treatment of the plunge bath in the river and the cold-water douche, which resulted in death in almost every case."[640]

By the time the disease burned itself out at the end of the following year, over a hundred of the Eastern Band had died from the Small Pox outbreak.[641] Their eyes now forced open by the successive events of war, famine, and now plague, the community collectively began reevaluating their situation. Choosing to rekindle their own traditional views, the downward spiral of unfortunate and ill-timed events

devolved into divine punishment and, by association, the ill omens for
the faltering leadership abilities of their Caucasian Cherokee Chief.
Similar to many southern citizens of the period, a number of the Eastern Band members suddenly were gripped by a sense of nostalgia for
the antebellum period, wishing for the quiet, productive, forward-
moving community that had preceded Colonel Thomas's rebellion,
the privations of war, and, most important, the increasing attraction of
their leader's private misfortune to their very public community.

Despite their February 1866 victory in the North Carolina General Assembly conferring on the inhabiting Cherokee the formal
right to remain within the state, when many of the businessman's
debts rose to an unconcealable level in 1867,[642] a number of formerly
loyal brethren had already warmed to the notion of escaping Quallatown's ashen ruins and Colonel Thomas's declining mental health in
favor of joining the Cherokee Nation.[643] While a few found justifica-
tion for their insecurities in the preachings of the anti-Thomas North
Carolina Cherokee upstart, Sergeant George Bushyhead,[644] others
looked back on Chief Yonajuska's old rival, Principal Chief John
Ross, and *his* wartime ministrations on behalf of *his* constituents.[645]

In July 1862, the United States President had feared the ramifications of the Cherokee Nation's potential alliance with the Confederate States of America to launch an operation to abduct Principal
Chief John Ross and convey him into northern-controlled territory
for consultation.[646] After Stand Watie was elected as his replacement
later that August, Principal Chief Ross continued to argue for remuneration for wrongs the federal government had perpetrated against
his people.[647] Where Colonel Thomas had severed his ties with the
United States government and failed to win a justifiable sum from
the Confederate government to take its place, Principal Chief Ross
had played a diplomatic chess game with both sides and seemed
likely to win an additional monetary allowance. In the postwar world,
the ancient ways practiced in the distant virgin territory of the west
seemed to be a far superior choice to the uncertain fate of Principal
Chief Thomas's Eastern Band.

In almost syncopation with his past several years of trouble and heartbreak, shortly thereafter he initiated the paperwork for his formal petition of forgiveness for taking up arms against the United States. Colonel Thomas's tenuous mental health unspooled further. At one point in 1867, the North Carolina businessman grabbed hold of a hatchet and raising the object above his wife's head menacingly, compelled Sarah to play their piano.[648] Fearing for herself, their children, and her ninety-year-old mother-in-law, Sarah summoned two of her brothers and the local sheriff to the house. Upon their arrival, the company of men seized the sixty-two-year-old colonel and conveyed him to the state's recently completed state hospital for North Carolina's insane located in Raleigh, called Dix Hill,[649] a project Colonel Thomas had, ironically, approved as a state senator in 1848.[650]

Diagnosed with a form of dementia, the colonel remained incarcerated for nearly a month in the facility until lucidity, savvy words, and repeated assurances were made that he had returned to his logical and competent self. On April 8th, he was declared sane, released into the custody of his brother-in-law, and charged twenty-five dollars for his room and board.[651] Colonel Thomas continued to burn with resentment for his apparent betrayers, but, after a brief time, the Western North Carolina businessman lapsed once more into violent dementia.

In rapid succession, the complex weaving of business transactions, social initiatives, financial records, owed debts, curried favors, and old alliances crashed to the ground and shattered. In 1867, Colonel William Holland Thomas was forced to resign as Chief of the Eastern Band of North Carolina Cherokee.[652] Shortly thereafter, the colonel was forced to transfer ownership of the Quallatown operation in its entirety to James Terrell.[653] In 1869 his creditors moved to have all real estate holdings in his name confiscated by the county sheriff to pay off his unrecoverable debts, and consequently, in 1870, the Eastern Band under the guidance of their new Principal Chief, Flying Squirrel (Chief Yonaguska's son-in-law),[654] won the right to sue Colonel Thomas for their entitlement to the land he had amassed over the previous several decades for their "Qualla Boundary" reservation.[655]

When the Eastern Band had met in 1868, they incorporated a number of the virtues their adopted brother had advocated, first as their Cherokee Agent and again as their Chief, in the formation of their new constitution (including the continual integrity of their North Carolina reservation,[656] the decision of the ruling council to hold festivals and fairs and control production assets,[657] the rationality of presenting a strong public image,[658] and the wisdom of an Eastern Band leader who frequently walks among his brethren[659]), but in requiring Cherokee blood and limiting the Principal Chief's term of office the group also excluded the possibility of Colonel Thomas or another like him directing Chief Yonaguska's legacy ever again.[660] With the land Chief Yonaguska and his followers had purchased now in jeopardy, the new leadership saw little recourse but to bring suit against their former Chief and longtime benefactor.

On July 15th, 1870, the protected group co-existing within the borders of North Carolina, but not yet citizens of the United States, won from the United States Congress the right to sue Colonel William Holland Thomas in North Carolina's circuit court.[661] After failing to meet a deal brokered by James Terrell (calling for Thomas creditor and new owner of the land William Johnston to grant them the land for $30,000—the Eastern Band was barely able to collect $6,500),[662] in May 1873 the Eastern Band filed papers against the colonel, his business associate James Terrell, and William Johnston to recover the balance of their owed federal money and settle their account with the present landowner.[663]

Much to the consternation of Terrell,[664] the former Chief reacted positively when he received news of the suit. He felt poorly about leaving his brethren mired in his financial quagmire and would have likely followed the same course of legal action had he not fallen ill. Yet, the adopted Cherokee could still serve a beneficial end towards firmly establishing Chief Yonaguska's dream.[665] In the absence of formal notes and business journals, Colonel Thomas devoted his more lucid hours of convalescence to providing facts, figures, and histories to explain his real estate transactions on behalf of the Eastern Band between his adoption by the tribe in 1836 and the suspension of Terrell's legal ministrations at the onset of the War of The Rebellion.[666] By the time the colonel's semblance of mental clarity evaporated and the "raving, furious maniac"[667] returned to disrupt the proceedings, the case had already moved well into the arbitration phase.

In October 1874, the court reached a decision. Finding in favor of the plaintiffs, the court divested the Thomas family of nearly their entire real estate holding, awarded the Cherokee their land, and laid out the means by which the Johnston family would be compensated for their troubles.[668]

The colonel, now a broken and impoverished man, was returned to his home at the conclusion of the trial and welcomed back into the company of his family with reassurances that the old man and his much younger bride would now finally have time to share unimpeded together. Over the next several years, however, as Sarah Thomas continued to care for her husband and his affairs at Stekoa Fields (one of only two pieces of property that managed to be spared from the state's liquidation process), the retirement time both had long promised together continued to be marred by ill-fortune. Now unable to care for both Colonel William Thomas and their few surviving business ventures, the family signed the entirety of his first store at Quallatown over to James Terrell. Following hard upon the transfer and the court finding, in October 1874 William's mother, Temperance, died at the age of 100.[669] In the following months, Colonel William Thomas's bursts of expression grew more frequent and increasingly unmanageable, forcing Sarah to send their children off to live with her sister Maria and her new husband, Major William Stringfield, in Waynesville.[670]

When it seemed the situation could not grow any worse, Sarah Thomas weakened under the constant strain and fell ill several times. In an 1876 letter to her eldest son, Willie, the forty-three-year-old woman confided that "your mother has almost been in eternity for several times during the last weeks, and if I have a recurrence of the same disease it may prove fatal, as I am in quite a delicate and critical situation."[671]

Since the colonel had returned from the war, she had taken on the burden of her husband's illness, his failing business, and the daily chore of sheltering her children from the potential harm their father might bring. Even though her mind remained resolutely dedicated to the recuperation of her husband, her equally suffering body was failing more and more with each passing episode. Less than a year later, on May 15th, 1877, the brief young light of Colonel William Holland Thomas's life died.[672]

After Sarah Thomas was interred next to her mother-in-law, the Loves had the now despondent husband admitted to the Raleigh facility. The sudden shock of his incarceration jarred Colonel Thomas to action once more. Reportedly accusing Robert and Samuel Love of placing him in the "Lunatic Asylum"[673] to escape the debts they owed him,[674] the former businessman commenced one final letter-writing campaign to win his freedom. The colonel denied the presence of dementia and begged Governor Zebulon Vance to use his influence to keep him from "wearing out [his] remaining days in a mad man's prison."[675] Eventually, the colonel was able to win partial freedom to visit the Stringfields and his children, but continued manifestations of dementia* ensured his permanent residence in the facility he had helped create.

DURING THE MID-1880s, a young anthropologist, named James Mooney, began to tour the mountains of Western North Carolina on assignment from the Department of the Interior. Charged with documenting the rich oral tradition, cultural practices, and ancient myths of the Cherokee people before the details could fade in the final stages of western assimilation, Mooney interviewed the Eastern

---

* Likely caused by venereal infection from a youthful sexual indiscretion.

Band's new Principal Chief, Nimrod Smith Jarrett. As the sessions drew on, the anthropologist learned about the differences between the eastern- and western-residing Cherokee, Chief Yonaguska, and an aging Caucasian mountain man who had risen to become Cherokee Chief of the Eastern Band and led the Cherokee against the Union Army.[676] After the Principal Chief, Mooney moved on to interview Captain James Terrell, who in turn added further details about the most influential advocate the Cherokee people had ever had.

As he continued to travel about the countryside following his list of interviewees, the young anthropologist time and again found William Holland Thomas the topic of conversation. By 1889, James Mooney realized that he now *had* to interview the former Eastern Band Chief. Tracking the colonel to Morganton, North Carolina's Western Insane Asylum, Mooney solicited an interview but was discouraged to find the man "subject to continued paraoxysms of excitement when he is very noisy, abusive, and destructive."[677]

When next passing through the area in 1890, James Mooney once more attempted to engage the aged shut-away man in conversation.[678] Instead of rebuffing Mooney, this time Colonel Thomas indicated for the anthropologist to stay. The two talked several times about the history of the North Carolina Cherokee; Thomas's predecessor and mentor, Chief Yonaguska; the foundation of the Eastern Band at Quallatown; Thomas's involvement in tracking down Tsali; the exploits of the Thomas Legion; and life amidst the Smoky Mountains. When the interview series was completed, James Mooney thanked the man and departed to complete his report, but the colonel continued to linger on the past.

In the early morning hours of May 10th, 1893, twenty-eight years and less than a day after the disbanding of the Thomas Legion, Colonel William Holland Thomas closed his eyes for the last time. Once his body was claimed, Lieutenant Colonel William Stringfield and the Loves conveyed the body to Waynesville's cemetery for burial.[679]

Now near his wife and mother, the mountain leader's gravestone reads:

WILLIAM HOLLAND THOMAS

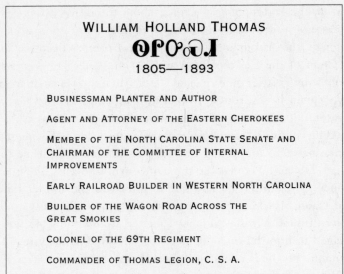

1805—1893

BUSINESSMAN PLANTER AND AUTHOR

AGENT AND ATTORNEY OF THE EASTERN CHEROKEES

MEMBER OF THE NORTH CAROLINA STATE SENATE AND
CHAIRMAN OF THE COMMITTEE OF INTERNAL
IMPROVEMENTS

EARLY RAILROAD BUILDER IN WESTERN NORTH CAROLINA

BUILDER OF THE WAGON ROAD ACROSS THE
GREAT SMOKIES

COLONEL OF THE 69TH REGIMENT

COMMANDER OF THOMAS LEGION, C. S. A.

FRIEND AND BENEFACTOR OF THE CHEROKEE PEOPLE

Conclusion: Thomas Reconsidered

Throughout his life, Colonel William Holland Thomas struggled hard to provide his family, friends, and constituents with the physical, emotional, and metaphysical comforts which had been robbed from the Thomas family by the untimely watery demise of his father, Richard Thomas.

In a time and place where education was considered a luxury, the young man grew into adulthood with skills that rivaled and even surpassed those of many of his superiors. In form, William Thomas may have been slow, but in the application of logic and the acquisition of pattern recognition the man was a master. Focusing his senses on the surrounding landscape, Thomas exploited more frontier niche markets and provided more skilled services than most of his frontier contemporaries. In little time, Colonel Thomas became not only a self-made man and mercantile pioneer but also a master of the new currency of the nation taking shape around him, legal contracts, and the reputable personal contacts which gave them value.

Yet, without Chief Yonaguska's Eastern Band of North Carolina Cherokee, Thomas's potential would have likely remained unrecognized. At first holding a sense of obligation towards the Native Americans for their efforts in supporting his business enterprise with *their* skills, William Thomas rapidly grew to appreciate the serenity of the Cherokee culture, the simplicity of their designs and the integrity of their motions.

In little time, he came to identify his own feelings of abandonment with these self-exiled people. When he first went to work for Chief Yonaguska mediating between the Eastern Band and their estranged former associates, he rapidly came to realize that he had stepped into his long desired world of influential figures and the policies they shaped for millions of residents. When he began dealing with national players, it quickly became apparent that mixing and matching his legal associates and business proposals made sense economically, politically, and socially.

Before long, the poor fatherless young man had parlayed his mother's inherited assets into a booming frontier franchise, a renowned legal business, and a strong alliance with his adopted brethren among the Eastern Band. His frequent trips to New York, Washington, Raleigh, and points south were, indeed, tiring and sometimes hazardous to his health, but there was profit to be made, places to see, and deals to be brokered. Soon Colonel Thomas managed to parlay his newfound connections into enhanced communal status and, much to the consternation of North Carolina's aristocracy, regional renown. By the 1830s, there seemed to be nothing the young man could not master. When the mantle of Eastern Band leadership was unexpectedly thrust upon him by the dying Chief Yonaguska, the young man bore his new responsibility with strength and conviction far beyond his years.

In thought, he stood as a cool and calculating advocate for his clients. Like early American pioneers of territory and invention, whenever the colonel met an impasse on one issue he took hold of the next available opportunity, rode it as far as he could, and reinvested his new skills, assets, and contacts in solving the situation. Still, the weight of serving everyone's needs soon wore on the man. His body grew weak with fatigue. His business enterprises faltered. His patience waned and, consequently, miscalculations were made. Whether by strength of character, quixotic desire, or simple hubris, the man refused to bend from his responsibilities. Instead of cutting his losses and delegating authority, however, Colonel William rose to the occasion and used his connections to draw himself and his allies out of the morass of bureaucracy.

Yet, the colonel's rise into the upper echelon of North Carolina society also brought new obstacles and enemies. Old money had little use for the upstart. New money felt threatened by him. Eastern politicians saw him as a threat. Northern governmental entities found the man to be a complication to their national plans. Rapidly, winning hands turned into unilaterally losing propositions. In entering the State Senate, he found the reward of power but was often kept from its application. In the secessionist crisis, his legal-minded sense of democracy took a backseat to the southern militants and supremacists. And in the War of the Rebellion, the colonel was the victim of several power plays.

In action, he was a stalwart symbol of southern resolve. When the War of the Rebellion started, William Holland Thomas had been fighting for his political survival. Gambling on the fortune a Confederate uniform coat-tails might bring him in the new American order he dreamt would follow, he had enlisted in the Confederate Army and actively sought the means of his own deliverance in theater actions and battlefield successes. As the Confederate Army disintegrated from gross mismanagement and the application of overwhelming Union force, Colonel Thomas remained as committed to the sworn cause as he was to the Eastern Band.

In defeat, he remained an honest and noble character, dutifully returning home with his charges to assess the damage and rebuild his community. Yet, an undiagnosed illness (likely tertiary syphilis),[680] probably contracted while visiting the Red Light District of an outlying urban center, robbed him of a clear mind, a supporting family, and the opportunity to put right what coastal and southern politics had nearly ruined. Where the aging colonel failed to find parity between Western North Carolina and the more advanced eastern counterparts, several of his former employee protégés and family members, including later state senators Captain James Wharey Terrell, Joseph Keener, James Bryson, Colonel James Robert Love (holding seats in first North Carolina and later Tennessee), and Lieutenant Colonel Major William Stringfield, did. The long neglected wilderness was finally coming into its own.

Although the precedents Colonel Thomas set in life would remain binding influences upon the development of the Eastern Band, his home, and the state legal system, the Thomas family failed to find the security the colonel had struggled to attain for his children. While the young orphans (Andrew Patton, William Hyde, and Angelina) Colonel Thomas cared for in his years prior to marrying his wife disappeared from the record, after the demise of their mother and the committal of their father, his first child, William Holland Thomas Jr. married Evelyn Bryson, but after her death (from complications birthing their fifth child) the son followed the father into poverty, ill health, and despair. He died at age thirty-eight. James Robert Thomas fared little better. When he was old enough, the second child took charge of both his father's affairs and his brother's orphaned children, which continued until his death in 1936. William and Sarah Thomas's third child, Sarah Love Thomas, however, fared better than her brothers. Marrying her own father figure, Alphonso Avery (a North Carolina attorney and eventual state senator), she died in relative comfort at the age of ninety-three.

In retrospect, Colonel William Holland Thomas may have supported a number of losing propositions, but he also contributed to the rise of the southern Appalachian mountain community, was responsible for helping modernize Western North Carolina, and saved the Eastern Band from destruction. Shortly after his demise, the Eastern Band won the money their Caucasian Cherokee Chief had long fought to have appropriated for their use. A few years later, North Carolina received its first over-mountain railroad. After that, gold and other precious metals were discovered among the mountains. Shortly thereafter, botanists and herbalists began mining the area's native plant life for generative and medicinal resources. In the twentieth century a Democratic President of the United States orchestrated the transformation of Western North Carolina into an easily accessible, nationally protected natural paradise with all the rights and protections the Eastern Band's Native American adversaries had long denied. Although he died an almost forgotten footnote of nineteenth-century North Carolina current events, the lasting words and works of Colonel William Holland Thomas continue to be felt in the shadows of the Smoky Mountains and the American nation beyond.

ENDNOTES

A few of the older texts cited here do not have page numbers. In this case, a chapter title or section header has been provided.

In the first instance of usage, sources accrued from on-line repositories of Internet links have been provided. For a general reference, please see the following bibliography.

Many of the following notations include digitally provided primary source material. They are permanently located at the following Web sites/repositories:

AM Library of Congress On-Line American Memory Database. http://memory.loc.gov.

CM The William Thomas Papers and Diaries at the Museum of the Cherokee Indian, Cherokee, North Carolina. Galileo On-Line: http://www.galileo.usg.edu/express?link=zlna&hp=1

CMHUSA Center for Military History. United States Army. http://www.army.mil/cmh-pg/books/.

GML The Governor McMinn Letters at the Tennessee State Library and Archive, Nashville. Galileo On-Line: http://www.galileo.usg.edu/express?link=zlna&hp=1

GU Gutenberg Digital Archives. http://promo.net/pg/.

IVP The Captain Isaac Vincent Papers at the Hargrett Rare Book and Manuscript Library, University of Georgia, Athens. Galileo On-Line: http://www.galileo.usg.edu/express?link=zlna&hp=1

PAM	The Printed At Globe Printing Office at the Hargrett Rare Book and Manuscript Library, University of Georgia, Athens. Galileo On-Line: http://www.galileo.usg.edu/express?link=zlna&hp=1

TCC	The Telamon Cuyler Collection at the Hargrett Rare Book and Manuscript Library, University of Georgia, Athens. Galileo On-Line: http://www.galileo.usg.edu/express?link=zlna&hp=1

UNC	University of North Carolina at Chapel Hill Libraries. Documenting the American South Collection. http://docsouth.unc.edu/nc/.

WT	The William Holland Thomas Collection at the Hoskins Special Collections Library, University of Tennessee, Knoxville. Galileo On-Line: http://www.galileo.usg.edu/express?link=zlna&hp=1

WTP	The William H. Thomas Papers at the Hargrett Rare Book and Manuscript Library, University of Georgia, Athens. Galileo On-Line: http://www.galileo.usg.edu/express?link=zlna&hp=1

1. Index Card of the Confederate Record of William H. Thomas, Thomas Legion. April 9, 1862. Colonel William Holland Thomas Personnel Record. National Archives Collection.
2. Mattie Russell. *William Holland Thomas, White Chief of the North Carolina Cherokee.* P. 1.
3. North Carolina has a varied topography. It can be segmented into the following east to west lying regions: the coastline (bordering the Atlantic Ocean), the Lower Piedmont (characterized by the region's few ocean-leading rivers and lush forests), the Upper Piedmont (extending deep into the territory's hilly woodland terrain), and the Mountain region (bordering modern Tennessee).
4. As Mattie Russell illustrated in her doctoral dissertation, a great deal of confusion has arisen in researching Temperance Thomas's ancestry, with multiple period spellings among Thomas family records alone. While variances such as "Colvard" and "Calvert" have been found, William Thomas apparently wrote his mother's maiden name as "Colvard." This last spelling will be used throughout this work. Mattie Russell. *William Holland Thomas, White Chief of the North Carolina Cherokee.* P. 2.
5. John Lawson. *A New Voyage to Carolina.* GU. *Dedication.* John Lawson's 1709 narrative of one man's journey through the southern American

colonies was widely distributed throughout the English-speaking world. Similar in aim to later North Carolina settler and pioneer Daniel Boone's pseudo-autobiography, *The Adventures of Colonel Daniel Boone; Containing a Narrative of the Wars of Kentucke.* Lawson's story was employed by English aristocracy as a guidebook/literary showcase for prospective colonial settlers. John Filson. *The Adventures of Colonel Daniel Boone.* GU.

6. Soon after the publication of *A New Voyage to Carolina,* John Lawson died under suspicious circumstances. According to William Gilmore Simms's *The Life of Francis Marion,* Lawson "fell a victim to his official duties. He was confounded, by the savages, with the government which he represented and sacrificed to their fury, under the charge of depriving them, by his surveys, of their land." William Gilmore Simms. *The Life of Francis Marion.* GU.

7. John Lawson. *A New Voyage to Carolina.* GU. *Dedication.*

8. While the Mountain and Upper Piedmont regions of North Carolina held negligible serviceable roadways, the inland region of the state featured a plentitude of foot-worn paths that had been utilized by Native Americans for centuries.

9. James Mooney. *History, Myths, and Sacred Formulas of the Cherokees.* P. 160.

10. Jack Clairborne and William Price, eds. *Discovering North Carolina: a Tar Heel Reader.* P. 30.

11. North Carolina furnished many tradeable goods, including hardwood lumber (used in furniture construction and shipbuilding), the sealant tar, the minerals gold, silver, and copper, the explosive compound saltpeter, and the ubiquitous agrarian products of grain, tobacco, cotton, and corn.

12. Mattie Russell. *William Holland Thomas, White Chief of the North Carolina Cherokee.* P. 3.

13. During the colonial period, North Carolina was home to four distinct professional classes: the gentry (landowners, large plantation farmers, and large scale coastal businessmen); the merchants; the large middle class, consisting of craftsmen and small farmers, and finally the lower class, which included the day-laborers, indentured servants, slaves, and tenant farmers. After the American Revolution, these distinctions began to degrade, allowing the lucky and ingenious to rise beyond their station in the new, less restrictive American society.

14. According to Archibald Henderson in *The Conquest of the Old South West: The Romantic Story of the Early Pioneers into Virginia, the Carolinas, Tennessee*

and Kentucky 1740–1790, by the time of the American Revolution most of the elder and more heavily trafficked American colonies were beginning to raise their land rates to meet with the rising demand. For example, in Pennsylvania the price of a hundred acre allotment soared from almost five pounds and eight shillings quit-rent to fifteen pounds and ten shillings quit-rent within the space of just thirteen years. For lower and middle class members of the new American society, North Carolina's deal of three shillings proclamation money for 640 acres of land seemed ideal. Archibald Henderson. *The Conquest of the Old South West: The Romantic Story of the Early Pioneers into Virginia, the Carolinas, Tennessee and Kentucky 1740–1790.* GU. *Chapter 1.*

15. North Carolina Board of Agriculture. *North Carolina and Its Resources.* UNC. P. 14.
16. E. Stanley Goldbold Jr. and Mattie U. Russell. *Confederate Colonel and Cherokee Chief: The Life of William Holland Thomas.* P. 1.
17. Robert K. Wright Jr. *The Continental Army.* CMHUSA. *"Virginia"* P. 16. Mattie Russell. *William Holland Thomas, White Chief of the North Carolina Cherokee.* P. 3–4.
18. Mattie Russell. *William Holland Thomas, White Chief of the North Carolina Cherokee.* Pp. 3–4.
19. Robert K. Wright Jr. *The Continental Army.* CMHUSA. *"Virginia."* P. 108.
20. Trevor N. Dupuy, Curt Johnson, and David L. Bongard, eds. *The Harper's Encyclopedia of Military Biography.* Pp. 524–525.
21. Robert K. Wright Jr. *The Continental Army.* CMHUSA. *"Virginia."* P. 108.
22. E. Stanley Godbold Jr. and Mattie U. Russell. *Confederate Colonel and Cherokee Chief: The Life of William Holland Thomas.* P. 2.
23. Robert K. Wright Jr. *The Continental Army.* CMHUSA. *"Virginia."* P. 16.
24. Major Patrick Ferguson had been ordered by his superiors to recruit and train the raw colonial recruits during his convalescence for an injury obtained during the Battle of Brandywine.
25. *Historical Statements Concerning the Battle of Kings Mountain and the Battle of the Cowpens South Carolina. Part II Gathering of the Patriots—The Battle.* CMHUSA. P. 17. http://www.army.mil/cmh-pg/books/RevWar/KM-Cpns/AWC-KM2.htm.
26. On the May 29th, 1780, battlefield at the Waxhaws, British colonel Banastre Tarleton of the Sixteenth British Light Dragoons reportedly slaughtered surrendering Continentals, earning him the battlefield appellation "Tarleton's Quarter."

27. *Historical Statements Concerning the Battle of Kings Mountain and the Battle of the Cowpens South Carolina. Part II Gathering of the Patriots—the Battle.* CMHUSA. Pp. 30–31.

28. The record remains unclear if Richard Thomas was once more captured as a prisoner-of-war or remained at large during this period of the war. Robert K. Wright Jr. *The Continental Army.* CMHUSA *"Virginia."*

29. There is much confusion about Richard Thomas's postwar profession. Most sources make no mention of the man's occupation, but, according to Mattie Russell, descendants of the Thomas family claim Richard was either a Civil Engineer or a Horse Trader. Mattie Russell. *William Holland Thomas, White Chief of the North Carolina Cherokee.* P. 1.

30. E. Stanley Godbold Jr. and Mattie Russell. *Confederate Colonel and Cherokee Chief: The Life of William Holland Thomas.* P. 2.

31. Ibid.

32. Mattie Russell. *William Holland Thomas, White Chief of the North Carolina Cherokee.* P. 2.

33. E. Stanley Godbold Jr. and Mattie Russell. *Confederate Colonel and Cherokee Chief: The Life of William Holland Thomas.* P. 2.

34. According to an 1896 report released by the North Carolina Board of Agriculture, the 1790 census listed the state's populace at 397,751. By 1800, the populace rose to 478,103. By the time William Thomas had reached the age of six in 1810 North Carolina had reached a reported population density of 555,500 inhabitants. North Carolina Board of Agriculture. *North Carolina and Its Resources.* UNC. P. 14.

35. John Lawson. *A New Voyage to North Carolina.* GU. Preface.

36. Haywood County was named for North Carolina's late eighteenth and early nineteenth century Treasurer, John Haywood. In the bestowing of the name, it was hoped that Haywood's colleagues in the General Assembly might look favorably on future legislated improvements to the area.

37. Waynesville County is named for American Revolutionary general Anthony Wayne.

38. Mattie Russell. *William Holland Thomas, White Chief of the North Carolina Cherokee.* P. 7.

39. Ibid. P. 4.

40. Ibid. P. 12.

41. Ibid. P. 10–11.

42. Congressman Felix Walker Sr., first elected in 1817 and reelected to

two successive terms by Western North Carolina's Buncombe and Haywood counties, is also renowned for the introduction of the expression "talking for buncombe" and the likely subsequent addition of the word "bunk" to the English dictionary. Hence, the man's nickname stemmed from his ability to captivate his audience in highly involved orations. Walker's tenure in the United States Congress ended in 1823. *Southwestern Historical Quarterly On-line.* Volume 8. Number 3. P. 263. http://www.tsha.utexas.edu/publications/journals/shq/online/v008/n3/ 0008003263.html. http://www.uschs.org/03_education/subs/subs_lessons/ 06_b.html.

43. Vicki Rozema. *Footsteps of the Cherokees: A Guide to the Eastern Homelands of the Cherokee Nation.* P. 207.

44. North Carolina Board of Agriculture. *North Carolina and Its Resources.* UNC. P. 157.

45. John Lawson. *A New Voyage to Carolina.* GU. *"Hunting of the Savages."*

46. North Carolina Board of Agriculture. *North Carolina and Its Resources.* UNC. P. 64–65.

47. Ibid. Pp. 21, 62–63.

48. James Mooney. *History, Myths, and Sacred Formulas of the Cherokees.* P. 14.

49. John Lawson. *A New Voyage to Carolina.* GU. *"Hunting of the Savages."*

50. Ibid. *"Rum."*

51. Many of the roots and herbs obtained by William Thomas and his contemporaries remained unable to be cultivated outside their natural Western North Carolina environment until the 1880s and 1890s.

52. E. Stanley Godbold Jr. and Mattie U. Russell. *Confederate Colonel and Cherokee Chief: The Life of William Holland Thomas.* P. 10.

53. Mattie Russell. *William Holland Thomas, White Chief of the North Carolina Cherokee.* P. 14.

54. John Lawson. *A New Voyage to Carolina.* GU. *"Corn."*

55. Richard Foreman and James W. Mahoney. *The Cherokee Physician . . .* UNC. P. 39.

56. Ibid. P. 248.

57. Ibid. P. 219.

58. Ibid.

59. James Mooney. *History, Myths, and Sacred Formulas of the Cherokees.* P. 160.

60. Ibid. Pp. 239–240.

61. Ibid. P. 20.

62. Ibid. Pp. 298–302, 407.

63. Vicki Rozema. *Footsteps of the Cherokees: A Guide to the Eastern Homelands of the Cherokee Nation*. P. 190.

64. Ibid. Pp. 23–27.

65. James Mooney. *History, Myths, and Sacred Formulas of the Cherokees*. Pp. 408–409. Vicki Rozema. *Footsteps of the Cherokees: A Guide to the Eastern Homelands of the Cherokee Nation*. P. 11.

66. Throughout the colonial and post–American Revolutionary period, most residents of North Carolina's backcountry escaped the paying of taxes. In the aftermath of their victory over British taxation, few state leaders could reasonably justify taxing a people without reasonable representation in their state assembly. With the state's coastal elite having no intention of providing the Upper Piedmont and Mountain regions' taxed investments with the erection of schools and roads, there was little reason for either party to dilute their semi-autonomy.

    Were the North Carolina tax code enforced in the western region, Felix Hampton Walker Jr. would have, however, likely found himself the occupant of one of Waynesville's new jail cells.

67. In her thesis, Mattie Russell stated that she believed the tract of land to have come from a piece of farmland Temperance bought in 1820 east of Waynesville, but the record remains unclear as to how she originally came by this property. Mattie Russell. *William Holland Thomas, White Chief of the North Carolina Cherokee*. P. 24.

68. These points of contention largely revolved around issues of blood purity and a lack of accommodation/assimilation with the European lifestyle. Ironically, the pure bloods of the North Carolina Cherokee largely endorsed assimilation into the world the Europeans and Americans offered, leaving the purported half-bloods of the Cherokee Nation (Cherokee who had taken up European mates) to maintain a strict policy of segregation, which they often enacted with the resounding approval of the majority of the nation's leadership.

69. There are several spellings of the name of Chief Yonaguska of the Kituhwa (later referred to as the "Oconaluftee Indians" or "Qualla Indians"), including "Yonagusta" and "Yonu-gunski." In some sources he is also referred to as the Principal Chief of the Mountain Cherokee.

70. Within the hierarchical structure of the Cherokee, a series of political checks and balances existed that divided governance duties into two leadership roles (Peace and War Chiefs), each assuming certain authorized tribal powers in response to the changing nature of Cherokee society.

While the War Chief was a powerful leader in times of trouble and matters of tribal security, when not engaged in an armed conflict or hostile action the Peace or Principal Chief held the reins of power for each Cherokee community. By the nineteenth century, the arguably divisive role of the War Chief had given way to the more proactive role of methodology of diplomacy.

71. Mattie Russell. *William Holland Thomas, White Chief of the North Carolina Cherokee.* P. 15.

72. Contrary to previous biographical accounts of William Thomas's adoption into the ranks of the Cherokee, Chief Yonaguska likely did not adopt Thomas out of pity or a sense of communal responsibility. Instead, Yonaguska chose to include Thomas in the tribe as the next step in shepherding the tribe through the process of western assimilation and acculturation.

73. E. Stanley Godbold Jr. and Mattie U. Russell. *Confederate Colonel and Cherokee Chief: The Life of William Holland Thomas.* P. 10.

74. Mattie Russell. *William Holland Thomas, White Chief of the North Carolina Cherokee.* P. 16. The name "Little Will" was likely bestowed upon the man as a play of words concerning his short stature compared to six-foot, two-inch Chief Yonaguska.

75. Ibid.

76. Mattie Russell. *William Holland Thomas, White Chief of the North Carolina Cherokee.* P. 13.

77. Ibid.

78. Ibid.

79. Doctors, lawyers, and wealthy managers of large agrarian tracks comprised the preponderance of the Professional Sector of North Carolina society. According to Guion Griffis Johnson, many middle and lower class men similar to Thomas began to find refuge from agrarian work in the legal and medical fields. Guion Griffis Johnson. *Antebellum North Carolina: A Social History.* UNC. P. 60.

80. Ibid. P. 61.

81. Ibid. P. 78.

82. William Powell briefly describes the process in *North Carolina Through Four Centuries.* William S. Powell. *North Carolina Through Four Centuries.* P. 318.

83. John Ehle. *Trail of Tears: The Rise and Fall of the Cherokee Nation.* P. 16.

84. The Cherokee Nation originally occupied much of modern Virginia,

North Carolina, South Carolina, Georgia, and Tennessee as well as parts of Alabama and Kentucky.

85. James Mooney. *History, Myths, and Sacred Formulas of the Cherokees*. P. 162.

86. The Cherokee inhabiting the modern day Qualla Boundary have also been called the Qualla Indians, but, for purposes of simplicity, they will hence be referred to as the Eastern Band.

87. Letter from Joseph McMinn to Secretary of State Daniel Graham. December 11, 1818. GML 010. http://www.galileo.usg.edu/express?link=zlna&hp=1.

88. Letter from Joseph McMinn to Hon. Daniel Graham. October 1, 1818. GML 007.

89. Initially, colonial and American leaders saw the Native American nations as sovereign entities requiring treaties for the exchange of goods, services, and land. Eventually, however, haste and expediency encouraged the United States to see the Native American nations as a collection of individuals granted the protection of the United States and allowed to live *on* United States land.

90. John Dillard would also later serve as a Justice of the Peace for the area. Dillard and Thomas remained legal business associates for some time. Deposition of Joseph Keener, Sworn to Before John L. Dillard. August 22nd, 1838. WT 194. http://www.galileo.usg.edu/express?link=zlna&hp=1.

91. E. Stanley Godbold Jr. and Mattie U. Russell. *Confederate Colonel and Cherokee Chief: The Life of William Holland Thomas*. P. 13.

92. James Mooney. *History, Myths, and Sacred Formulas of the Cherokees*. P. 163.

93. According to E. Stanley Godbold Jr. and Mattie Russell, William Thomas actually spent about nine hundred dollars in currency and $1,400 in the valued ownership of three slaves on his Soco Creek purchase. E. Stanley Godbold Jr. and Mattie U. Russell. *Confederate Colonel and Cherokee Chief: The Life of William Holland Thomas*. Pp. 17–18.

94. With the acquisition of each new store, Thomas promoted his more reliable store personnel to a greater managerial level in the enterprise's distant outposts. For example, when Johnson King was promoted to the management of another Thomas store, he was replaced by his brother, H. P. King, who was, in turn, succeeded by George W. Hughes. Finally, Thomas's partner and store manager James Wharey Terrell was granted custodial management of Thomas's flagship Indiantown/Quallatown store.

95. By the end of the next decade, William Thomas would own a total of seven stores. They were most notably tended by the following clerks: James W. Terrell, H. P. King, Allen Fisher, Johnson King, and James Bryson.

96. Deposition of Joseph Keener, Sworn to Before John L. Dillard. August 22nd, 1838. WT 194.

97. Ibid.

98. Deposition of Ute Hyatt. Sworn to Before Samuel Gibson. August 24th, 1838. WT 192.

99. Deposition of Ebenezer Newton, Sworn to Before George W. Hayes. August 24th, 1838. WT 193.

100. Deposition of Joseph Keener, Sworn to Before John L. Dillard. August 22nd, 1838. WT 194.

101. While William Thomas likely understood few of the demands that would be placed upon him as an Indian Agent when he agreed to the position, the preparations that Chief Yonaguska had made in maneuvering the young man into Dillard's position, coupled with the establishment/legal machinations of the Eastern Band over the preceding decades, made Chief Yonaguska and his leadership council well aware of the vital role the young man would soon play in their fate.

102. With the Native American territories indirectly conceded as sovereign entities in the Friday, October 26th, 1787, *Journal of the Continental Congress,* Congress, as afforded by the Articles of Confederation and later, the Constitution of the United States, could enter into treaties/seal with the Native Americans on behalf of its affected states and territories.

     This situation led to the appointment of federal representatives and state commissioners to initially deal with boundary disputes among the Native American territories. Later, the Commission for Indian Affairs was created under the Department of War to fill this void. It was subsequently succeeded by the Bureau of Indian Affairs. Later administrations ignored this precedent (primarily the Andrew Jackson Administration) and Supreme Court decisions, relegating the Cherokee to the level of a "protected peoples" devoid of national autonomy and integrity. *A Century of Lawmakers, 1774–1873.* Item 34 of 500. *Journals of the Continental Congress.* Friday, October 26, 1787. AM. Pp. 708–712. http://memory.loc.gov/cgi-bin/query/D?hlaw:1:./temp/~ammem_ Qc4W::.

103. Letter from George Washington to the Senate. August 22, 1789. "Negotiations with Southern Indians." John C. Fitzpatrick, ed. *The Writings of*

George Washington from the Original Manuscript Sources, 1745–1799. AM. http://memory.loc.gov.

104. Most of President Jefferson's direct communications with elements of the Cherokee Nation contained variations of this word and fed directly from a Native American attribution towards George Washington as their "Great White Father." Letter from Thomas Jefferson to the Cherokees, May 4, 1808. Images 521 and 522 of 1,370. *Thomas Jefferson Papers Series 1. General Correspondence. 1651–1827.* AM. http://memory.loc.gov.

105. Thomas Jefferson Letter to Benjamin Hawkins, February 18, 1803. Paul Leicester Ford, ed. *The Works of Thomas Jefferson in Twelve Volumes.* Federal Edition. AM.

106. Charles Kappler, ed. "Treaty of Hopewell." Document Number BT2352000756. *Indian Treaties, 1778–1883.* Washington, D.C.: 1904, Pp. 8–11. Reproduced in History Resource Center. Farmington Hills, MI: Gale Group. http://galenet.galegroup.com/servlet/HistRC/.

107. *Supreme Court Decisions,* 1832, *Worcester v. Georgia,* 31 U.S. 518. A subsequent treaty, signed on June 26th, 1794, in Philadelphia, served as a supplement to the Treaty of Holston and more precisely qualified the boundaries of the Cherokee Nation's landholdings.

108. According to John R. Finger in *The Eastern Band of Cherokees, 1819–1900,* this decision was instrumental in allowing Chief Yonaguska to break away from the Cherokee Nation and establish his own distinct territory. The court case also indirectly led to the Eastern Band's hiring of John Dillard as their Cherokee Agent. John R. Finger. *The Eastern Band of Cherokees, 1819–1900.* P. 11.

109. Mattie Russell. *William Holland Thomas, White Chief of the North Carolina Cherokee.* P. 45.

110. Ibid.

111. Ibid. P. 44.

112. According to Vicki Rozema, clusters of brilliant lights have been seen moving about Brown Mountain for centuries. The Cherokee reportedly believed the lights were the undying spirits of the ancient Catawba and Cherokee warriors who had fought on the great mountaintop around 1200 C.E. Vicki Rozema. *Footsteps of the Cherokees: A Guide to the Eastern Homelands of the Cherokee Nation.* P. 223.

113. James Mooney. *History, Myths, and Sacred Formulas of the Cherokees.* P. 349.

114. John Lawson. *A New Voyage to Carolina.* GU. *"The Beasts of Carolina Are the . . ."*

115. Mattie Russell. *William Holland Thomas, White Chief of the North Carolina Cherokee.* Pp. 28–29.

116. Ibid. P. 50.

117. Ibid.

118. Ibid. P. 5.

119. George Bancroft. *History of the United States, volume II: History of the Colonization of the United States of America. Chapter VI, "The Languages and Manners of the Red Men."*

120. Mattie Russell. *William Holland Thomas, White Chief of the North Carolina Cherokee.* P. 51.

121. Ibid.

122. As a direct result of their various faulty dealing with Europeans and Americans over the prior centuries, the Cherokee Nation had recently placed within their constitution that Cherokee land could never be granted to Caucasian.

123. Cherokee Indians: Memorial of a Delegation of the Cherokee Tribe of Indians. 22nd Congress, 1st Session. H. R. Doc. 45. January 9th, 1832. PAM 009. http://www.galileo.usg.edu/express?link=zlna&hp=1.

124. Sometimes referred to as "Ridge" alone, the man is not to be confused with his son and dissident successor John Ridge.

125. *Supreme Court Decisions*, 1831, *Cherokee Nation v. Georgia*, 30 U.S. 1.

126. *Memorial of the Cherokee Indians Living in North Carolina Praying the Payment of Their Claims, Agreeably to the 8th and 12th Articles of the Treaty of 1835.* 29th Congress, 1st Session. Senate Doc. 408. June 25th, 1846. Pp. 2–3. http://www.1st-hand-history.org/Congress/sd408/01.jpg.

127. *Supreme Court Decisions*, 1832, *Worcester v. Georgia*, 31 U.S. 518.

128. Sympathizers with the Cherokee in their plight brought several reports before the floor of Congress on behalf of the Cherokee Nation, but after each document was read into the congressional record, they were repeatedly transferred to the Indian Affairs office for study. Once the matter was there the point of contention was effectively neutralized. *Memorial of John Ross and Others on Behalf of the Cherokee Nation of Indians, Praying Protection from the United States . . .* 23rd Congress, 2nd Session, Doc. 71. January 21st, 1835.

129. James Mooney. *History, Myths, and Sacred Formulas of the Cherokees.* P. 120.

130. *An Appeal of the Cherokee, to the People of the United States.* PAM 005.

131. *Journal of the House of Representatives of the United States, 1789–1873.* Friday,

November 15, 1811. *A Century of Lawmakers, 1774–1873*. Item 23 of 500. http://memory.loc.gov.

132. Ibid.

133. In *Cherokee Nation v. Georgia*, it was stated that a Cherokee national by the name of Corn Tassel had been arrested, taken from the Cherokee Nation sovereign territory, tried, and executed by Georgia officials. In 1832 the Supreme Court ruled that as the Cherokee Nation was a sovereign nation governed by their own internal judiciary system, Georgia had grossly overstepped its bounds. *Supreme Court Decisions*, 1831, *Cherokee Nation v. Georgia*, 30 U.S. 1. *Supreme Court Decisions*, 1832, *Worcester v. Georgia*, 31 U.S. 515.

134. John R. Finger. *The Eastern Band of Cherokees, 1819–1900*. Pp. 14 and 63.

135. *Memorial of the Cherokee Indians Living in North Carolina Praying the Payment of Their Claims. Agreeably to the 8th and 12th Articles of the Treaty of 1835*. Senate Doc. 408. 29th Congress, 1st Session, June 25th, 1846. P. 8.

136. Memorial of John Ross and Others, on Behalf of the Cherokee Nation of Indians, Praying Protection from the United States, and Protesting Against Certain Articles of Agreement Between the Agent of the United States and a Certain Part of said Cherokee Nation of Indians. 23rd Congress, 2nd Session. Doc. 71. January 21st, 1835. http://www.1st-hand-history.org/Congress/ cd71/albuml.html.

137. While the Eastern Band were considered quasi members of the State of North Carolina, there is no record of members attempting to vote in elections outside their community until well after the Civil War.

138. Deposition of Johnson W. King, Sworn to Before G. W. Hayes. November 27th, 1838. WT 178. Mattie Russell. *William Holland Thomas, White Chief of the North Carolina Cherokee*. P. 73.

139. Deposition of Joseph Keener, Sworn to Before John L. Dillard. August 22nd, 1838. WT 194. Deposition of Ute Hyatt, Sworn to Before Samuel Gibson. August 24th, 1838. WT 192. Deposition of Ebenezer Newton, Sworn to Before George W. Hayes, August 24th, 1838. WT 193. Deposition of Johnson W. King, Sworn to Before G. W. Hayes. November 27th, 1838. WT 178.

140. "Memorial of the Wife and Child of Arkaooki (Reserve no. 229) circa 1835" WT 197. Letter from Nicholas Peck to William Holland Thomas. June 18, 1840. WTP 005. Document Certifying the Appointment of Power of Attorney Granted to William Holland Thomas. Harry Morris, signatory. March 13, 1850. Document Certifying the Appointment of

Power of Attorney to William Holland Thomas for the Cherokees of Paint Town, Wolf Town, and Bird Town. November 2, 1850. WTP 047. Document Certifying the appointment of Power of Attorney to William Holland Thomas. Mason Barkley, signatory. March 22, 1851. WTP 051.

141. *Memorial of the Cherokee Indians Living in North Carolina Praying the Payment of Their Claims, agreeably to the 8th and 12th Articles of the Treaty of 1835.* Senate Doc. 408. 29th Congress, 1st Session, June 25th, 1846.

142. Given the gravity, Major Ridge and his followers were occupied with the dual role of Cherokee face-saving and providing for the continuance of their populace's way of life (a situation made even more grave by the implied threat of death at the hands of their brothers for violating the Blood Law, which forbid the selling of Cherokee land to the Americans). Although believing the Eastern Band to be wayward siblings of his government, Principal Chief Ross could similarly not expend the energy, time, or political capital at the time to argue the point with Thomas, Chief Yonaguska, or the federal government. He was fighting for his political future.

143. *Memorial of the Cherokee Indians Living in North Carolina Praying the Payment of Their Claims, Agreeably to the 8th and 12th Articles of the Treaty of 1835.* Senate Doc. 408. 29th Congress, 1st Session, June 25th, 1846. P. 2.

144. A seemingly insignificant point at the time, the timely move actually laid the groundwork for later appeals to expand the role of Eastern Band Cherokee with the great context of the North Carolina populace and the entire United States citizenry. Ibid. P. 4.

145. Mattie Russell. *William Holland Thomas, White Chief of the North Carolina Cherokee.* Pp. 62–64.

146. According to E. Stanley Godbold Jr. and Mattie Russell, during this period Thomas also expanded his business enterprise into Cherokee County, Valleytown, Murphy, Cheoch, and Fort Cass in Tennessee. E. Stanley Godbold Jr. and Mattie U. Russell. *Confederate Colonel and Cherokee Chief: The Life of William Holland Thomas.* P. 28.

147. Deposition of Joseph Keener, Sworn to Before John L. Dillard. August 22nd, 1838. WT 194. Deposition of Ute Hyatt, Sworn to Before Samuel Gibson. August 24th, 1838. WT 192. Deposition of Ebenezer Newton Sworn to Before George W. Hayes. August 24th, 1838 WT 193. Deposition of Johnson W. King, Sworn to Before George W. Hayes. November 27th, 1838. WT 178.

Reverend John Freeman Schermerhorn also instructed other

merchant friends to supply the "destitute Conditions of the Cherokees" in a similar fashion. John Schermerhorn Letter to Elbert Herring, Commissioner of Indian Affairs. July 4th, 1836. WT 177. Diary of William Holland Thomas. 1840–1842. Pp. 1,47,49 CM 001. http://www.galileo. usg.edu/express?link=zlna&hp=1

148. James Mooney. *History, Myths, and Sacred Formulas of the Cherokees*. P. 127.

149. Mattie Russell. *William Holland Thomas, White Chief of the North Carolina Cherokee*. P. 66.

150. Fragment of Letter from William Holland Thomas, 1835–1860. CM 148. Letter from William Holland Thomas to Brigadier General John E. Wool. November 20, 1839. WT 110.

151. E. Stanley Godbold Jr. and Mattie U. Russell. *Confederate Colonel and Cherokee Chief: The Life of William Holland Thomas*. P. 34.

152. Mattie Russell. *William Holland Thomas, White Chief of the North Carolina Cherokee*. P. 66.

153. This pretext of quasi-isolation was not provided by the United States military roughly a hundred years later, when President Franklin D. Roosevelt chose to enact the removal of Japanese citizens and Japanese-Americans from the Western Defense Command at the onset of World War II.

154. General Winfield Scott. *Memoirs of Lieutenant-General Scott, LL.D. In Two Volumes*, P. 318.

155. Order No. 25 of Major General Winfield Scott. Headquarters, Eastern Division. Cherokee Agency, Tennessee. May 17, 1838. IVP 0001. http://www.galileo.usg.edu/express?link=zlna&hp=1.

156. Letter from Augustus Crawford to Georgia governor William Schley. June 20, 1836. TCC 580. http://www.galileo.usg.edu/express?link=zlna&hp=1.

157. Letter from Carey A. Harris to William Holland Thomas. July 19, 1839. WT 186.

158. According to E. Stanley Godbold Jr. and Mattie Russell, although Chief Yonaguska and his group did not sign on with Reverend Schermerhorn, 3,250 members of the Cherokee Nation living in North Carolina (likely the southernmost settlements) followed their Georgia affiliates. E. Stanley Godbold Jr. and Mattie U. Russell. *Confederate Colonel and Cherokee Chief: The Life of William Holland Thomas*. P. 24.

159. General Winfield Scott Memorandum. Headquarters, Eastern Division. Athens, Tennessee. November 9, 1838. CH0 64. http://www.galileo. usg.edu/express?link=zlna&hp=1.

160. Letter from George Cumming to Governor William Schley of Georgia. May 24, 1836. TCC 574.

161. Ibid.

162. General Winfield Scott. *Memoirs of Lieutenant-General Scott, LL.D. In Two Volumes.* P. 319.

163. Order No. 30 of Major General Winfield Scott. Headquarters, Eastern Division. New Echota. May 20, 1838. IVP 013.

164. General Winfield Scott. *Memoirs of Lieutenant-General Scott, LL.D. In Two Volumes.* P. 320.

165. Order No. 25 of Major General Winfield Scott. Headquarters, Eastern Division. Cherokee Agency, Tennessee. May 20, 1838. IVP 001.

166. General Winfield Scott. *Memoirs of Lieutenant-General Scott, LL.D. In Two Volumes.* P. 326.

167. While Mooney claims that only a single soldier was killed in the initial conflict with Tsali, further evidence shows that at least two soldiers were indeed killed in the hostile action. James Mooney. *History, Myths, and Sacred Formulas of the Cherokees.* P. 131. Letter from William Holland Thomas to Major General Winfield Scott. March 9, 1846. WTP 023.

168. Tsali is also referred to as "Charley" in some sources. James Mooney. *History, Myths, and Sacred Formulas of the Cherokees.* P. 130.

169. There are significant differences between accounts of this situation. I have chosen the most logical and earliest accounts, taking into account the lack of clarity encumbered by the passage of decades and Thomas's eventual decline into madness as well as the limited scope of the junior officers involved in the incident.

170. Letter from William Holland Thomas to Major General Winfield Scott. March 9, 1846. WTP 023.

171. James Mooney. *History, Myths, and Sacred Formulas of the Cherokees.* P. 131.

172. Letter from William Holland Thomas to Major General Winfield Scott. March 9, 1846. WTP 023.

173. Ibid.

174. The State of North Carolina was not entirely altruistic in their 1830s-legislated protection of the North Carolina Cherokee. If any Cherokee sold their land to any party, the state stood a chance of losing control of the land to unqualified private investors or, worse, the United States government.

175. There is some discrepancy between the sources concerning Thomas's

pursuit of Tsali, but it is likely that Major General Scott ordered Thomas a small guard to accompany him for the duration of the incident as E. Stanley Godbold Jr. and Mattie Russell claim. E. Stanley Godbold Jr. and Mattie U. Russell. *Confederate Colonel and Cherokee Chief: The Life of William Holland Thomas.* P. 38.

176. Ibid.

177. Letter from William Holland Thomas to Major General Winfield Scott. March 9, 1846. WTP 023.

178. Ibid.

179. *Letter from the Secretary of the Interior in Response to Resolution of the House of February 25, 1882, relative to the Lands and Funds of the Eastern Band of North Carolina Cherokee.* Executive Doc. 196. 47th Congress. February 25th, 1882. P. 16.

180. Ibid.

181. According to Mooney, Major General Winfield Scott stayed the execution of Tsali's youngest son on account of his age. James Mooney. *History, Myths, and Sacred Formulas of the Cherokees.* P. 131.

182. Letter from Duncan G. Campbell to the Chiefs, Headmen and Warriors of the Cherokee Nation. January 20, 1823. TCC 054.

183. E. Stanley Godbold Jr. and Mattie U. Russell. *Confederate Colonel and Cherokee Chief: The Life of William Holland Thomas.* P. 13.

184. Had William Thomas led the Cherokee towards a full assimilation with the general populace of North Carolina, the argument may well have eventually been made against the retention of Eastern Band landholdings as protected reservations. Furthermore, such an action would have placed the Cherokee within a situation similar to the Cherokee Nation's standing against Georgia.

185. Letter from William Holland Thomas to H. P. King. July 8, 1839. WT 025.

186. James Mooney. *History, Myths, and Sacred Formulas of the Cherokees.* P. 179.

187. Letter from William Holland Thomas to Commissioner of Indian Affairs T. Hartley Crawford. June 28, 1839. WT 017.

188. James Mooney. *History, Myths, and Sacred Formulas of the Cherokees.* P. 161. When Euchella was inducted into the Eastern Band, he was awarded the position of Wolf Town Chief.

189. Letter from William Holland Thomas to J. W. King. July 8, 1839. WT 026.

190. Letter from William Holland Thomas to H. P. King. July 12, 1839. WT 029.

191. *Memorial of the Cherokee Indians Living in North Carolina Praying the*

Payment of Their Claims, Agreeably to the 8th and 12th Articles of the Treaty of 1835. Senate Doc. 408. 29th Congress, 1st Session. June 25th, 1846. P. 3.

192. Letter from William Holland Thomas to Felix Axeley. December 9, 1839. WT 126.

193. John R. Finger. *The Eastern Band of Cherokees, 1819–1900.* P. 13.

194. John Lawson. *A New Voyage to Carolina.* GU. *"The Hunting of Savages."*

195. George Bancroft. *History of the United States, Volume II: History of the Colonization of the United States of America. Chapter VI, "The Languages and Manners of the Red Men."*

196. Sequoya was also known as Sikwayi, Sikwaji, Sequoia, Sogwili, George Gist, George Guest, and George Guess. He was part of Major Ridge's Cherokee delegation. For details on the Cherokee syllabary language, see James Mooney's *History, Myths, and Sacred Formulas of the Cherokees.* Pp. 219–220.

197. Among others, the *Cherokee Phoenix* (1828) and the *Cherokee Advocate* (1844).

198. John R. Finger. *The Eastern Band of Cherokees, 1819–1900.* P. 15.

199. *Memorial of the Cherokee Indians Living in North Carolina Praying the Payment of Their Claims, Agreeably to the 8th and 12th Articles of the Treaty of 1835.* Senate Doc. 408. 29th Congress, 1st Session. June 25th, 1846. P. 12.

200. According to an 1890s North Carolina Board of Agricultural report, there were 3,829 followers of the Moravian faith, 146,040 (white and black) members of the Methodist Episcopal Church South, 16,416 Methodist Protestants, and 265,579 Missionary-oriented Baptists within the state. North Carolina Board of Agriculture. *North Carolina and Its Resources.* P. 226.

201. Reverend William Henry Foote. *Sketches of North Carolina, Historical and Biographical, Illustrative of the Principles of a Portion of Her Early Settlers.* P. 368.

202. Clavin Jones. "The Cherokee Indians." 1818. PAM 007. http://www.galileo.usg.edu/express?link=zlna&hp=1.

203. Contrary to the assertions of E. Stanley Godbold Jr. and Mattie Russell, Chief Yonaguska was not a possessor of Christian ethics but a naturalist and a benevolent father figure for his tribal membership when viewed within ancestral, hierarchical, and traditional teachings of the Cherokee. E. Stanley Godbold Jr. and Mattie U. Russell. *Confederate Colonel and Cherokee Chief: The Life of William Holland Thomas.* P. 11.

204. James Mooney. *History, Myths, and Sacred Formulas of the Cherokees.* P. 163.

205. Guion Griffis Johnson. *Antebellum North Carolina: A Social History.* UNC. P. 92.

206. E. Stanley Godbold Jr. and Mattie U. Russell. *Confederate Colonel and Cherokee Chief: The Life of William Holland Thomas.* P. 31.

207. John R. Finger. *The Eastern Band of Cherokees, 1819–1900.* P. 62.

208. Ibid. P. 70.

209. Ibid. P. 61.

210. North Carolina Board of Agriculture. *North Carolina and Its Resources.* UNC. P. 157.

211. John Lawson. *A New Voyage to North Carolina. "A Journal of a Thousand Miles Traveled Among the Indians from South to North Carolina."* GU.

212. *Cherokee Indians: Memorial of a Delegation of the Cherokee Tribe of Indians.* H. R. Doc. 45. 22nd Congress, 1st Session. January 9th, 1832. PAM 009.

213. Ibid.

214. Although not mentioning them by name, Thomas makes reference in his correspondence to the challenges some of his "white neighbors" had raised against the presence of the Eastern Band. Letter from William Holand Thomas to Felix Axeley. December 9, 1839. WT 126.

215. There are several other stories concerning Chief Yonaguska's episode covered in Mattie Russell's dissertation, but James Mooney's appears to be the most accurate. Mattie Russell. *William Holland Thomas, White Chief of the North Carolina Cherokee.* Pp. 40–41. James Mooney. *History, Myths, and Sacred Formulas of the Cherokees.* P. 163.

216. Ibid.

217. Ibid.

218. According to James Mooney, Chief Yonaguska was prone to astral visions, but deprived of details that might place his revelations within a scheduled context for causal-effect relationship study, the origins, character, and quality of these experiences can solely be viewed through the lens of established bio-chemical interactions. James Mooney. *History, Myths, and Sacred Formulas of the Cherokees.* P. 163.

219. Ibid.

220. There is an abundance of literature on the effects of alcohol ingestion. *The Merck Manual—Second Home Edition* asserts: "Because alcohol is absorbed faster than it is processed (metabolized) and eliminated from the body, alcohol levels in the blood rise rapidly." This can lead to the inducement of tremors, blackouts, coma, and even death. The United Kingdom's Institute for Alcohol Studies in a June 2000 on-line piece

attributes the inducement of coma in an individual to a catastrophic fall in blood sugar. As a result, the body is unable to metabolize the consumed beverage's sugar content and the body enters into a state of neurological shock. Marc Galanter, MD, Merck contributor. *The Merck Manual—Second Home Edition Section 7. "Mental Health Disorders." Chapter 108. "Drug Use and Abuse."* Http://www.merck.com/pubs/mmanual_ home2/ sec07/ch108/ch108b.htm, United Kingdom's Institute for Alcohol Studies. June 2000. http://www.ias.org.uk/factsheets/medsoc3.htm.

221. *Memorial of the Cherokee Indians Living in North Carolina Praying the Payment of Their Claims, Agreeably to the 8th and 12th Articles of the Treaty of 1835.* Senate Doc. 408. 29th Congress, 1st Session. June 25th 1846. P. 13.

222. Mattie Russell. *William Holland Thomas, White Chief of the North Carolina Cherokee.* P. 41.

223. Letter from William Holland Thomas to H. P. King. January 1, 1840. WT 143.

224. Mattie Russell. *William Holland Thomas, White Chief of the North Carolina Cherokee.* Pp. 43–44.

225. *Memorial of the Cherokee Indians Living in North Carolina Praying the Payment of Their Claims, Agreeably to the 8th and 12th Articles of the Treaty of 1835.* Senate Doc. 408. 29th Congress, 1st Session. June 25th, 1846. P. 12.

226. Letter from William H. Thomas to H. P. King. August 20, 1839. WT 051. Letter from William H. Thomas to H. P. King. August 9, 1839. WT 047.

227. Letter from William H. Thomas to Colonel Nicholas Peck. November 25, 1839. WT 117.

228. Letter from William Holland Thomas to Commissioner T. Hartley Crawford. December 23, 1839. WT 140. Letter from William Holland Thomas to Commissioner T. Hartley Crawford. December 23, 1839. WT 141.

229. Letter from William Holland Thomas to Capt. C. O. Collins. July 17, 1839. WT 033. Letter from William Holland Thomas to Maj. Gen. Thomas S. Jesup. July 30, 1839. WT 039.

230. Given Welch's past experience with Thomas, it is likely that either or both clients mentioned knew about Thomas's prior dispute with breveted Brigadier General Wool and the contrasting influence Thomas had on the succeeding operational commander, Major General Scott.

231. Letter from William Holland Thomas to Commissioner T. Hartley Crawford. December 23, 1839. WT 140. Letter from William Holland Thomas to Commissioner T. Hartley Crawford. December 23, 1839. WT 141.

232. Letter from William Holland Thomas to Maj. Gen. Thomas S. Jesup. July 30, 1839 WT 039.

233. Ibid.

234. Letter from William Holland Thomas to John G. Dunlap. July 1839. WT 024. Letter from William Holland Thomas to John G. Dunlap. July 7, 1839. WT 019.

235. Letter from William Holland Thomas to Hyatt McBurney and Co. July 7, 1839. WT 023.

236. Letter from William Holland Thomas to Secretary of War Joel Poinsett. September 9, 1839. WT 057. Letter from William Holland Thomas to Silas Perry. September 28, 1838. WT 078. Letter from William Holland Thomas to T. Hartley Crawford. August 7, 1839. WT 048.

237. Letter from William Holland Thomas to Clarke, McTier and Company. November 23, 1839. WT 115.

238. Letter from William Holland Thomas to James Bryson. December 6, 1839. WT 125. Letter from William Holland Thomas to T. Hartley Crawford. November 12, 1839. WT 103.

239. The Diary of William Holland Thomas. 1840–1842. CM 001.

240. E. Stanley Godbold Jr. and Mattie U. Russell. *Confederate Colonel and Cherokee Chief: The Life of William Holland Thomas.* P. 53.

241. The Diary of William Holland Thomas. 1840–1842. CM 001. P. 6.

242. Letter from William Holland Thomas to Allen Fisher. November 22, 1839. WT 113.

243. The Diary of William Holland Thomas. 1840–1842. CM 001. P. 11. Letter from William Holland Thomas to H. P. King. October 21, 1839. WT 088.

244. Ibid.

245. Letter from William Holland Thomas to Dr. Isaac Heylin. November 22, 1839. WT 114.

246. The Diary of William Holland Thomas. 1840–1842. CM 001. P. 2.

247. According to his surviving travel diaries, William Thomas visited the Bank of Farmers and Merchants, the Bank of North Carolina, and the Bank of Baltimore. The Diary of William Holland Thomas. 1840–1842. CM 001. Pp. 10, 13.

248. *Schermerhorn Genealogy and Family Chronicles. Chapter II, "Descendants of Ryer Jacobse Schermerhorn (Part 3 of 4)."* The Schenectady Digital History Archive. http://www.schenectadyhistory.org/families/schermerhorn/chronicles/2c.html.

249. Letter from William Holland Thomas to Gen. B. S. Britain. December 17, 1839. WT 135.

250. Letter from William Holland Thomas to Rev. John F. Schermerhorn. July 13, 1839. WT 032. Letter from William Holland Thomas to Rev. John F. Schermerhorn. December 19, 1839. WT 137. Letter from William Holland Thomas to Rev. John F. Schermerhorn. July 31, 1839. WT 040. Letter from William Holland Thomas to J. K. Rogers. August 5, 1839. WT 044.

251. Letter Extract from William Holland Thomas to an Unnamed Store Clerk. June 4, 1839. WT 006.

252. Ibid.

253. Letter from William Holland Thomas to Secretary of War Joel Poinsett. September 17, 1839. WT 061. Letter from William Holland Thomas to John F. Gillespie. April 22, 1839. WTP 002. Letter from William Holland Thomas to T. Hartley Crawford. June 28, 1839. WT 017. Letter from William Holland Thomas to Hyatt MacBurney and Co. July 7th, 1839. WT 023.

254. Letter from William Holland Thomas to Secretary of War Joel Poinsett. September 9, 1839. WT 057.

255. *Memorial of the Cherokee Indians Living in North Carolina Praying the Payment of Their Claims, to the 8th and 12th Articles of the Treaty of 1835.* Senate Doc. 408. 29th Congress, 1st Session. June 25th, 1846. P. 14.

256. Ibid. P. 13. It is presumed, therefore, that the Senate either did not know or overlooked the fact that Thomas sometimes sold up to half a gallon of whisky to his Cherokee customers. Mattie Russell. *William Holland Thomas, White Chief of the North Carolina Cherokee.* Pp. 43–44.

257. President Andrew Jackson's 7th Annual Message to the United States Congress. December 7, 1835. *Messages and Papers of Andrew Jackson.*

258. Letter from William Holland Thomas to Preston Starritt. September 6, 1839. WT 055.

259. Letter from William Holland Thomas to J. W. King. December 13, 1839. WT 127.

260. Letter from William Holland Thomas to Felix Axeley. December 9, 1839. WT 126.

261. Letter from William Holland Thomas to the Cherokee at Quallatown. July 12, 1839. WT 030.

262. Letter from William Holland Thomas to Gideon F. Harris and Cherokee Friends. April 22, 1839. WT 003.

263. Letter from William Holland Thomas to the Cherokee at Quallatown. July 12, 1839. WT 030.

264. Letter from William Holland Thomas to Colonel Nicholas Peck. November 25, 1839. WT 117.

265. James Mooney. *History, Myths, and Sacred Formulas of the Cherokees.* P. 163.

266. Ibid.

267. Ibid. P. 173.

268. Letter from William Holland Thomas to John F. Gillespie. April 22, 1839. WT 002.

269. Ibid.

270. Letter from William Holland Thomas to Allen Fisher. June 28, 1839. WT 014.

271. Letter from William Holland Thomas to Price, Newlin Co., Philadelphia, PA. January 16, 1840. WT 154.

272. Letter from William Holland Thomas to Jas H. Bryson, Quallatown. November 22, 1839. WT 112.

273. Letter from William Holland Thomas to Price, Newlin Co., Philadelphia, PA. January 16, 1840. WT 154.

274. The Diary of William Holland Thomas, 1840–1842. CM 0001. P. 4.

275. Letter from William Holland Thomas to Jno. Gillespie, Athens, GA. December 2, 1839. WT 122.

276. Ibid.

277. Letter from William Holland Thomas to Nicholas Woodfin. June 6, 1839. WT 007.

278. E. Stanley Godbold Jr. and Mattie U. Russell. *Confederate Colonel and Cherokee Chief: The Life of William Holland Thomas.* P. 54.

279. The Diary of William Holland Thomas. 1842. CM 002. P. 7. E. Stanley Godbold Jr. and Mattie U. Russell. *Confederate Colonel and Cherokee Chief: The Life of William Holland Thomas.* Pp. 54–55.

280. E. Stanley Godbold Jr. and Mattie U. Russell. *Confederate Colonel and Cherokee Chief: The Life of William Holland Thomas.* P. 54.

281. Letter from William Holland Thomas to Capt. N. S. Jarrett, Franklin, N.C. November 11, 1839. WT 101.

282. "Memorial of the Wife and Child of Arkaooki (Reservee No. 229) circa 1835." WT 197. Letter from Nicholas Peck to William Holland Thomas. June 18, 1840. WTP 005. Document Certifying the Appointment of Power of Attorney Granted to William Holland Thomas. Harry Morris,

signatory. March 13, 1850. Document Certifying the Appointment of Power of Attorney to William Holland Thomas for the Cherokees of Paint Town, Wolf Town, and Bird Town. November 2, 1850. WTP 047. Document Certifying the Appointment of Power of Attorney to William Holland Thomas. Mason Barkley, signatory. March 22, 1851. WTP 051.

283. Letter from William Holland Thomas to John Gillespie. July 1, 1839. WT 021.

284. Neither Thomas nor Chief Yonaguska ever signed this treaty, but it remained an uncontested and binding article concerning the Cherokee Nation and the Eastern Band. Had Thomas pitched this idea prior to requesting a legal separation between the Eastern and Western Cherokee, his critics would have been able to utilize the maneuver to force the armed transport of the Qualla Boundary residents onto western reservations.

285. Letter from William Holland Thomas to the Cherokee of Quallatown. November 15, 1839. WT 107. Mattie Russell. *William Holland Thomas, White Chief of the North Carolina Cherokee.* P. 126.

286. Mattie Russell. *William Holland Thomas, White Chief of the North Carolina Cherokee.* P. 107.

287. Letter from William Holland Thomas to General Thomas Jessup. July 30, 1839. WT 039. Letter from William Holland Thomas to Captain C. O. Collins. July 17, 1839. WT 033.

288. Letter from William Holland Thomas to Dr. Isaac Heylin. November 22, 1839. WT 114.

289. Letter from William Holland Thomas to H. P. King. July 30, 1839. WT 038.

290. Ibid.

291. Letter from James Graham to William Holland Thomas. September 7, 1834. WT 175.

292. Letter from William Holland Thomas to James Porter. November 25, 1839. WT 118.

293. Letter from William Holland Thomas to J. W. King. June 28, 1839. WT 016.

294. Letter from William Holland Thomas to Ja. Perry. December 18, 1839. WT 133.

295. Ibid.

296. Letter from William Holland Thomas to H. P. King. July 30, 1839. WT 038.

297. Ibid.

298. Eventually, it was discovered that a long-held feeling of animosity towards the Ridge family and his associates (for having perpetrated the
grievous sin of, in essence, selling Cherokee land to non–Native Americans, carrying the penalty of death) had turned to bloody vengeance.
The bitter irony of the situation, however, was undoubtedly lost on
most of Thomas's governmental contemporaries, as Major Ridge several years prior had lobbied for the institution of such a statute within
the Cherokee Nation. The approved Cherokee National legislation was
called the Blood Law.

299. Letter from William Holland Thomas to Col. Nicholas S. Peck. November 25, 1839. WT 117.

300. Letter from William Holland Thomas to the Cherokee of Cheoih and
Valley River. October 25, 1839. WT 072.

301. Letter from William Holland Thomas to J. Porter. November 25, 1839.
WT 118.

302. Article of Agreement Between Betsy Woodward and Nicholas Peck.
December 21, 1838. WT 179.

303. Letter from William Holland Thomas to Col. Nicholas S. Peck. Novem-
ber 25, 1839. WT 117. Letter from William Holland Thomas to John
Gillespie. December 17, 1839. WT 131. Letter from William Holland
Thomas to T. Hartley Crawford. January 20, 1840. WT 158.

304. Letter from William Holland Thomas to Col. Nicholas S. Peck. November 25, 1839. WT 117.

305. Letter from William Holland Thomas to Allen Fisher. November 13,
1839. WT 104.

306. Letter from William Holland Thomas to John Schermerhorn. July 1,
1839. WT 018. Letter from William Holland Thomas to John Schermerhorn. July 13, 1839. WT 032. Letter from William Holland Thomas
to John Schermerhorn. July 31, 1839. WT 040. Letter from William
Holland Thomas to Reverend John Schermerhorn. August 15, 1839.
WT 050. Letter from William Holland Thomas to Reverend John
Schermerhorn. December 19, 1839. WT 137.

307. Letter from William Holland Thomas to the Postmaster of the City of
Utica, New York. September 5, 1839. WT 052.

308. Letter from William Holland Thomas to Reverend John F. Schermerhorn.
September 14, 1839. WT 059.

309. Ibid.

310. Letter from William Holland Thomas to Reverend John Schermerhorn. September 28, 1839. WT 079.

311. Ibid.

312. Letter from William Holland Thomas to Price, Newlin, and Company. July 24, 1839. WT 035.

313. Letter from William Holland Thomas to Maj. J. Porter. September 18, 1839. WT 062.

314. Ibid.

315. Letter from William Holland Thomas to the Cherokee of Quallatown. November 15, 1839. WT 107.

316. Letter from William Holland Thomas to Maj. Jas. P. H. Porter. September 18, 1839. WT 062.

317. Letter from William Holland Thomas to Preston Starritt. December 29, 1839. WT 138.

318. Mattie Russell. *William Holland Thomas, White Chief of the North Carolina Cherokee*. P. 105.

319. Ibid. Pp. 139–140.

320. Letter from William Holland Thomas to H. P. King. July 12, 1839. WT 029. Letter from William Holland Thomas to Temperance Thomas. July 12, 1839. WT 031. Letter from William Holland Thomas to H. P. King. July 12, 1839. WT 065.

321. Mattie Russell. *William Holland Thomas, White Chief of the North Carolina Cherokee*. P. 170.

322. Letter from William Holland Thomas to E. D. Cook. November 23, 1839. WT 116.

323. Yet, according to E. Stanley Godbold Jr. and Mattie Russell's *Confederate Colonel,* during the time William Thomas worked as a dispersing agent in Western North Carolina, he gathered $17,797.50 for his Cherokee clients and only managed to collect $401 for his own services. As a result of past client-agent agreements, Thomas may well have been paid his ten percent fee upon the claimants' receipt of their funds. In this light, Thomas would have been honoring the integrity of his agreements with both his clients and Indian Affairs. E. Stanley Godbold Jr. and Mattie U. Russell. *Confederate Colonel and Cherokee Chief: The Life of William Holland Thomas*. P. 43.

324. Letter from William Holland Thomas to H. P. King. January 17, 1840. WT 153.

325. Letter from William Holland Thomas to MacBurney Hyatt and Company. December 17, 1839. WT 132.

326. Letter from William Holland Thomas to Duff Green. December 30, 1844. WT 180. Letter from Ben and Duff Green to Honorable A. K. Parris. May 3, 1849 WTP 038. Letter from William Holland Thomas to Duff Green. September 19, 1844. CM 147.

327. Mattie Russell. *William Holland Thomas, White Chief of the North Carolina Cherokee.* P. 177.

328. Article of Agreement Between James Terrell and William Holland Thomas. January 6, 1854. WT 187.

329. Letter from William Holland Thomas to Allen Fisher and H. P. King. WT 084.

330. Letter from William Holland Thomas to James H. Bryson. December 6, 1839. WT 125.

331. Letter from William Holland Thomas to Allen Fisher. October 23, 1839. WT 089.

332. Letter from William Holland Thomas to H. P. King. January 1, 1840. WT 143.

333. Mattie Russell. *William Holland Thomas, White Chief of the North Carolina Cherokee.* Pp. 183–185, 174.

334. As William Thomas entered the 1840s and liquid funds became increasingly scarce, the man's staff members often went for months and even years without remuneration in cash. Mattie Russell. *William Holland Thomas, White Chief of the North Carolina Cherokee.* Pp. 183–185.

335. Ibid. Pp. 183–184.

336. Ibid. P. 175.

337. Ibid. P. 134.

338. E. Stanley Godbold Jr. and Mattie U. Russell. *Confederate Colonel and Cherokee Chief: The Life of William Holland Thomas.* P. 67. Mattie Russell. *William Holland Thomas, White Chief of the North Carolina Cherokee.* P. 177.

339. E. Stanley Godbold Jr. and Mattie U. Russell. *Confederate Colonel and Cherokee Chief: The Life of William Holland Thomas.* P. 65.

340. Mattie Russell. *William Holland Thomas, White Chief of the North Carolina Cherokee.* Pp. 138–139.

341. Ibid. John Finger goes as far as to claim the entire affair to be a Thomas-orchestrated scam to secure Cherokee land for the Eastern Band under their own name as a corporate entity. John R. Finger. *The Eastern Band of Cherokees, 1819–1900.* Pp. 44–45.

342. Although there was indeed interest in removing the Catawba to the

West, the idea was abandoned at the politically driven concept stage when Chief Thomas extended an offer of Eastern Band incorporation to the estranged native populace that had long before been mortal enemies. John R. Finger. *The Eastern Band of Cherokees, 1819–1900*. Pp. 47–48.

343. North Carolina Board of Agriculture. *North Carolina and Its Resources*. UNC. Pp. 122–123.

344. The proposed turnpike was to be named after the river Chief Yonaguska's people settled near when they broke from the Cherokee Nation. The name also held the additional distinction of an implied distancing of the North Carolina Cherokee (referred to as the Oconaluftee Indians prior to becoming the Eastern Band) from their Georgia counterparts.

345. Guion Griffis Johnson. *Antebellum North Carolina: A Social History*. UNC. P. 26.

346. North Carolina Board of Agriculture. *North Carolina and Its Resources*. UNC. P. 117.

347. Guion Griffis Johnson. *Antebellum North Carolina: A Social History*. UNC. Pp. 26–27.

348. Ibid.

349. Ibid.

350. Ibid.

351. Letter from William Holland Thomas to J. W. King. June 24, 1839. WT 124. Letter from William Holland Thomas to Preston Starritt. September 6, 1839. WT 055.

352. Letter from William Holland Thomas to H. P. King. September 28, 1839. WT 065.

353. Letter from William Holland Thomas to Nicholas Woodfin. June 6, 1839. WT 007. Letter from William Holland Thomas to Felix Axeley [Axley] December 9, 1839. WT 126. A Deed Between George Mingus, William H. Thomas and Allen Fisher. November 13, 1840. WT 190.

354. John R. Finger. *The Eastern Band of Cherokees, 1819–1900*. P. 43.

355. *Memorial of the Cherokee Indians Living in North Carolina Praying the Payment of Their Claims, Agreeably to the 8th and 12th Articles of the Treaty of 1835*. Senate Doc. 408. 29th Congress, 1st Session. June 25th, 1846.

356. Thomas Notes on the Census of 1840. WTP 002.

357. The Appointment North Carolina Cherokee Power of Attorney to William Holland Thomas January 9, 1845. WTP 018.

358. Letter from William Holland Thomas to E. B. Dudley. September 22, 1839. WT 070.

359. "A Resolution Relating to the Cherokee Indians Residing in North Carolina." January 9, 1845. WTP 022.

360. The Diary of William Holland Thomas, 1840–1842. CM 001. P. 4.

361. Letter from Duff Green to William Holland Thomas. December 13, 1844. WT 180.

362. Letter from James Guthrie to James Terrell. January 19, 1855. CM 146. Letter from James Terrell to the First Auditor of the Treasury. July 22, 1856. CM 41.

363. Mattie Russell. *William Holland Thomas, White Chief of the North Carolina Cherokee.* P. 122.

364. Ibid. P. 124.

365. Letter from William Holland Thomas to Major General Winfield Scott. July 5, 1844. WTP 011. Letter from William Holland Thomas to Brigadier General John Wool. November 30, 1839. WT 110.

366. E. Stanley Godbold Jr. and Mattie U. Russell. *Confederate Colonel and Cherokee Chief: The Life of William Holland Thomas.* P. 51.

367. According to Guion Griffis Johnson, every free white between the ages of eighteen and forty-five was required by law to take part in militia exercises at least twice a year. A number of William Thomas's collected letters indicate that he took the matter of militia mustering and equipment very seriously. Guion Griffis Johnson. *Antebellum North Carolina: A Social History.* Pp. 102–105.

368. Mattie Russell. *William Holland Thomas, White Chief of the North Carolina Cherokee.* P. 288.

369. Ibid. Pp. 282–283.

370. With the exception of a single term, William Thomas would remain on the Internal Improvements committee for the duration of his time in office. He served four times as the committee's chairman. Mattie Russell. *William Holland Thomas, White Chief of the North Carolina Cherokee.* P. 289.

371. Ibid.

372. E. Stanley Godbold Jr. and Mattie U. Russell. *Confederate Colonel and Cherokee Chief: The Life of William Holland Thomas.* P. 69.

373. "A Bill to Provide Relief for the Purchasers of the Cherokee Lands at the Sale of 1838, and Secure a Portion of the Debts to the State." North Carolina Assembly. 1848. WTP 167.

374. Mattie Russell. *William Holland Thomas, White Chief of the North Carolina Cherokee.* P. 283.

375. Ibid.

376. Ibid. P. 292.

377. North Carolina Board of Agriculture. *North Carolina and Its Resources.* UNC. P. 93.

378. Mattie Russell. *William Holland Thomas, White Chief of the North Carolina Cherokee.* P. 304.

379. Guion Griffis Johnson. *Antebellum North Carolina: A Social History.* UNC. P. 25.

380. North Carolina Board of Agriculture. *North Carolina and Its Resources.* UNC. P. 213.

381. John Inscoe. *Mountain Masters: Slavery and the Sectional Crisis in Western North Carolina.* P. 171.

382. A notion only realized in the twentieth century through President Franklin D. Roosevelt's extensive WPA Project.

383. Mattie Russell. *William Holland Thomas, White Chief of the North Carolina Cherokee.* P. 302.

384. There is some evidence to support a level of malfeasance on the part of State Senator William Holland Thomas in the creation of the region's rail lines. William Thomas and his staff often loaned out their stock of slaves for public works. According to John Inscoe in *Mountain Masters: Slavery and the Sectional Crisis in Western North Carolina,* at one point Johnson King was remunerated the sum of $5,000 for the use of his slave labor force in the construction of a courthouse. John Inscoe. *Mountain Masters: Slavery and the Sectional Crisis in Western North Carolina.* P. 78.

385. Frontis V. Johnston. *The Papers of Zebulon Baird Vance,* Volume I: *1843–1862.* P. xxii.

386. Ibid. P. 28.

387. E. Stanley Godbold Jr. and Mattie U. Russell. *Confederate Colonel and Cherokee Chief: The Life of William Holland Thomas.* P. 73.

388. Frontis V. Johnston. *The Papers of Zebulon Baird Vance,* Volume I: *1843–1862.* P. 67.

389. E. Stanley Godbold Jr. and Mattie U. Russell. *Confederate Colonel and Cherokee Chief: The Life of William Holland Thomas.* P. 73.

390. Frontis V. Johnston. *The Papers of Zebulon Baird Vance.* Volume I: *1843–1862.* P. 67n.

391. Letter from William Holland Thomas to MacBurney Hyatt. June 22, 1839. WT 011. Letter from William Holland Thomas to Dillard Love. June 30, 1839. WT 020. Letter from William Holland Thomas to James Robert Love. January 14, 1840. WT 152.

392. Letter from William Holland Thomas to Sarah Thomas. December 13, 1857. WT 182.

393. Mattie Russell. *William Holland Thomas, White Chief of the North Carolina Cherokee.* P. 267.

394. Ibid. P. 266.

395. Ibid.

396. Ibid. P. 268.

397. Guion Griffis Johnson. *Antebellum North Carolina: A Social History.* UNC. P. 203.

398. Mattie Russell. *William Holland Thomas, White Chief of the North Carolina Cherokee.* P. 269.

399. Ibid. P. 271.

400. Letter from William Holland Thomas to Sarah Love Thomas. December 13, 1857. WT 182.

401. Ibid. The alluded to gift of entertainment was a Washington-bought piano. Mattie Russell. *William Holland Thomas, White Chief of the North Carolina Cherokee.* P. 274.

402. Letter from William Holland Thomas to Governor Thomas Bragg. September 26, 1856. WTP 071. Letter from William Holland Thomas to the Honorable Alfred B. Greenwood. February 1, 1856. WTP 175.

403. Letter from William Holland Thomas to Governor Thomas Bragg of North Carolina. September 26, 1855. WTP 071.

404. "A Resolution Relating to the Cherokee Indians Residing in North Carolina." January 9, 1845. WTP 022.

405. Letter from William Holland Thomas to Governor Thomas Bragg of North Carolina. September 26, 1855. WTP 071.

406. "A Report of the Judiciary Committee on the North Carolina Cherokees, 1859." WTP 176.

407. Ibid.

408. Hinton Rowan Helper. *The Impending Crisis of the South: How to Meet It.* UNC. P. 205.

409. James M. McPherson. *Battle Cry of Freedom: The Civil War Era.* Pp. 199–200.

410. The Diary of William Holland Thomas. 1840–1842. CM 001. P. 70. John Inscoe. *Mountain Masters: Slavery and the Sectional Crisis in Western North Carolina*. P. 266.

411. John Inscoe. *Mountain Masters: Slavery and the Sectional Crisis in Western North Carolina*. P. 77.

412. Ibid. Pp. 70, 78.

413. Ibid. P. 90. James Mooney. *History, Myths, and Sacred Formulas of the Cherokees*. P. 163.

414. John Inscoe. *Mountain Masters: Slavery and the Sectional Crisis in Western North Carolina*. P. 90.

415. The Diary of William Holland Thomas. 1840–1842. CM 001. P. 4.

416. John Inscoe. *Mountain Masters: Slavery and the Sectional Crisis in Western North Carolina*. P. 90.

417. Ibid. P. 98.

418. Mattie Russell. *William Holland Thomas, White Chief of the North Carolina Cherokee*. P. 233.

419. E. Stanley Godbold Jr. and Mattie U. Russell. *Confederate Colonel and Cherokee Chief: The Life of William Holland Thomas*. P. 73.

420. According to Hinton Helper, by 1850 the populace of the northern states totaled approximately 13,434,922, with the combined slave, freeman, and white populace of the south tallying at 9,612,979. Hinton Rowan Helper. *The Impending Crisis of the South: How to Meet It*. UNC. P. 144.

421. Mattie Russell. *William Holland Thomas, White Chief of the North Carolina Cherokee*. P. 324.

422. Ibid. P. 325.

423. Ibid. P. 328.

424. Ibid.

425. E. Stanley Godbold Jr. and Mattie U. Russell. *Confederate Colonel and Cherokee Chief: The Life of William Holland Thomas*. P. 91.

426. Hinton Rowan Helper. *The Impending Crisis of The South: How to Meet It*. UNC.

427. Frontis V. Johnston. *The Papers of Zebulon Baird Vance*, Volume I: *1843–1862*. Pp. 61n, 84.

428. E. Stanley Godbold Jr. and Mattie U. Russell. *Confederate Colonel and Cherokee Chief: The Life of William Holland Thomas*. Pp. 92–93.

429. Frontis V. Johnston. *The Papers of Zebulon Baird Vance*, Volume I: *1843–1862*. P. 75.

430. Ibid.

431. Mattie Russell. *William Holland Thomas, White Chief of the North Carolina Cherokee.* P. 330.
432. Ibid. P. 292.
433. Ibid.
434. Ibid. P. 294.
435. Frontis V. Johnston. *The Papers of Zebulon Baird Vance*, Volume I: *1843–1862.* P. 87.
436. William Holland Thomas likely nicknamed his son Junaluska in deference towards his Cherokee brethren who long revered the Cherokee National who had helped turn the tide against the Creek at the now infamous Battle of Horseshoe Bend.
437. Mattie Russell. *William Holland Thomas, White Chief of the North Carolina Cherokee.* P. 276.
438. E. Stanley Godbold Jr. and Mattie U. Russell. *Confederate Colonel and Cherokee Chief: The Life of William Holland Thomas.* Pp. 83–84.
439. The hiring of James Terrell a decade prior to take care of the Qualla store and the Eastern Band had actually freed William Thomas from having to deal with much of the day-to-day business of running the Eastern Band to better service his constituents' political and legal needs.
440. Frontis V. Johnston. *The Papers of Zebulon Baird Vance*, Volume I: *1843–1862.* P. 80.
441. Ibid. P. 75.
442. While William Thomas would have to wait several more decades for his Western North Carolina dreams to see partial fruition, Zebulon Vance's views were Pyrrhicly on target. In May 1861 the Confederate States of America transferred their capital to the northerly lying city of Richmond, Virginia.
443. The meeting of the convention was in actuality a formality of democratic procedures, allowing time for the state to set up a new provisional government and more closely assess their level of commitment to the new Confederate States of America.
444. Jack Clairborne and William Price, eds. *Discovering North Carolina: A Tar Heel Reader.* P. 44.
445. Mattie Russell. *William Holland Thomas, White Chief of the North Carolina Cherokee.* P. 337.
446. Ibid. P. 336.
447. E. Stanley Godbold Jr. and Mattie U. Russell. *Confederate Colonel and Cherokee Chief: The Life of William Holland Thomas.* P. 88.

448. Like his railroad and roadway projects in the State Senate, however, a final resolution with the United States government on the matter was consistently sidetracked by the disappearance of appropriable congressional funds, sporadic political in-fighting, suddenly vacant positions in key administrative offices, and the increasingly hostile southern climate stemming from the secessionist crisis.

449. Letter from William Thomas to Thomas Bragg. September 26, 1855. WTP 071. E. Stanley Godbold Jr. and Mattie U. Russell. *Confederate Colonel and Cherokee Chief: The Life of William Holland Thomas.* Pp. 58–59. William Thomas had been advocating the assertion of his Eastern Band brethren's rights as United States citizens for decades, but, disregarding their taxable status (to which William Thomas himself annually tended from his own pocket), there is little direct evidence to support their actual testing/full utilization of these rights before local authorities (e.g., voting or legal representation in criminal proceedings).

450. Frontis V. Johnston. *The Papers of Zebulon Baird Vance*, Volume I: *1843–1862.* P. 216.

451. E. Stanley Godbold Jr. and Mattie U. Russell. *Confederate Colonel and Cherokee Chief: The Life of William Holland Thomas.* Pp. 99–100.

452. Mattie Russell. *William Holland Thomas, White Chief of the North Carolina Cherokee.* P. 339. Ironically, in a previous capacity, as President Franklin Pierce's Secretary of War, Jefferson Davis had shown little sympathy for the plight of Native Americans and oversaw a large portion of the removal of the Cherokee from Georgia.

453. John R. Finger. *The Eastern Band of Cherokees, 1819–1900.* P. 83.

454. Period sources are vague as to the sequence of events surrounding the initial meeting between Major Washington Morgan and William Thomas. As John R. Finger asserts in *The Eastern Band of Cherokees, 1819–1900,* William Thomas was visiting Richmond in early 1862. James Mooney lists the encounter as "early in 1862" with the Cherokee enrolling in military service with Thomas alone. According to his Confederate personnel records, William Thomas was inducted into Confederate Service on April 9th, 1862. Consequently, the record is also vague as to the exact date Major Morgan assumed command of the unit. John R. Finger. *The Eastern Band of Cherokees, 1819–1900.* Pp. 83–84. James Mooney. *History, Myths, and Sacred Formulas of the Cherokees.* P. 169. Colonel William Holland Thomas Personnel Record, National Archives.

455. James Mooney. *History, Myths, and Sacred Formulas of the Cherokees.* P. 168.

456. Ibid. P. 169.

457. Some authors, like James Mooney, have claimed that William Thomas feared the reckless reputation that seemed to follow the Confederate major as the discouraging factor of the 1862 offer of enlistment. Far more likely, however, is the rationale that Thomas could return the offer with one which favored his own continued influence, the integrity of the Eastern Band, *and* the relative protection of his warriors under his own command. Ibid.

458. Ibid.

459. Ibid. Pp. 168–169.

460. John R. Finger. *The Eastern Band of Cherokees, 1819–1900.* P. 84.

461. Aside from his date of induction, William Thomas's personnel record offers few personal facts, but the document does note his formal occupation as "merchant" and his residence as Jackson County (given Temperance and Sarah's continued maintenance of their Stekoa Fields home, this may be explained as a result of either a redistricted county line or a plot of land Thomas utilized as a legal address to continue to service both Haywood *and* Jackson counties). Colonel William Holland Thomas Personnel Record. National Archives.

462. James Mooney. *History, Myths, and Sacred Formulas of the Cherokees* P. 170.

463. Mattie Russell. *William Holland Thomas, White Chief of the North Carolina Cherokee.* P. 353.

464. It is unlikely this meant that the original company's members would be unable to transfer into the other company, but rather the distinction Thomas made served to reinforce the integral importance of the region's southern Appalachian communities.

465. Astoogatogeh was the grandson of the revered warrior Junaluska.

466. Mattie Russell. *William Holland Thomas, White Chief of the North Carolina Cherokee.* P. 357.

467. E. Stanley Godbold Jr. and Mattie U. Russell. *Confederate Colonel and Cherokee Chief: The Life of William Holland Thomas.* P. 101.

468. John R. Finger. *The Eastern Band of Cherokees, 1819–1900.* P. 85.

469. Mattie Russell. *William Holland Thomas, White Chief of the North Carolina Cherokee.* P. 355–356.

470. Ibid. P. 356.

471. Noel C. Fisher. *War at Every Door: Partisan Politics and Guerrilla Violence in East Tennessee, 1860–1869.* P. 6. Florette Henri. *Southern Indians and Ben Hawkins.* P. 53.

472. W. Todd Groce. *Mountain Rebels: East Tennessee Confederates and the Civil War, 1860–1870*. P. 6.

473. Mattie Russell. *William Holland Thomas, White Chief of the North Carolina Cherokee*. P. 358.

474. E. Stanley Godbold Jr. and Mattie U. Russell. *Confederate Colonel and Cherokee Chief: The Life of William Holland Thomas*. P. 102.

475. One such businessman, Colonel John C. Vaughn, had actually fired one of the posted artillery batteries against Fort Sumter, then had to race home to place his vote for secession. His vote cast, Vaughn then returned to Confederate military service, raised a group of Tennessean volunteers, and led them in the First Battle of Manassas. W. Todd Groce. *Mountain Rebels: East Tennessee Confederates and the Civil War, 1860–1870*. P. 68.

476. Ibid. P. 77.

477. Captain William Holland Thomas Hand Written Supply Requisition. May 6, 1862. National Archives.

478. Captain William Holland Thomas Munitions, Ammunition and Supply Requisitions. May 27, 1862. National Archives.

479. John R. Finger. *The Eastern Band of Cherokees, 1819–1900*. P. 85.

480. Ibid.

481. Ibid. Pp. 85–86.

482. With very few rules, the game was often played competitively within the tribe. James Mooney *History, Myths, and Sacred Formulas of the Cherokees*. P. 170.

483. Mattie Russell. *William Holland Thomas, White Chief of the North Carolina Cherokee*. P. 361.

484. Noel C. Fisher. *War at Every Door: Partisan Politics and Guerrilla Violence in East Tennessee, 1860–1869*. P. 35.

485. John R. Finger. *The Eastern Band of Cherokees, 1819–1900*. P. 86.

486. Ibid.

487. E. Stanley Godbold Jr. and Mattie U. Russell. *Confederate Colonel and Cherokee Chief: The Life of William Holland Thomas*. P. 103.

488. *Official Records*. Series I. Volume XXVIII. Operations in Kentucky, Middle and East Tennessee, North Alabama, and Southwest Virginia, June 10–October 31, 1862. Part II. Chapter XXVIII. "Morgan's First Kentucky Raid, Perryville Campaign." P. 716.

489. Mattie Russell. *William Holland Thomas, White Chief of the North Carolina Cherokee*. P. 361.

490. Walter Clark, ed. *Histories of Several Regiments and Battalions from North Carolina in the Great War 1861–1865*. Volume III. P. 732.
491. Ibid.
492. Ibid.
493. Mattie Russell. *William Holland Thomas, White Chief of the North Carolina Cherokee*. P. 365.
494. John R. Finger. *The Eastern Band of Cherokees, 1819–1900*. P. 86.
495. James Mooney. *History, Myths, and Sacred Formulas of the Cherokees*. P. 170.
496. John R. Finger. *The Eastern Band of Cherokees, 1819–1900*. P. 93.
497. Mattie Russell. *William Holland Thomas, White Chief of the North Carolina Cherokee*. P. 359. James Terrell's postwar comments are rather curious, as there were no later reported reoccurrences of the conduct at Baptist Gap. It is likely that, given the later business difficulties he and William Thomas would suffer, James Terrell either carefully concealed his personal views on the Cherokee to work under Thomas, grew somewhat bitter upon reflection of his involvement in ministering to the Eastern Band, or participated in a combination of both.
498. Colonel William Holland Thomas Personnel Record. National Archives.
499. Colonel William Holland Thomas Personnel Record. National Archives.
500. The sappers, and miners were officially added to the unit's complement in 1863 with Levi's Light Battery of artillery.
501. Walter Clark, ed. *Histories of Several Regiments and Battalions from North Carolina in the Great War 1861–1865*. Volume III. P. 730.
502. Mattie Russell asserts in her research that the Thomas Legion eventually came to hold as many as 2,083 officers and men. Yet, the National Parks Service holds only 1,770 personnel records for the "infantry regiment, Thomas's North Carolina Legion." This discrepancy can be accounted for given the fluid nature of battlefield command, Thomas's later losses of command during several court-martial proceedings, and the loss of several records to fire and enemy. Mattie Russell. *William Holland Thomas, White Chief of the North Carolina Cherokee*. P. 367. National Park Service. *Civil War Soldiers and Sailors System*. http://www.itd.nps.gov/cwss/template.cfm?unitcode=CNCTHOMRI&unitname=Infantry%20Regiment%2C%20Thomas%27%20North%20Carolina%20Legion.
503. *Southern Historical Society Papers*. Volume I. P. 295. *"A Modern Horatius."*
504. Ibid.
505. Ibid. P. 296.

506. Walter Clark, ed. *Histories of Several Regiments and Battalions from North Carolina in the Great War 1861–1865.* Volume III. Pp. 735–736.

507. After a long period of indecisiveness, on October 28th, 1861, Principal Chief John Ross finally acceded to an alliance between the Cherokee Nation and the Confederacy, but before formative measures could be taken, the Cherokee National was abducted by Union troops and conveyed to Washington, D.C. In his stead, Stand Watie assumed command of the Cherokee Nation, quickly marshaled his supporters, and led his Cherokee volunteers unwaveringly against the enemy. By the time Colonel Thomas had been granted command of the legion, the Cherokee Nation's actions had already attracted national attention and positive propagandist permanence offered by the southern press. Thomas Osmond Summers, ed. *The Confederate States Almanac for the Year of Our Lord 1862. Being the Second After Bissextile, or Leap Year, the Eighty-sixth of American Independence, and the Second of the Confederate States.*

508. Stanley Godbold Jr. and Mattie U. Russell. *Confederate Colonel and Cherokee Chief: The Life of William Holland Thomas.* P. 361.

509. Mattie Russell. *William Holland Thomas, White Chief of the North Carolina Cherokee.* Pp. 368–370.

510. E. Stanley Godbold Jr. and Mattie U. Russell. *Confederate Colonel and Cherokee Chief: The Life of William Holland Thomas.* P. 110.

511. Ibid. P. 110. Although originally considered a major component in the Confederacy's war effort, by the time Colonel Thomas offered his unsolicited ideas the Kentucky salt facility was actually a declining interest for the beleaguered southern cause.

512. Frontis V. Johnston. *The Papers of Zebulon Baird Vance,* Volume I, *1843–1862.* Pp. 385–386.

513. Like William Thomas and his Mountain region neighbors, Governor Vance could trace much of America's history through his ancestors. Unlike Richard Thomas, however, Vance's progenitors had a greater scope of options and broader experiences. His grandfather Colonel David Vance served under General George Washington at Valley Forge, Brandywine, and Monmouth. Zebulon's own father, David Vance, rose to the rank of captain in the War of 1812. His father's brother, Robert B. Vance, and years later Zebulon's brother of the same name, Robert Brank Vance, had used their family's acquired influence to gain seats in the United States Congress. http://statelibrary.dcr.state.nc.us/nc/bio/public/vance.htm, http://bioguide.congress.gov/scripts/biodisplay.pl?

index=V000018, http://bioguide.congress.gov/scripts/biodisplay.pl?index=V000019.

514. http://statelibrary.dcr.state.nc.us/nc/bio/public/vance.htm. Frontis V. Johnston. *The Papers of Zebulon Baird Vance*, Volume I: *1843–1862*. Pp. 7–8.

515. Frontis V. Johnston. *The Papers of Zebulon Baird Vance*, Volume I: *1843–1862*. Pp. 3–6.

516. http://bioguide.congress.gov/scripts/biodisplay.pl?index=V000021.

517. Mattie Russell. *William Holland Thomas, White Chief of the North Carolina Cherokee*. Pp. 327, 362.

518. For information regarding North Carolina's period fishing industry, see the 1896 North Carolina Board of Agriculture's report *North Carolina and Its Resources*. UNC. Pp. 141–147. For agricultural resources, see *North Carolina and Its Resources*. UNC. Pp. 155–186.

519. A full list and description of North Carolina's regional geological morphology and locations of discovered period mining assets can be found in the 1896 North Carolina Board of Agriculture's report *North Carolina and Its Resources*. UNC. Pp. 73–117.

520. Beside the region's antiquated agrarian and fishing industries, antebellum North Carolina had little to offer in industry and refinery. However, evidence of a sudden surge in postwar industries throughout the occupied state can be seen in the 1896 North Carolina Board of Agriculture's report *North Carolina and Its Resources*. UNC. Pp. 187–213.

521. Frontis V. Johnston. *The Papers of Zebulon Baird Vance*, Volume I: *1843–1862*. P. 388.

522. Mattie Russell. *William Holland Thomas, White Chief of the North Carolina Cherokee*. P. 370.

523. Ibid.

524. The term "Tory" appears throughout numerous southern-leaning volumes published during and after the War of the Rebellion, characterizing the southern dissenters against secession and Unionist insurgents as second-generation allies of America's long-standing enemy, the British Crown.

525. Much like the southern guerrilla patriots of the American Revolution, these paramilitary factions largely traveled light, struck hard at poorly defended targets of opportunity, and retreated to territory which would give them safe haven from the enemy. Unlike the Francis Marion, Thomas Sumter, and Andrew Pickins forces, these factions rarely altered their rally points and seldom ventured outside their home territory.

They were thus easy prey for skilled trackers and a comparably armed Confederate hunting party.

526. E. Stanley Godbold Jr. and Mattie U. Russell. *Confederate Colonel and Cherokee Chief: The Life of William Holland Thomas.* P. 91.

527. General Jackson was granted the memorable name "Mudwall" to better distinguish him from the already legendary Confederate general Thomas Jonathan "Stonewall" Jackson, tearing through Union lines throughout the Virginia theater of battle.

528. E. Stanley Godbold Jr. and Mattie U. Russell. *Confederate Colonel and Cherokee Chief: The Life of William Holland Thomas.* Pp. 113–115.

529. Ibid. P. 113.

530. Ibid. Pp. 114–115.

531. E. Stanley Godbold Jr. and Mattie U. Russell. *Confederate Colonel and Cherokee Chief: The Life of William Holland Thomas.* P. 115. During the invasion, a number of the Thomas Legion's complement (Lieutenant Colonel William C. Walker's men) were reportedly encamped at Greenville, Tennessee. They were quickly attached to several nearby commands. Walter Clark, ed. *Histories of Several Regiments and Battalions from North Carolina in the Great War 1861–1865.* Volume III. P. 737.

532. Ibid.

533. E. Stanley Godbold Jr. and Mattie U. Russell. *Confederate Colonel and Cherokee Chief: The Life of William Holland Thomas.* P. 115.

534. Walter Clark, ed. *Histories of Several Regiments and Battalions from North Carolina in the Great War 1861–1865.* Volume III. P. 738.

535. Ibid. P. 739.

536. Ibid.

537. Ibid.

538. Ibid. P. 745.

539. Ibid. P. 736.

540. Ibid.

541. Ibid. P. 739.

542. Ibid. P. 745.

543. According to W. Todd Groce, General Vaughn had fired one of the first shots of Fort Sumter, participated in the Confederate victory at the Battle of First Manassas, raised the first Confederate regiment in the East Tennessee region, and served as the Third Tennessee commander of Lieutenant General Longstreet's Corps. W. Todd Groce. *Mountain Rebels: East Tennessee Confederates and the Civil War, 1860–1870.* Pp. 60, 68.

544. Mattie Russell. *William Holland Thomas, White Chief of the North Carolina Cherokee.* Pp. 380–381.

545. Sean Michael O'Brien. *Mountain Partisans: Guerrilla Warfare in the Southern Appalachians, 1861–1865.* P. 33. John R. Finger. *The Eastern Band of Cherokees, 1819–1900.* Pp. 87–88.

546. *Official Records.* Series I. Volume XXXI. Operations in Kentucky, Southwest Virginia, Tennessee, Mississippi, North Alabama, North Georgia, October 20–December 31, 1863. Part I. Chapter XLIII. "Skirmish in Cherokee County, N.C." P. 235.

547. Ibid.

548. Ibid.

549. Ibid.

550. John R. Finger. *The Eastern Band of Cherokees, 1819–1900.* P. 94.

551. Sean Michael O'Brien. *Mountain Partisans: Guerrilla Warfare in the Southern Appalachians, 1861–1865.* P. 27.

552. *Official Records.* Series I. Volume XXXI. Operations in Kentucky, Southwest Virginia, Tennessee, Mississippi, North Alabama, North Georgia, October 20–December 31, 1863. Part I. Chapter XLIII. "Skirmish in Cherokee County, N.C." Pp. 438–440.

553. On one occasion, Colonel William J. Palmer was reportedly captured behind enemy lines in civilian clothes, trying to ascertain troop movements for McClellan's army. Mistaken for a civilian, he was promptly conducted to Richmond's Castle Thunder and was later exchanged for a southern civilian prisoner. http://www.swcivilwar.com/ 15PalmerBiography.html.

554. *Official Records.* Series I. Volume XXXI. Operations in Kentucky, Southwest Virginia, Tennessee, Mississippi, North Alabama, North Georgia, October 20–December 31, 1863. Part I. Chapter XLIII. "Skirmish in Cherokee County, N.C." P. 438.

555. Ibid. P. 439.

556. Ibid.

557. Ibid.

558. Ibid.

559. Sean Michael O'Brien. *Mountain Partisans: Guerrilla Warfare in the Southern Appalachians, 1861–1865.* P. 31.

560. Noel C. Fisher. *War at Every Door: Partisan Politics and Guerrilla Violence in East Tennessee, 1860–1869.* P. 103.

561. *Official Records.* Series I. Volume XXXI. Operations in Kentucky, Southwest Virginia, Tennessee, Mississippi, North Alabama, North Georgia,

October 20–December 31, 1863. Part I. Chapter XLIII. "Skirmish in Cherokee County, N.C." P. 439.

562. Sean Michael O'Brien. *Mountain Partisans: Guerrilla Warfare in the Southern Appalachians, 1861–1865.* P. 27.

563. Ibid. P. 28.

564. Ibid. P. 26.

565. Virgil Carrington Jones. *Grey Ghosts and Rebel Raiders.* P. 209.

566. Mattie Russell. *William Holland Thomas, White Chief of the North Carolina Cherokee.* P. 398.

567. James Mooney. *History, Myths, and Sacred Formulas of the Cherokees.* P. 171.

568. Sean Michael O'Brien. *Mountain Partisans: Guerrilla Warfare in the Southern Appalachians, 1861–1865.* P. 30.

569. Mattie Russell. *William Holland Thomas, White Chief of the North Carolina Cherokee.* P. 385.

570. Sean Michael O'Brien. *Mountain Partisans: Guerrilla Warfare in the Southern Appalachians, 1861–1865.* P. 28.

571. Mattie Russell. *William Holland Thomas, White Chief of the North Carolina Cherokee.* P. 386.

572. Ibid. Pp. 387–388.

573. Similar to Colonel Thomas's Civil War beginnings, Robert Brank Vance's entry in military service was through the creation of his own unit, the Buncombe Life Guards. Unlike Colonel Thomas, however, Robert Vance had managed to fully utilize his family's personal and political resources to rapidly rise through the ranks and, by 1863, command the Western District of North Carolina. John Wheeler. *Reminiscence and Memoirs of North Carolina and Eminent North Carolinians.* P. 68. *Official Records.* Series I. Volume XXXI. Operations in Kentucky, Southwest Virginia, Tennessee, Mississippi, North Alabama, North Georgia, October 20–December 31, 1863. Part III. Chapter XLIII. P. 711.

574. John H. Wheeler. *Reminiscence and Memoirs of North Carolina and Eminent North Carolinians.* P. 69. http://www.researchonline.net/nccw/bios/ wheeler.htm#p69.

575. Mattie Russell. *William Holland Thomas, White Chief of the North Carolina Cherokee.* P. 382.

576. John Wheeler. *Reminiscence and Memoirs of North Carolina and Eminent North Carolinians.* P. 69. http://www.researchonline.net/nccw/bios/ wheeler.htm#p69.

577. Mattie Russell. *William Holland Thomas, White Chief of the North Carolina Cherokee.* P. 382.

578. There is some disagreement among secondary sources regarding the number of Union wagons spotted by Brigadier General Vance. Mattie Russell claims seventeen, but John Inscoe and Gordon McKinney claim twenty-eight. Since Inscoe and McKinney misidentified Lieutenant Colonel James L. Henry as "Colonel James Henry" in the same context, seventeen seems the likelier number. Ibid. John Inscoe and Gordon McKinney. *The Heart of Confederate Appalachia: Western North Carolina in the Civil War.* P. 132.

579. Mattie Russell. *William Holland Thomas, White Chief of the North Carolina Cherokee.* P. 383.

580. Ibid.

581. Ibid.

582. Ibid. P. 384.

583. John Wheeler. *Reminiscence and Memoirs of North Carolina and Eminent North Carolinians.* P. 68. http://www.researchonline.net/nccw/bios/wheeler.htm#p68.

584. *Official Records.* Series I. Volume XXXII. Operations in Kentucky, Middle and East Tennessee, North Alabama, and Southwest Virginia, June 10–October 31, 1862. Part II. P. 76.

585. Ibid.

586. Ibid.

587. Sean Michael O'Brien. *Mountain Partisans: Guerrilla Warfare in the Southern Appalachians, 1861–1865.* P. 31.

588. Lieutenant Colonel Walker had been sent home to recuperate from wounds sustained in the field. E. Stanley Godbold Jr. and Mattie U. Russell. *Confederate Colonel and Cherokee Chief: The Life of William Holland Thomas.* P. 118.

589. Mattie Russell. *William Holland Thomas, White Chief of the North Carolina Cherokee.* Pp. 384–385.

590. Vicki Rozema. *Footsteps of the Cherokees: A Guide to the Eastern Homelands of the Cherokee Nation.* Pp. 59–60.

591. Sean Michael O'Brien. *Mountain Partisans: Guerrilla Warfare in the Southern Appalachians, 1861–1865.* P. 31. Apparently, Dr. Hilliard was widely known throughout Western North Carolina for having dueled with *Spectator* editor John D. Hyman in 1855 over the poor status of

regional mail service (Hilliard was the Postmaster of the time). http://www.ls.net/~newriver/nc/wncduel.htm. http://toto.lib.unca.edu/ findingaids/mss/sherrills_inn/clarke_history.htm.

592. Sean Michael O'Brien. *Mountain Partisans: Guerrilla Warfare in the Southern Appalachians, 1861–1865.* P. 31.

593. *Official Records.* Series I. Volume XXXII. Operations in Kentucky, Middle and East Tennessee, North Alabama, and Southwest Virginia, June 10–October 31, 1862. Part II. P. 712.

594. Ibid. P. 811.

595. Ibid. P. 853.

596. Ibid. Pp. 853–854.

597. By May 1864, Colonel Love was being ordered to return to Asheville, North Carolina, collect approximately four hundred soldiers, and race to join the main Confederate line moving through Virginia's Shenandoah Valley, before finally being allowed to return home for good in December 1864. In October 1864 Major Stringfield had likewise found his way to Colonel Thomas's Quallatown headquarters. Ibid. P. 856. Sean Michael O'Brien. *Mountain Partisans: Guerrilla Warfare in the Southern Appalachians, 1861–1865.* Pp. 28, 32.

598. *Official Records.* Series I. Volume XXXII. Operations in Kentucky, Middle and East Tennessee, North Alabama, and Southwest Virginia, June 10–October 31, 1862. Part II. P. 854.

599. Sean Michael O'Brien. *Mountain Partisans: Guerrilla Warfare in the Southern Appalachians, 1861–1865.* P. 31.

600. Mattie Russell. *William Holland Thomas, White Chief of the North Carolina Cherokee.* Pp. 388–389.

601. Ibid. P. 390.

602. Sean Michael O'Brien. *Mountain Partisans: Guerrilla Warfare in the Southern Appalachians, 1861–1865.* P. 31.

603. Thomas Legion Special Requisition. September 3rd, 1864. National Archives.

604. According to Mattie Russell, Colonel Thomas's attempt to quell dissension between southern Unionists and ardent Confederates was "myopic." Yet, it can be argued that Colonel Thomas was once again looking beyond his immediate comforts in favor of postwar regional stability. Mattie Russell. *William Holland Thomas, White Chief of the North Carolina Cherokee.* P. 392.

605. *A Century of Lawmakers, 1774–1873* (Item 114 of 500), Volume 4: *Journal*

of the Congress of the Confederate States of America, 1861–1865. Wednesday May 18, 1864. AM. P. 53. http://lcweb2.loc.gov/cgi_bin/query/D?hlaw: 4:./temp/~ammem_8HVc:: *A Century of Lawmakers, 1774–1873* (Item 2 of 100), Volume 4: *Journal of the Congress of the Confederate States of America, 1861–1865.* Wednesday, December 21, 1864. AM. http://lcweb2.loc. gov/cgi_bin/query/D?hlaw:2:./temp/~ammem_8HVc::. *Southern Historical Society Papers.* Pp. 34, 2588.

606. Letter clarifying the duties of Colonel William Holland Thomas. Signed by Confederate States of America War Department Adjutant and Inspector General's Office. Richmond, Va. November 9, 1864. National Archives.

607. W. Buck Yearns and John G. Barrett. *North Carolina Civil War Documentary.* Pp. 165, 179–180, 209–212, 214.

608. Colonel William Holland Thomas personnel record. National Archives Collection.

609. E. Stanley Godbold Jr. and Mattie U. Russell. *Confederate Colonel and Cherokee Chief: The Life of William Holland Thomas.* P. 125.

610. Mattie Russell. *William Holland Thomas, White Chief of the North Carolina Cherokee.* P. 395.

611. E. Stanley Godbold Jr. and Mattie U. Russell. *Confederate Colonel and Cherokee Chief: The Life of William Holland Thomas.* P. 127.

612. John R. Finger. *The Eastern Band of Cherokees, 1819–1900.* P. 88.

613. Vicki Rozema. *Footsteps of the Cherokees: A Guide to the Eastern Homelands of the Cherokee Nation.* P. 185.

614. Mattie Russell. *William Holland Thomas, White Chief of the North Carolina Cherokee.* P. 396.

615. Walter Clark, ed. *Histories of Several Regiments and Battalions from North Carolina in the Great War 1861–1865.* Volume III. P. 758.

616. Ibid. P. 759.

617. Ibid.

618. Ibid.

619. Vicki Rozema. *Footsteps of the Cherokees: A Guide to the Eastern Homelands of the Cherokee Nation.* P. 207.

620. E. Stanley Godbold Jr. and Mattie U. Russell. *Confederate Colonel and Cherokee Chief: The Life of William Holland Thomas.* P. 127.

621. Walter Clark, ed. *Histories of Several Regiments and Battalions from North Carolina in the Great War 1861–1865.* Volume III. P. 758.

622. *Operational Records.* Chapter LVIII, "North and South East Virginia, North Carolina." P. 195.

623. Sean Michael O'Brien. *Mountain Partisans: Guerrilla Warfare in the Southern Appalachians, 1861–1865.* P. 35.

624. Ibid.

625. For the sake of clarity of command and as a demonstration of the sovereign nature of Eastern Band society, the Cherokee warriors guarding Chief William Thomas remained militarily apart from their Confederate-enrolled brethren. The Cherokee were not Confederate soldiers.

626. Sean Michael O'Brien. *Mountain Partisans: Guerrilla Warfare in the Southern Appalachians, 1861–1865.* P. 35.

627. Mattie Russell. *William Holland Thomas, White Chief of the North Carolina Cherokee.* P. i.

628. According to Union wartime policy, as a landowner and rebel leader Colonel William Holland needed to file a plea of forgiveness to the President of the United States, await a verdict to accept his penitence, and publicly swear an oath of loyalty to the United States.

629. John Inscoe. *Mountain Masters: Slavery and the Sectional Crisis in Western North Carolina.* P. 266.

630. According to John Inscoe, at the time of the secessionist crisis Colonel Thomas held reportedly an amassed real estate holding valued at $22,725. John Inscoe. *Mountain Masters: Slavery and the Sectional Crisis in Western North Carolina.* P. 266.

631. E. Stanley Godbold Jr. and Mattie U. Russell. *Confederate Colonel and Cherokee Chief: The Life of William Holland Thomas.* P. 130.

632. Ibid.

633. Ibid.

634. According to E. Stanley Godbold Jr. and Mattie Russell, in 1867 Colonel Thomas hired on his old slave and adjutant, Major Bartlett Wells, at a rate of ten dollars a month. Ibid.

635. James Mooney. *History, Myths, and Sacred Formulas of the Cherokees.* P. 172.

636. According to the United States Center for Disease Control, Small Pox has

an incubation period during which people do not have any symptoms and may feel fine. This incubation period averages about 12 to 14 days but can range from 7 to 17 days. During this time, people are not contagious.

The first symptoms of smallpox include fever, malaise, head and body aches, and sometimes vomiting. The fever is usually high, in the range of 101 to 104 degrees Fahrenheit. At this time, people are usually too sick to carry on their normal activities. This is called the prodrome phase and may last for 2 to 4 days.

http://www.bt.cdc.gov/agent/smallpox/overview/disease_facts.asp.

637. Letter from William Holland Thomas to Dr. Jno. Mingus. November 20, 1865. CM 150.

638. E. Stanley Godbold Jr. and Mattie U. Russell. *Confederate Colonel and Cherokee Chief: The Life of William Holland Thomas.* P. 131.

639. James Mooney. *History, Myths, and Sacred Formulas of the Cherokees.* P. 172.

640. Ibid.

641. Ibid.

642. By 1867, Colonel Thomas owed his primary creditor, the Johnson estate, nearly $34,000. *Letter from the Secretary of the Interior in Response to Resolution of the House of February 25, 1882, Relative to the Lands and Funds of the Eastern Band of North Carolina Cherokee.* Executive Doc. 196. 47th Congress. February 25, 1882. P. 3. *The Eastern Band of Cherokees v. The United States and The Cherokee Nation.* No. 13828 United States Court of Claims 20 Ct. Cl. 449; 1885 U.S. Ct. Cl. Stanley Godbold Jr. and Mattie U. Russell. *Confederate Colonel and Cherokee Chief: The Life of William Holland Thomas.* P. 131.

643. Letter from William Holland Thomas to the Chiefs of the North Carolina Cherokee. March 31, 1871. WT 191.

644. During the War of The Rebellion, George Bushyhead served as a sergeant for Company B of the Thomas Legion. After the war, he became a firebrand for North Carolina's Cherokee populace to remove westward. http://www.itd.nps.gov/cwss/Personz_Detail.cfm?PER_NBR= 1348777.

645. James Mooney. *History, Myths, and Sacred Formulas of the Cherokees.* P. 151.

646. Letter from William F. Cloud to Cherokee Nation August 3, 1862. Lincoln Studies Center, Knox College. *Abraham Lincoln Papers at the Library of Congress.* Galesburg, Illinois. Letter from James G. Blunt to President Abraham Lincoln. August 13, 1862. Lincoln Studies Center, Knox College. *Abraham Lincoln Papers at the Library of Congress.* Galesburg, Illinois. AM. http://memory.loc.gov/cgi_bin/query/r?ammem/mal:@field(DO-CID+@lit(d1762800)). Letter from William G. Coffin to Principal Chief John Ross. June 16, 1862. Lincoln Studies Center, Knox College. *Abraham Lincoln Papers at the Library of Congress.* Galesburg, Illinois. AM. http://memory.loc.gov/cgi_bin/query/r?ammem/mal:@field(DOCID+@lit (d1650800)). Letter from Mark W. Delahay to President Abraham

Lincoln. August 21, 1862. Lincoln Studies Center, Knox College. *Abraham Lincoln Papers at the Library of Congress.* Galesburg, Illinois. AM. http:// memory.loc.gov/cgi_bin/query/r?ammem/mal: @field(DO-CID+@lit(d1785800)).

647. Letter from Principal Chief John Ross to President Abraham Lincoln. September 16, 1862. Lincoln Studies Center, Knox College. *Abraham Lincoln Papers at the Library of Congress.* Galesburg, Illinois. AM. http://memory.loc.gov/cgi_bin/query/r?ammem/mal:@field(DOCID+@lit (d1845200)). Letter from President Abraham Lincoln to Principal Chief John Ross. September 25, 1862. Lincoln Studies Center, Knox College. *Abraham Lincoln Papers at the Library of Congress.* Galesburg, Illinois. AM. http://memory.loc.gov/cgi_bin/query/r?ammem/mal:@field (DOCID+@lit(d1862600)).

648. E. Stanley Godbold Jr. and Mattie U. Russell. *Confederate Colonel and Cherokee Chief: The Life of William Holland Thomas.* P. 132.

649. Ibid.

650. "Asylums." *Laws of the State of North Carolina, Passed by the General Assembly at the Session of 1848–1849.* Tmos. J. Lemay, Printer-Star Office. 1849. The hospital actually opened in January 1856. Senator Henson P. Barnes. *Work in Progress: The North Carolina Legislature.* North Carolina Legislature. 1993.

651. E. Stanley Godbold Jr. and Mattie U. Russell. *Confederate Colonel and Cherokee Chief: The Life of William Holland Thomas.* P. 132.

652. Ibid. P. 133.

653. Ibid.

654. *The Eastern Band of Cherokees v. The United States and The Cherokee Nation.* No. 13828 United States Court of Claims. 20 Ct. Cl. 449; 1885 U.S. Ct. Cl. Lexis 22. June 1885. P. 451.

655. According to an 1882 congressional document, the proposed Qualla Boundary covered 50,000 acres and comprised large portions of Jackson and Swain counties in North Carolina. *Letter from the Secretary of the Interior in Response to Resolution of the House of February 25, 1882. Relative to the Lands and the Funds of the Eastern Band of North Carolina Cherokee.* Executive Doc. 196. 47th Congress, 1st Session. February 25, 1882. P. 2.

656. *The Eastern Band of Cherokees v. The United States and The Cherokee Nation.* No. 13828 United States Court of Claims. 20 Ct. Cl. 449; 1885 U.S. Ct. Cl. Lexis 22. June 1885. 453.

657. Ibid. 451.

658. Ibid. 455.

659. Ibid. 454.

660. Ibid. 454.

661. *Letter from the Secretary of the Interior in Response to Resolution of the House of February 25, 1882. Relative to the Lands and the Funds of the Eastern Band of North Carolina Cherokee.* Executive Doc. 196. 47th Congress, 1st Session. February 25, 1882. P. 2.

662. Ibid. P. 3.

663. Ibid. According to E. Stanley Godbold Jr. and Mattie Russell, a second suit filed shortly after the first was entered against the same parties as well as A. J. Murray and J. B. Allison (sureties on the bonds Terrell dispersed as Colonel Thomas's replacement as Cherokee Agent.), but the two suits were later combined into one. E. Stanley Godbold Jr. and Mattie U. Russell. *Confederate Colonel and Cherokee Chief: The Life of William Holland Thomas.* P. 136.

664. James Terrell shared Colonel Thomas's vision of a prosperous future for the Western North Carolina Native Americans but also harbored certain prejudiced opinions against the Eastern Band, including such beliefs as that "the war brought out the latent indian in their nature" as well as their comparative inability to master fire arms over bows and arrows. James Mooney. *History, Myths, and Sacred Formulas of the Cherokees.* P. 170. Sean Michael O'Brien. *Mountain Partisans: Guerrilla Warfare in the Southern Appalachians, 1861–1865.* P. 26.

665. Letter from James W. Terrell and Thomas Johnson to Judge Robert P. Dick. November 15, 1879. WT 189.

666. *Letter from the Secretary of the Interior in Response to Resolution of the House of February 25, 1882. Relative to the Lands and the Funds of the Eastern Band of North Carolina Cherokee.* Executive Doc. 196. 47th Congress, 1st Session. February 25, 1882. P. 2. E. Stanley Godbold Jr. and Mattie U. Russell. *Confederate Colonel and Cherokee Chief: The Life of William Holland Thomas.* P. 137. Letter from Thomas L. Clingman to William Holland Thomas. January 9, 1855. CM 145. Letter from James Guthrie to James W. Terrell. January 9, 1855. CM 156. Letter from James W. Terrell to the First Auditor of the Treasury, Washington, D.C. July 22, 1856. CM 141. Letter from Howell Cobb to James W. Terrell. January 20, 1858. CM 143. Letter from James W. Terrell to William Holland Thomas. January 19, 1860. CM 144.

667. E. Stanley Godbold Jr. and Mattie U. Russell. *Confederate Colonel and Cherokee Chief: The Life of William Holland Thomas.* P. 139.

668. *Letter from the Secretary of the Interior in Response to Resolution of the House of February 25, 1882, Relative to the Lands and the Funds of the Eastern Band of North Carolina Cherokee.* Executive Doc. 196. 47th Congress, 1st Session. February 25, 1882.

669. E. Stanley Godbold Jr. and Mattie U. Russell. *Confederate Colonel and Cherokee Chief: The Life of William Holland Thomas.* P. 141.

670. Ibid.

671. Ibid.

672. Ibid.

673. Ibid.

674. Ibid. P. 144.

675. Ibid. P. 145.

676. James Mooney. *History, Myths, and Sacred Formulas of the Cherokees.* P. 9.

677. Ibid. P. 16.

678. Ibid. P. 16.

679. E. Stanley Godbold Jr. and Mattie U. Russell. *Confederate Colonel and Cherokee Chief: The Life of William Holland Thomas.* P. 149.

680. While the United States had made great strides in caring for the mentally ill, the true source of Colonel Thomas's illness eluded both diagnostic techniques and treatments of nineteenth-century medicine. Given the nature of his symptoms (early fevers followed by alternating periods of lucidity and increasing mental imbalance), the colonel likely contracted *Treponema pallidum* (also known as syphilis) at some point during his mid-life travels. If left untreated by antibiotics, the sexually transmitted disease, prevalent throughout the period, would have progressed through three stages of symptomology (first the manifestation of chancre sores, followed by fever, and ending in latency). According to the United States Center for Disease Control, the latent or the tertiary stage "begins when secondary symptoms disappear. Without treatment, the infected person will continue to have syphilis events though there are no signs or symptoms . . . It may subsequently damage the internal organs, including the brain, nerves, eyes, heart, blood vessels, liver, bones, and joints . . . Signs and symptoms . . . include difficulty coordinating muscle movement, paralysis, numbness, gradual blindness, and dementia." Had they the knowledge, Colonel Thomas could have easily been cured in the first few months of the STD's manifestation through the administration of antibiotics http://www.cdc.gov.std/syphilis/STDFact-Syphilis.htm.

BIBLIOGRAPHY

PRIMARY SOURCES

Collections

The Captain Isaac Vincent Papers at the Hargrett Rare Book and Manuscript Library, University of Georgia, Athens. Galileo On-Line: http://www.galileo.usg.edu/express?link=zlna&hp=1.

Colonel William Holland Thomas and Thomas Legion Papers. National Archives Collection.

The Governor McMinn Letters at the Tennessee State Library and Archive, Nashville. Galileo On-Line: http://www.galileo.usg.edu/express?link=zlna&hp=1.

Messages and Papers of Andrew Jackson. Electronic Edition. American Reference Library. Western Standard Publishing Company. 1998.

National Parks Service. *Civil War Soldiers and Sailors System.* http://www.itd.nps.gov/cwss/template.cfm?unitcode=CNCTHOMRI&unitname=Infantry%20Regiment%2C%20Thomas%27%20North%20Carolina%20Legion.

The Printed At Globe Printing Office at the Hargrett Rare Book and Manuscript Library, University of Georgia, Athens. Galileo On-Line: http://www.galileo.usg.edu/express?link=zlna&hp=1.

The Telamon Cuyler Collection at the Hargrett Rare Book and Manuscript Library, University of Georgia, Athens. Galileo On-Line: http://www.galileo.usg.edu/express?link=zlna&hp=1.

Thomas Jefferson Papers Series 1. General Correspondence. 1651–1827. United States Library of Congress American Memory Digital Collection. http://memory.loc.gov.

The William H. Thomas Papers at the Hargrett Rare Book and Manuscript Library, University of Georgia, Athens. Galileo On-Line: http://www.galileo.usg.edu/express?link=zlna&hp=1.

The William Holland Thomas Collection at the Hoskins Special Collections Library, University of Tennessee, Knoxville. Galileo On-Line: http://www.galileo.usg.edu/express?link=zlna&hp=1.

The William Thomas Papers and Diaries at the Museum of the Cherokee Indian, Cherokee, North Carolina. Galileo On-Line: http://www.galileo.usg.edu/express?link=zlna&hp=1.

Periodicals

Cherokee Phoenix and the *Cherokee Advocate. 1828–1834.*

Government/Legal Documentation
"Asylums." *Laws of the State of North Carolina, Passed by the General Assembly at the Session of 1848–1849.* Tmos. J. Lemay, Printer-Star Office. 1849.

Cherokee Indians: Memorial of a Delegation of the Cherokee Tribe of Indians. H.R. Document 45. 22nd Congress, 1st Session. January 9th, 1832.

The Eastern Band of Cherokees v. The United States and The Cherokee Nation. No. 13828 United States Court of Claims 20 Ct. Cl. 449; 1885 U.S. Ct. Cl. The Cherokee Trust Funds; *Eastern Band of Cherokee Indians v. United States and Cherokee Nation, Commonly Called Cherokee Nation West.* United States Supreme Court. 117 U.S. 299; 6 S. Ct. 718; 29 L. Ed. 880; 1886 U.S.

Historical Statements Concerning the Battle of Kings Mountain and the Battle of the Cowpens South Carolina. Part II Gathering of the Patriots—the Battle, House Document No. 328. 70th Congress, 1st Session. United States Government Printing Office, Washington, D.C., 1928. http://www.army.mil/cmh-pg/books/RevWar/KM-Cpns/AWC-KM2.htm.

Kappler, Charles, ed. "Treaty of Hopewell." Document Number BT2352000756. *Indian Treaties, 1778–1883.* Washington, D.C., 1904, pp 8–11. Reproduced in History Resource Center. Farmington Hills, MI: Gale Group. http://galenet.galegroup.com/servlet/HistRC/.

Letter from the Secretary of the Interior in Response to Resolution of the House of February 25, 1882, Relative to the Lands and Funds of the Eastern Band of North Carolina Cherokee. Executive Document 196. 47th Congress. February 25th, 1882.

Memorial of John Ross and Others, on Behalf of the Cherokee Nation of Indians, Praying Protection from the United States, and Protesting Against Certain Articles of Agreement Between the Agent of the United States and a Certain Part of Said Cherokee Nation of Indians. Document 71. 23rd Congress, 2nd Session. January 21st, 1835.

Memorial of the Cherokee Indians Living in North Carolina Praying the Payment of Their Claims, Agreeably to the 8th and 12th Articles of the Treaty of 1835. Senate Document 408. 29th Congress, 1st Session. June 25th, 1846.

Supreme Court Decisions, 1831, *Cherokee Nation v. Georgia*, 30 U.S.

Supreme Court Decisions, 1832, *Worcester v. Georgia*, 31 U.S.

Books

Bancroft, George. *History of the United States. Volume II: History of the Colonization of the United States of America. Chapter VI, "The Languages and Manners of the Red Men."* Little, Brown, and Co., 1856. Electronic Edition. *Multimedia U.S. History.* Bureau of Electronic Publishing. 1995.

Brock, R. A. *Southern Historical Society Papers.* Volume XXI. Southern Historical Society, 1893. Electronic Edition. H-Bar Enterprises. 1997.

Clairborne, Jack, and Price, William, eds. *Discovering North Carolina: A Tar Heel Reader.* University of North Carolina Press. 1991.

Clark, Walter, ed. *Histories of Several Regiments and Battalions from North Carolina in the Great War 1861–1865.* Volume III. Nash Brothers, Book and Job Printers, 1901.

Filson, John. *The Adventures of Colonel Daniel Boone.* Electronic Edition. Project Gutenberg Etext #909. May 1997. http://promo.net/pg/.

Fitzpatrick, John C., ed. *The Writings of George Washington from the Original Manuscript Sources, 1745–1799.* United States Library of Congress American Memory Digital Collection. http://memory.loc.gov.

Ford, Paul Leicester, ed. *The Works of Thomas Jefferson in Twelve Volumes.* Federal Edition. United States Library of Congress American Memory Digital Collection. http://memory.loc.gov.

Ford, Worthington C. et al., eds. *A Century of Lawmakers, 1774–1873.* United States Library of Congress American Memory Digital Collection. http://memory.loc.gov.

Foreman, Richard, and Mahoney, James W. *The Cherokee Physician, or Indian Guide to Health, As Given by Richard Foreman, A Cherokee Doctor; Comprising a Brief View of Anatomy, with General Rules for Preserving Health Without the Use of Medicine. The Diseases of the U. States, with Their Symptoms,*

Causes, and Means of Prevention, Are Treated On in a Satisfactory Manner. It Also Contains a Description of a Variety of Herbs and Roots, Many of Which Are Not Explained in Any Other Book, and Their Medical Virtues Have Hither To Been Unknown to the Whites; to Which Is Added a Short Dispensatory. Asheville, North Carolina; Edney & Dedman, 1849. Electronic Edition. University of North Carolina at Chapel Hill. 2001. http://docsouth.unc.edu/nc/forman/menu.html.

Helper, Hinton Rowan. *The Impending Crisis of the South: How to Meet It.* Burdick Brothers, 1857. Electronic Edition. University of North Carolina at Chapel Hill. 2001. http://docsouth.unc.edu/nc/helper/helper.html.

Johnston, Frontis V. *The Papers of Zebulon Baird Vance,* Volume I: 1843–1862. Raleigh State Department Archives and History. 1963.

Journal of the Congress of the Confederate States of America, 1861–1865. United States Library of Congress American Memory Digital Collection. http://memory.loc.gov.

Journal of the House of Representatives of the United States, 1789–1873. United States Library of Congress American Memory Digital Collection. http://memory.loc.gov.

Journal of the Senate of the United States, 1789–1873. United States Library of Congress American Memory Digital Collection. http://memory.loc.gov.

Lincoln Studies Center, Knox College. *Abraham Lincoln Papers at the Library of Congress.* Galesburg, Illinois. United States Library of Congress American Memory Digital Collection. http://memory.loc.gov.

Mooney, James. *History, Myths, and Sacred Formulas of the Cherokees.* Bright Mountain Books. 1992.

North Carolina Board of Agriculture. *North Carolina and Its Resources.* Winston: M. I. & J. C. Stewart, Public Printers and Binders, 1896. Electronic Edition. University of North Carolina at Chapel Hill. 2001. http://docsouth.unc.edu/nc/state/state.html.

Scott, General Winfield. *Memoirs of Lieutenant-General Scott, LL.D. In Two Volumes.* New York: Sheldon & Co. 1864.

Scott, Robert, ed. *The War of the Rebellion: A Compilation of the Official Records of the Union and Confederate Armies.* 1880–1901. Electronic Edition. H-Bar Enterprises. 1995.

Summers, Thomas Osmond, ed. *The Confederate States Almanac for the Year of Our Lord 1862. Being the Second After Bissextile, or Leap Year, the Eighty-sixth of American Independence, and the Second of the Confederate States.* Nashville, Tenn.: Southern Methodist Publishing House, 1862. Electronic Edition.

University of North Carolina at Chapel Hill. 2000. http://docsouth. unc.edu/imls/almanac/menu.html.

Wheeler, John H. *Reminiscences and Memoirs of North Carolina and Eminent North Carolinians*. Columbus, Ohio; Columbus Printing Works, 1884. Electronic Edition. University of North Carolina at Chapel Hill. 2001. http://www.researchonline.net/nccw/bios/wheeler.htm#p69.

Yearns, Buck W., and Barrett, John G., eds. *North Carolina Civil War Documentary*. University of North Carolina Press. 1980.

SECONDARY SOURCES

Barnes, Senator Henson P. *Work in Progress: The North Carolina Legislature*. North Carolina Legislature. 1993.

Biographical Directory of the United States Congress. 1774–Present. http:// bioguide.congress.gov/biosearch/biosearch.asp.

Center for Disease Control. *STD Prevention: STD-Facts*. 2003. http://www. cdc.gov/std/Syphilis/STDFact-Syphilis.htm.

Dowd, Gregory Evans. *A Spirited Resistance: The North American Indian Struggle for Unity, 1745–1815*. John Hopkins University Press. 1992.

Dupuy, Trevor N., Johnson, Curt, and Bongard, David L., eds. *The Harper's Encyclopedia of Military Biography*. Castle Books. 1995.

Ehle, John. *Trail of Tears: The Rise and Fall of the Cherokee Nation*. Anchor Books. 1988.

Finger, John R. *The Eastern Band of Cherokees, 1819–1900*. University of Tennessee Press. 1984.

Fisher, Noel C. *War at Every Door: Partisan Politics and Guerilla Violence in East Tennessee, 1860–1869*. University of North Carolina Press. 1997.

Foote, Reverend William Henry. *Sketches of North Carolina, Historical and Biographical, Illustrative of the Principles of a Portion of Her Early Settlers*. New York: R. Craighead's Power Press, 1846. Electronic Edition. 2001. http://docsouth.unc.edu/nc/foote/foote.html.

Fulmores, Z. T. *Southwestern Historical Quarterly Online*. Volume 8. Number 3. January, 1905. http://www.tsha.utexas.edu/publications/journals/shq/online/v008/n3/008003265.html.

Galanter, Marc, M.D., contributor. *The Merck Manual—Second Home Edition* Section 7. "Mental Health Disorders." Chapter 108: "Drug Use and Abuse." Merck. 2003. http://www.merck.com/pubs/mmanual_home2/sec07/ch108/ch108b.htm.

Godbold, E. Stanley, Jr., and Russell, Mattie U. *Confederate Colonel and*

Cherokee Chief: The Life of William Holland Thomas. University of Tennessee Press. 1990.

Groce, W. Todd. *Mountain Rebels: East Tennessee Confederates and the Civil War, 1860–1870.* University of Tennessee Press. 1999.

Hayden, Deborah. *Pox: Genius, Madness, and the Mysteries of Syphilis.* Basic Books. 2003.

Henderson, Archibald. *The Conquest of the Old South West: The Romantic Story of the Early Pioneers into Virginia, the Carolinas, Tennessee and Kentucky 1740–1790.* Chapter 1. The Century Co., 1920. Electronic Edition. Project Gutenberg Etext #2390. November 2000. http:promo.net/pg/.

Henri, Florette. *Southern Indians and Ben Hawkins.* University of Oklahoma Press. 1986.

Inscoe, John. *Mountain Masters: Slavery and the Sectional Crisis in Western North Carolina.* University of Tennessee Press. 1989.

Inscoe, John, and McKinney, Gordon. *The Heart of Confederate Appalachia: Western North Carolina in the Civil War.* University of North Carolina Press. 2000.

Johnson, Guion Griffis. *Antebellum North Carolina: A Social History.* University of North Carolina Press, 1937. Electronic Edition. 2002. http://docsouth.unc.edu/nc/johnson/johnson_all.html.

Jones, Virgil Carrington. *Grey Ghosts and Rebel Raiders.* Promontory Press. 1995.

Kennedy, Frances, H, ed. *The Civil War Battlefield Guide.* Second Edition. Houghton Mifflin Co. 1998.

McLoughlin, William G. *After the Trail of Tears: The Cherokee's Struggle for Sovereignty, 1839–1880.* University of North Carolina Press. 1993.

McPherson, James M. *Battle Cry of Freedom: The Civil War Era.* Oxford University Press. 1988.

North Carolina State Library. *North Carolina Encyclopedia: Zebulon Baird Vance.* March 1997. http://statelibrary.dcr.state.nc.us/nc/bio/public/ vance.htm.

O'Brien, Sean Michael. *Mountain Partisans: Guerrilla Warfare in the Southern Appalachians, 1861–1865.* Praeger. 1999.

Powell, William S. *North Carolina Through Four Centuries.* University of North Carolina Press. 1989.

Rozema, Vicki. *Footsteps of the Cherokees: A Guide to the Eastern Homelands of the Cherokee Nation.* John F. Blair. 1995.

Russell, Mattie. *William Holland Thomas, White Chief of the North Carolina Cherokee.* Doctoral Thesis. Duke University. 1956.

Schermerhorn Genealogy and Family Chronicles. The Schenectady Digital History Archive. The Schenectady County Public Library. http://www. schenectadyhistory.org/families/schermerhorn/chronicles/2c.html.

Simms, William Gilmore. *The Life of Francis Marion.* Electronic Edition. Project Gutenberg Etext #847. March 1997. http://promo.net/pg/.

United Kingdom's Institute for Alcohol Studies. June 2000. http://www.ias. org.uk/factsheets/medsoc3.htm.

The United States Capitol Historical Society. *The Education Center.* http:// www.uschs.org/03_education/subs/subs_lessons/06_b.html.

Wright, Robert K, Jr. *The Continental Army.* Center For Military History United States Army. 1983. http://www.army.mil/cmh-pg/books/revwar/ contarmy/CA-fm.html

INDEX